BUS

Strategy

## Human Resource Management in Action

---

*Series Editor: Brian Towers*

*Successful Training Practice*
Alan Anderson

*Managing Performance Appraisal Systems*
Gordon Anderson

*European Employee Relations*
Jeff Bridgford and John Stirling

*Practical Employment Law*
Paul Lewis

*Managing the Team*
Mick Marchington

*The Japanization of British Industry*
Nick Oliver and Barry Wilkinson

*Strategy and the Human Resource*
Ken Starkey and Alan McKinlay

*Handbook of Human Resource Management*
Edited by Brain Towers

## Other HRM Books from Blackwell Business

*Successful Selection Interviewing*
Neil Anderson and Vivian Shackleton

*The Equal Opportunities Handbook*
Helen Collins

*Total Quality and Human Resources*
Barrie Dale and Cary Cooper

*The Handbook of Human Resource Planning*
Gordon McBeath

*Developments in the Management of Human Resources*
John Storey

*Women's Career Development*
Barbara White, Charles Cox and Cary Cooper

# Strategy and the Human Resource

*Ford and the Search for Competitive Advantage*

KEN STARKEY AND
ALAN McKINLAY

First published 1993

Blackwell Publishers
108 Cowley Road
Oxford OX4 1JF
UK

238 Main Street
Suite 501
Cambridge, Massachusetts 02142
USA



*British Library Cataloguing in Publication Data*

A CIP catalogue record for this book is available from the British Library.

*Library of Congress Cataloging-in-Publication Data*

Starkey, Ken,
Strategy and the human resource: Ford and the search for competitive advantage/Ken Starkey and Alan McKinlay.
p. cm. — (HRM in action)
Includes bibliographical references and index.
1. Ford Motor Company—Management. 2. Automobile industry and trade—United States—Management—Case studies. 3. Ford Motor Company Ltd.—Management. 4. Automobile industry and trade—Great Britain—Management—Case studies. I. McKinlay, Alan. II. Title. III. Series.
HD9710.U54F694 1993 338.7'6292'0973—dc20 92-43004

ISBN 0-631-186743

Typeset in 11 on 13 pt Plantin
by Best-set Typesetter Ltd., Hong Kong
Printed in Great Britain
by T.J. Press (Padstow) Ltd., Padstow, Cornwall

This book is printed on acid-free paper

*'We must throw a bridge between Europe and*
*the United States of America'* (*Henry Ford, 1924*)

*'The idea was to achieve a quick transfusion of the American experience*
*into the European company'* (*American Personnel manager on secondment*
*to Ford of Europe, 1989*)

*'I don't have a starry-eyed view of why we changed.*
*If we could have continued to run our business the old way and*
*still make money we'd have been much happier to do so'*
(*Ford of Europe Manufacturing manager, 1990*)

*'The unexamined life is not worth living'* (*Socrates, 470–399 BC*)

# Contents

# List of Figures

# Foreword

Ford is far more than a giant, multinational company which makes good value, popular cars. In its origins, business methods and rise to industrial prominence it has become an important ingredient of the history and folklore of the West, not least in the part that machine-paced work has played in the lives of millions which, though mostly baleful, was we were told the social price which had to be paid for widely-available and cheap private transportation. Beyond the factory and even today, Henry Ford retains his place as the image of the visionary, risk-taking US multi-millionaire and autocrat; and his name, when describing the organization and technology of his factories, has given a new word to the language – 'Fordism'. It is also a word which has been used much beyond car making and rarely with anything other than disapproval.

Within car manufacturing, and especially at Ford, it is now a matter of record that the domination of the 'line', job insecurity, and harsh, top–down management resulted in an explosive employee cocktail of anger, resentment and alienation, which determined the lives and industrial behaviour of successive generations of forgotten men and women at the bottom of Roosevelt's pyramid. The rationale for such a regime was commercial success. The first 'people's car' was the Model 'T', trundling through middle America three decades before Hitler's Volkswagen, in its post 1945 reincarnation, and five decades before the all-conquering 'beetle' took firm hold on the popular imagination.

But both before and since the beetle, the Ford adventure has at several times nearly come to tears, especially in the US. There was, in the fifties, the marketing and near corporate disaster of the Edsel, revealing that the Ford family's sclerotic hold was much like that of the ancien régime with the deluge approaching. Change was imperative. Ford did so, survived and prospered, and again faced near extinction in the eighties as the Japanese consolidated their industrial invasion of the US. Ford, like General Motors, faced the challenge by democratizing its management style. It also looked carefully at its management and production methods through the Japanese lens provided by its 25 per cent stake in Mazda.

Although some similar developments were taking place in the European car industry – as for example Honda's stake in Rover – for Ford, Europe, is another 'country'. The US survival strategy of the eighties did not travel. Nor did it appear to need to, given the continuing commercial success of the European operation. The deep and continuing recession of the recent decade has changed all that. Japan is once again inside the gates with ambitions to dominate Western European quality as well as volume car-production and to build bridgeheads into the potentially important (though much longer-term) markets of the emerging new democracies of Eastern Europe. Ford was not alone in hearing the alarm bells: they were also ringing loudly in the ears of the German prestige car-makers.

These were some of the imperatives behind Ford Europe's historic decision to follow the Japanese road and is the story told here by Starkey and McKinlay. The book has two themes. The first is to demonstrate that an organizational-change strategy can only succeed (and not always even then) if it is indelibly marked by an unswerving commitment to those who spend their lives working in the organization, and that this commitment can be best demonstrated through policies focusing on employee quality. The second is to record the experience of managers coming to terms with major change. Interestingly, in pursuing this second theme the authors acknowledge following Beynon, in his pioneering study of the experience of Ford workers, by allowing the 'actors' to tell the story in their own words.

But how will the story end? Will the Japanese road help Ford Europe to survive reasonably intact through the current perils besetting the whole industry – perils besetting the Japanese themselves? Whatever the outcome, this story is well-told with lessons to learn – for good or ill – for the motor vehicle industry and beyond.

*Brian Towers*

# Acknowledgements

We would like to thank the Economic and Social Research Council for funding the project upon which the book is based (award reference number R000221040). We would also like to thank: Peter Grinyer of the University of St Andrews who supported our research in its infancy; the School of Management and Finance and the Overseas Travel Fund Committee, University of Nottingham, and the Centre for Business History, University of Glasgow for assistance towards travel to North America; Paul Dobson of the University of Nottingham who provided advice and reassurance in the final stages of manuscript completion; and Sandra Mienczakowski, also of the University of Nottingham, for word-processing advice. In particular we would like to thank the many managers who gave so generously of their hard-pressed time to participate in our research. Previous experience with the Company had convinced us that Ford offered the opportunity of collaboration with a most willing, cordial and enthusiastic research partner, one whose learning and lessons had much to teach us and our readers about crucial business issues. We are happy to report that all our expectations were satisfied. The Ford experience was as rich a source of learning as we anticipated and the Company's participation in the project was all that we could have expected. We hope the reader finds the experience equally rewarding. Although Ford were strongly supportive of our research they neither sponsored nor commissioned it. The interpretation of the Ford experience is, of course, our own.

We dedicate the book to our long-suffering partners, Angela and Linda, in the hope that our next project will not require the same amount of time and travel, and to Catherine and Michael in the hope that the organizations they join in the twenty-first century will provide working environments that are both participative and involving.

# List of Abbreviations

AJ — After Japan

CAE — Computer Aided Engineering. The use of computer models in the design and prototype simulation process, thereby avoiding the need for 'physicals', and achieving higher accuracy in less time.

DVP — Design Verification and Prototype (sign-off). All major product features agreed – no further changes (other than for failures in test and development).

EI — Employee Involvement

FMEA — Failure Mode and Effect Analysis. One of the key quality planning tools, which requires systematic analysis of potential problems in the design stage.

MVGP — Mission, Value, and Guiding Principles

NVH — Noise, Vibration and Harshness – a total vehicle issue which can impact badly on customer satisfaction but can have its root cause in one or several of many inter-related component systems.

SLR — Surface Lines Release. Confirmation that the vehicle shape is firm so that tool design for body metal stamping can be progressed.

4P — The final pre-volume production vehicles built at the pilot stage but using approved production parts.

PM — Participative Management

PST — Program Steering Team. A group of managers or specialists drawn together from all relevant functions to ensure delivery of key elements of the product program.

# Introduction

> I then made a presentation to Manufacturing but because it got people interested it became a Ford of Europe presentation. So it developed into a presentation to all employees of Ford of Europe. And this became known as *After Japan*. Who invented the name beats the hell out of me. . . . There were all kinds of jokes at that time: one was the difference between the West and Japan is that they both have boats of eight but in Japan you have seven oarsmen and one cox whereas in the West you have one oarsman and seven coxes!

This is how Bill Hayden, Vice-President of Manufacturing Ford of Europe 1975–89 and Chairman of Jaguar 1989–92, describes the aftermath of a fateful visit to Japan in 1979.

Hayden's visit gave us the beginning for the book. In Ford of Europe *After Japan* was the name given to a series of change initiatives introduced into the company to prepare for what it saw as its major strategic threat of the 1980s, the imminent arrival of Japanese competition in the European arena. Our subject is contemporary changes in human resource management, corporate strategy, organizational structure and management processes 'after Japan'. At its heart is a critical examination of the complex relationship between corporate strategy and human resource management in the Ford Motor Company.

The link between strategy and human resource management (HRM) is crucial to effective business performance. The two are, in effect, the two sides of the one coin – corporate strategy/HRM. In the past this link too often has been ignored or taken for granted. Strategic decision-making should inform *and* be informed by human resource considerations. The quality of a firm's human resources will have a profound effect – enabling or constraining – upon its strategic potential, its ability to formulate and implement strategy.

Competitive advantage, the ultimate goal of strategy, is no longer defined in terms of high quality or low cost. HRM aims to achieve both best quality and lowest cost, technical innovation, design leadership and efficiency, and proposes a new managerial agenda based on organizational learning, strategic flexibility, the integration of managerial and employee interests and world class competitiveness. It attacks head-on old management traditions based on accepted but unexamined wisdom, over-specialization and conservatism.

While broadly endorsing the emerging agenda we do counsel against the 'quick fix' mentality that suggests that organizational change is non-problematic and can be easily introduced through embracing a set menu of readily achievable management practices. In this regard some management theory, including sometimes the most influential, has run ahead of best practice. While recognizing the lure of wishful thinking we do not think it helps us improve the performance of organizations. Real improvement in the way we manage, we contend, requires deep analysis rather than superficial prescription, concentrated reflection upon the way we act and often painful learning to undo existing patterns of thought and behaviour.

The answers to our management dilemmas are not yet fully clear. The issues, though, are becoming clearer. Our study offers a sober but hopefully entertaining account of the reality of the management process and its changing context. This is framed in the analysis of one particular company at a crucial turning point in its history. The new corporate strategy/HRM agenda, its genesis, its implications and its problems, is examined through the medium of the experience of the Ford Motor Company, in particular the experience of Ford in Europe.

Can one generalize from the experience of one company to capture the crucial management issues facing a multitude of companies? We think that this is possible and even desirable. To obtain the necessary depth of analysis in a study encompassing more than one company, particularly a multinational company of Ford's complexity, would be difficult and would require a mammoth tome. It was our original intention to compare Ford's experience with that of others. We save that study for another time and concentrate on Ford primarily because we became so fascinated by the issues Ford was addressing and by what we came to see as Ford's representative significance at a particular moment in the evolution of the Western approach to management.

Ford is one of the world's largest and most successful corporations. Furthermore, it is associated historically with the development of a distinctive approach to management which bears its name, Fordism, which some management theorists argue is *the* typical Western approach. One only has to 'dine' in any fast food outlet to appreciate the pervasiveness of the Fordist, 'machine bureaucracy' image of organization (Mintzberg, 1983; Morgan, 1986). The legacy of this approach is writ large across many industries. Ford's experience of the problems of the Fordist approach in a changing business environment, in particular its implications for manufacturing and product development, has much to teach other companies.

The automobile industry is the most representative of manufacturing industries and perhaps the best barometer of industrial health in a nation. In the UK, whose indigenous manufacturers have suffered major decline, it is Ford that has served as the model for solutions to the 'British disease' – poor productivity, bad industrial relations and declining market share (Marsden *et al.*, 1985). The Ford management approach has been much envied. Ford managers have been eagerly head-hunted by other companies hoping for the Ford magic to help them. The UK media have even labelled Ford the 'university of industry'.

Increasingly Western managers have turned to Japan for lessons in world-class manufacturing. It is in the car industry that the effect of Japanese competition has had the most far-reaching ramifications. Ford has led the way in responding to this threat and has been praised as the Western car company most advanced in its efforts to introduce 'lean production', Japan's 'secret weapon' in what has been termed a 'global auto war' (Womack *et al.*, 1990). Ford has been at the forefront of strategic change in an industry in which the need for change has been increasing dramatically. In the words of Ford Motor Company's 1985 Annual Report,

> Change is a permanent feature of the motor industry, but its present phase must rank as the most fluid since the earliest years. The process of restructuring within and between companies is bound to continue: our objective must be to manage and control that process.

In the 1980s Ford Motor Company in the US negotiated what is one of the most spectacular business turnarounds of all time, coming from the verge of extinction to a position of industry leader on a variety of performance indicators. At the core of this turnaround was a searching reanalysis of corporate strategy grounded in a successful attempt to come to terms with the legacy of Fordism, undoing its constraints, confirming its strengths, all the while redefining management practices at Ford in a radically new way. At the heart of Ford's transformation in the US was the development of a new approach to the management of its human resource. The new approach emphasized employee involvement and employee participation, key elements of the emerging HRM agenda.

For Ford in Europe the context was very different. For much of the 1980s Ford of Europe, the company's European arm, was enjoying great success. Unlike in the US, where increasingly successful Japanese automobile companies were changing the rules of competition, in Europe Japan posed a potential but not an actual threat. We now all appreciate that a major strategic objective of Japanese firms is to 'Europeanize' their activities in the 1990s. Ford of Europe however recognized the new Japanese challenge early – in 1979 to be precise, when Bill Hayden returned from a tour of Japanese factories in a state of shock at their productivity levels and the quality of their outputs. Out of this sense of shock and disbelief came *After Japan*.

Much of the organizational learning at Ford in the 1980s that we discuss in the book focused on understanding the Japanese challenge. This involved the company's managers in a searching analysis of accepted managerial practice in the company which led to a gradual 'unlearning' of its past competences and to the learning of new modes of managerial behaviour. Ford, therefore, provides a leading example of learning from Japan. Holding a 25 per cent equity stake in the Japanese automobile company Mazda has given it a rare window onto the sources of Japanese competitive advantage.

Ford of Europe management also had the example of Ford US to reflect upon and a change agenda developed in the USA that set out to redefine the relationship between business strategy and HRM philosophy and practice. Ford of Europe in the 1980s, therefore, as well as illustrating the importance of the Japanese 'model' in the framing of current management thinking and practice, also constitutes perhaps the key case for analyzing the diffusion of an American way of thinking about strategy and HRM to Europe. One of the major puzzles we address is why the problem of linking changes in strategy to a new HRM approach was more successfully managed by Ford in the US than in Europe.

To summarize, we chose Ford as our core case because it represented an organizational and industrial context in which many of the key business issues of the 1990s are being played out. Ford of Europe was established in 1967 to integrate Ford's UK and German companies. Ford effectively put in place with the establishment of Ford of Europe an organizational structure geared to the demands of 1992 and the single market 25 years before it became a reality. Ford thus also provides a key case of the integration of a complex business system across European national divides. Ford worldwide illustrates the complexity of managing strategy and HRM on a global scale.

## The Nature of the Managerial Experience

Underlying the focus on the link between corporate strategy and human resource management is our other major interest – the experience of managers in coming to terms with the new strategic issues of the 1990s. Huw Beynon, in his seminal sociological account of working for Ford (Beynon, 1984), argued that the experience of the people who work in factories was rarely examined while men like Henry Ford, founders of the companies who own the factories, were public figures. He set out to redress this imbalance and his and later work has gone a long way in correcting this deficiency in our knowledge.

Managers are one of a company's key human resources and the quality of the management process is crucial to strategic effectiveness. What is lacking, though, in analyses of management is serious consideration of the managerial experience – what the American poet Wallace Stevens, himself a senior executive in the insurance industry, described as the 'demnition grind day after day [that] keeps me well, cheerful, prosperous, overweight and sober' (Stevens, 1967: 766). Ford provides us with a microcosm of this experience – the effects of bureaucracy, the dismantling of bureaucracy, the relationships between bosses and between bosses and bossed, 'us and them' mind-sets, opposing cultures, sectionalism, competition, cooperation, status, power, politics, individualism, careerism, groupism, the sense of a common mission, opportunities, challenges, distrust and trust, the science of management, systems, rationality, structure, process, irrationality, cognition, emotions, pessimism, cynicism, fear, anger, enjoyment, hope, failure, success, resistance to change, learning, and change.

## Structure of the Text

We discuss our research methodology in the Appendix. Our major concern in the text is the lived experience of men and women wrestling with new complex managerial agendas. We attempted to capture this experience by an extensive and intensive process of interviewing over a four-year period. Unless otherwise attributed the quotations in the book are drawn from these interviews.

Chapter 1 introduces the conceptual framework underpinning our analysis. This provides an overview of the key issues of the strategic human resource management agenda 'after Japan'. Chapter 2 examines the development of the link between corporate strategy and human resource management in Ford in the US with its spectacularly successful outcome. Chapters 3 to 6 analyse Ford's experience in Europe. Chapter 3 discusses the HRM initiatives of the 1980s as they impacted upon employee relations. Chapter 4 shifts the attention to the experience of managers wrestling with the effects of a deeply embedded, traditional, highly successful management system and the growing sense of a need for change. Chapters 5 and 6 are concerned with the implications of new ways of thinking about strategic and human resource management for product development, in particular the daunting problem of integrating efforts across long-established bureaucratic organizational divides.

A major issue is the role of top management in strategic change initiatives. Chapter 7 critically examines the role of top management in such initiatives in the complex structures and management processes of the large multinational corporation in the context of an analysis of the top management process in Ford. In chapter 8, our concluding chapter, we ask what comes next – for Ford, and more generally?

# 1

# After Japan: Corporate Strategy/Human Resource Management

It has been claimed that human resource management (HRM) is a typically American way of thinking about personnel management. According to this point of view HRM has little to offer Europe because its roots lie in the 'American Dream' and a very different cultural context, where the emphasis is on the importance of strong leadership and where people believe in 'a kind of rugged entrepreneurial individualism reflected in and reinforced by a strong organizational culture' (Guest, 1990: 391). HRM also has its roots in the American Quality of Working Life movement, – with its desire to improve opportunities for people at work – which itself is rooted in the work of the human relations school and the writings of such luminaries as Mayo, Maslow and McGregor who share a peculiarly American belief in the human potential for psychological 'growth'.

We contest this view of HRM. We argue that issues addressed in the debate about HRM are relevant to Europe. It is also our contention, contrary to the view that sees HRM as a purely American phenomenon, that HRM in the European context is an amalgam of reactions to *both* American HRM practices *and* to the HRM practices of Japanese firms. Indeed we also contend that one cannot divorce American HRM in the 1980s from such Japanese influences. Our key case is the experience of the American automobile manufacturer Ford in Europe. Ford of Europe's exploration of HRM ideas and practices had a dual source – the experience of its American parent, and its own independent analysis of and reflection upon the sources of Japanese firms' success.

## Human Resource Management and Corporate Strategy

HRM, as defined in the seminal Harvard Business School book on the subject (Beer *et al.*, 1984), is designed to maximize organizational integration, employee commitment, flexibility and quality of work. Guest (1988) contrasts HRM with a 'production model' approach to personnel management – Ford is Guest's ideal-typical example of this – based on tough, consistent industrial relations practice, focusing on the maintenance of efficient continuity of production. This approach has much in common with Purcell and Gray's (1986) 'traditional/ consultative' style of employee relations in which labour is viewed merely as a factor of production and employee relations policies centre on the need for stability, control and the institutionalization of conflict through, for example, the recognition of unions and collective agreements. There is a strong emphasis on the 'right to manage' supported by a strong central personnel control function. In this traditional approach a key aim of personnel management is to minimize employee constraints on both operational (line) and strategic (corporate) management.

The traditional production model is based on the negotiation and enforcement of collective agreements. It emphasizes the need for the managerial definition of the nature of work, forms of control that support this definition and behaviours that conform to it. Employee compliance rather than commitment is the major managerial concern, and relationships of low trust between management and labour the result (Fox, 1973). By contrast, the HRM model is people-oriented with an emphasis on the maximization of individual skills and motivation through consultation with the workforce so as to produce high levels of commitment to company strategic goals. Labour is more than a factor of production to be minimized. It is an asset to be invested in. The emphasis is on the fostering of working conditions that encourage responsible autonomy rather than the need for direct control. Labour provides potential, not constraint. It is a resource to be used to its fullest capacity. In the conversion from traditional personnel practices to HRM a key transition to be made is that from a managerial emphasis on control to the facilitation of employee commitment (Walton, 1985). In terms of employee relations this represents a shift from a pluralist, collective, low trust approach to a unitarist one which emphasizes individuals, teamwork and high trust (Guest, 1987; Fox, 1973).

Emerging from both Japanese and American experience is a

growing *rapprochement* of thinking about corporate strategy and HRM. A successful strategy is based on the allocation of an organization's resources to create a unique and viable long-term position in its environment. HRM assumes strategic importance when the need for employee commitment becomes central to the implementation of corporate strategy, for example, commitment to strategic goals concerning efficiency, quality and innovation. A key policy goal underpinning HRM practice is to 'maximize organizational integration' (Guest, 1988: 503). Strategic integration 'refers to the ability of the organization to integrate HRM issues into its strategic plans' (Guest, 1989: 42). HRM emphasizes the strategic significance of strong culture in promoting a sense of purpose and commitment in the organization.

Proponents of strategic human resource management argue that it is desirable to integrate HRM and strategic management because integration provides a broader range of solutions for solving complex organizational problems and also

> ensures that human, financial, and technological resources are given consideration in setting goals and assessing implementation capabilities. Third, through integration organizations must explicitly consider the individuals who comprise them and must implement policies. Finally, reciprocity in integrating human resource and strategic concerns limits the subordination of strategic considerations to human resource preferences and the neglect of human resources as a vital source of organizational competence and competitive advantage. (Lengnick-Hall and Lengnick-Hall, 1988: 455–6)

The current growth of interest in HRM reflects past failings of the personnel function – 'a persistent failure of personnel departments to innovate on personnel policy and therefore to contribute to the pursuit of competitive advantage' (Guest, 1988: 10). HRM represents a policy agenda, in many cases, of personnel management in search of a new role and even a justification for its very existence. It presents us with a radical rethinking of the personnel function which has traditionally been seen as 'something performed on subordinates by managers'. HRM focuses not only on the development of employees but also on the development of managers themselves (Legge, 1989: 27).

Key skills for personnel specialists of the future comprise management and employee development, and manpower planning rather than traditional industrial relations activities where the shift is from collective to local bargaining (Cowans, 1986). In organization design the parallel change is from bureaucratic, centralized structures with highly defined, specialized roles to less bureaucratic, less centralized structures, with flexibility a key feature of job design and working practice agreements, and an ensuing emphasis on individual autonomy and innovating work practices.

Traditional personnel management is non-strategic, separate from the business, reactive, short-term and constrained by a limited definition of its role as dealing with unionized and lower-level employees (Miller, 1989). Personnel management becomes strategic when employees are managed in ways which recognize their key role in strategy implementation and a key goal of employee relations becomes the motivation of employees to fulfil strategic objectives. This view fits with the literature on strategic leadership where the most important top management function is to motivate employees to exceptional effort by fostering a sense of commitment to institutional purpose (Selznick, 1957; Wrapp, 1967; *Strategic Management Journal*, 1989). Selection, appraisal, rewards and employee development become strategic issues in guaranteeing the appropriate skill base to enable companies to fulfil their strategic visions and respond to new competition (Tichy et al. 1982; Porter, 1987; Abernathy et al., 1981). HRM is seen as long-term and proactive, aimed at the maximum utilization of the human resource; traditional personnel management as short-term, reactive and *ad hoc*, primarily interested in cost minimization, peripheral to strategy.

For Johnson (1988), reflecting on Ford's employee development programmes in the US, it is an important task for the personnel specialist

> to better identify where our HR systems impact and support corporate strategic issues . . . to demonstrate its competence in strategic planning and implementation. We need to clearly specify the value-added benefit of the HR function in formulating and implementing business strategy. We need to be able to surface the Human Resources implications of strategic alternatives and provide options for handling HR issues that are directly related to strategic planning issues. . . . In short, we need to evolve the role of Human Resources from an administrative role to a consultant one in running the business. (Johnson, 1988: 199)

## Strategic Frames of Reference

HRM can best contribute to strategy, its proponents claim, through the development of the 'frames of reference' of those managers who make strategy (Hendry and Pettigrew, 1990). In this section we examine those frames of reference that have dominated Western strategic thinking and also look at the emerging interest in the process of strategic management. Strategic management can be thought of in at least two distinct ways: as economic analysis and planning, and as a decision-making process strongly influenced by organizational, political, and cultural factors (Johnson and Scholes, 1989).

The literature on corporate strategy has, until recently, been dominated by the economic planning approach, exemplified by the work of Michael Porter and the portfolio planners. The major danger of this approach is an inherent one-dimensionality which encourages an early and rigid adoption of a single perspective (Wensley, 1982). In Porter's case, the focus is on either/or choices between mutually exclusive generic strategies. In portfolio planning, according to the most influential of its proponents, the Boston Consulting Group, the emphasis is on a single measure of the attractiveness of particular markets and this guides the decision to compete or to exit (Abell and Hammond, 1979).

According to Porter (1980, 1985) there are essentially two distinct sources of competitive advantage – cost leadership or differentiation. To compete on cost requires intense supervision of labour, tight cost control, frequent and detailed control reports, a highly structured organization and incentives based on strict quantitative targets. Successful differentiation demands a different approach to give products or services an edge, and HRM's emphasis on bringing the best out of employees through improving the quality of working life and cultivating employee commitment and initiative appears more suited to this strategy. Human resource policies that support the selection, training and retention of skilled labour are crucial here.

Porter's model refers to the basis of competitive advantage in single product or service organizations. In large diversified organizations the focus shifts to the management of multiple generic strategies. For this task the dominant tool has been portfolio management, which allocates strategic roles to each business unit on the basis of their product market growth rate and relative market share. The Boston Consulting Group categorization of roles is well-known

(Abell and Hammond, 1979). 'Cash cows' have dominant share of fast growing markets, 'problem children' have low share of fast-growing markets, 'stars' have high share of fast growing markets, and 'dogs' have low share of slow growing markets. Long-term strategic success hinges on the use of cash generated by cash cows to finance market share increases for 'problem children', which are then nurtured into new 'stars' before becoming 'cash cows' themselves. In product life cycle terms successful products tend to start out as 'problems', develop into 'stars', mature into 'cash cows' and deteriorate into 'dogs'.

Portfolio planning encourages different approaches to employee relations in different parts of the corporation (Purcell, 1989). In the cash cow the emphasis in personnel management is on cost control, efficiency and labour productivity. In dogs efficiency improvements are to be achieved by work intensification, demanning and cutting overhead costs. In the star innovation is the issue, a priority which entails HRM practices geared to stimulate individual creativity, teamwork and lateral communication (Guest, 1989: 78). The typical problem child is a small innovatory part of an organization where the key issues are generating innovation, then developing and stabilizing market share. Each category in the portfolio schema is based on a distinctive logic that dictates its unique and inevitable life-cycle. Just as management styles and workforce competencies are not transferable between categories so the units are locked into their fates by the self-fulfilling imagery of portfolio management. The approach prescribes harvesting mature businesses, discourages aggressive reinvestment and precludes the search for innovation to prolong the product life cycle (Pascale, 1984; Seeger, 1984).

There is a strong contrast between economic and process/organizational approaches to strategy (Carroll, 1987). Organizational approaches focus on issues that economic approaches usually assume away. A basic assumption of the organizational research is that organizational factors are problematic and that they severely constrain strategic decisions. Thus, Chandler's (1962) seminal view that strategy leads to structure is turned on its head. Structure and other organizational factors also severely limit strategy. The difference between organizational and economic approaches is more than one of emphasis. It is a central tenet of Porter's views on generic strategies that 'being stuck in the middle' will lead to failure. Yet an important finding of the organizational perspective is that many successful strategies develop out of early failures; as, for example, in the Honda case analysed by Pascale (1988). If these firms had not been able to 'muddle through', without prematurely embracing any one generic strategic prescription, they would not have succeeded in the long term (Carroll, 1987: 8–9).

HRM is a key concern in the strategic management literature that views strategy as a process to be managed rather than an exercise in rational planning and execution (Mintzberg and Quinn, 1991). The process perspective encourages us to think of strategic management as a form of organizational learning and focuses our attention on problems of strategy implementation and actually 'making it happen' (Harvey-Jones, 1988). It highlights the importance in strategy implementation of continuous attention to the fine-tuning of detail as strategies evolve and emphasizes leveraging resources and the development of core competencies as the essence of strategy.

The view of strategy as a process is best developed in the text of Quinn, Mintzberg and James (1988):

> in reality, [strategy] formulation and implementation are intertwined as complex interactive processes in which politics, values, organizational culture, and management styles determine or constrain particular strategic decisions. And strategy, structure, and systems mix together in complicated ways to influence outcomes. (Quinn, Mintzberg and James, 1988: xxii)

Peters and Waterman's seminal work can also be situated in this paradigm. They were crucial in bringing human resource concerns to the forefront of the management agenda with their astoundingly successful and very influential *In Search of Excellence* (1982). They situate their work in a tradition of organizational analysis stemming from the human relations school, Chester Barnard's work on the functions of management, and Simon's theories on decision-making (Starkey, 1992). Their '7-S framework' has as its central idea the claim that organizational effectiveness stems not just from the interaction of strategy and structure, the traditional concerns in organization design, but also from the relationship between a number of other Ss – systems, management style, as seen in an organization's culture, the organization's skills base, its staff and its superordinate goals. Excellence is equated with HRM ('productivity through people'). Employees are to be trusted, respected and inspired to become 'winners'.

According to Peters and Waterman senior executives resolve the problem of employee commitment by creating a stable, unifying value system: organizations are to be guided by a clear sense of shared values, a sense of mission and identity and inspirational leadership rather than bureaucratic control. The goal of top management is to inculcate a sense of strategic vision. Drucker (1973) argues that the most common reason for business failure is the lack of a clear sense of mission. Mission statements help to articulate the unique purposes of organizations and provide a clear sense of purpose for employees, thus serving an important motivational role. David (1989) argues that developing and communicating a clear business mission is one of the most commonly neglected tasks in strategic management.

Peter Senge emphasizes the importance of shared vision as a key aspect of the learning organization. The impetus to learning is to foster an environment in which people share their visions of the organization and through this process of sharing create a common future. Through the creation of a common vision, organizations can overcome the sectionalism that is inimical to the sense of shared responsibility for the organization's fate.

> Getting started is as simple as sitting people in small circles and asking them to talk about 'what's really important to them'. . . . When people begin to state and hear each other's visions, the foundation of the political environment begins to crumble – the belief that all we care about is self-interest. Organizations that fail to foster genuinely shared visions, or that foist unilateral visions on their members and pretend that they are shared, fail to tap this broader commitment. Though they decry internal politics, they do nothing to nurture a nonpolitical environment. (Senge, 1990: 275)

It is only in a nonpolitical environment that responsibility for the common good can be generated. One of the deepest desires underlying shared vision, Senge argues, is the desire to be connected, to a larger purpose *and* to one another. He also reminds us that the spirit of connection is difficult to create and, once created, fragile.

## Fordism, Markets and HRM

Driving the changes in corporate strategy and HRM are changes in the nature of industrial markets. The relationship between markets and the organization of production has been most systematically analyzed in debates about Fordism (Sabel, 1982). The emblematic significance of the Ford Motor Company derives from the seminal role of Henry Ford in developing an organizational system which became synonymous with modern large-scale factory production in general. Under the Fordist management regime – with its integration of scientific management principles and the major technological innovation of the assembly line – organization is geared to mass production (Womack *et al.*, 1990). One sees the progressive development of specialized machinery operated by closely supervised, deskilled labour to mass produce a standardized product for stable, homogeneous mass markets. Cost reduction is perceived as the main source of competitive advantage and radical product and process innovations are systematically sacrificed in favour of efficiency. In essence, Porter's cost leadership strategy rules supreme.

Fordism rests on the assumption that large numbers of customers have identical wants to be serviced by a rationalized and product-specific manufacturing procedure. The dominant Fordist marketing and production strategies before 1980 were predicated upon product market stability and the maximization of scale economies through a highly integrated division of labour based on dedicated machinery, deskilling of labour and direct managerial control, with finely defined tasks and the detailed, centralized planning of work. This approach has important implications for personnel management. Beynon (1984) argues that two elements, productivity and continuity of production, were at the heart of Ford's industrial relations policy in the 1970s, as they were in many other companies.

In the 1980s the nature of the strategic challenges facing firms changed radically. The key strategic task became responsiveness to new forms of fast-changing demand and the key organizational task the efficient and innovative management of a portfolio of associated rather than standardized products in fluctuating batch sizes and specifications. These demands placed a premium upon increased work organization flexibility and the active cooperation of an upskilled, more versatile workforce. The achievement of these new forms of work organization, in turn, placed a premium upon a rethinking of human resource management practices.

The new emphasis is on economies of scope which demand flexible technology flexibly used and an adaptable workforce that adjusts quickly to new patterns of organization, rather than dedicated machines and semi-skilled workers (Piore and Sabel, 1984).

Flexibility, the capacity to produce a range of different products at the lowest total cost, is increasingly seen as more important than reducing the cost of any one product to the technically attainable minimum (Sabel, 1982: 202). At the very least economies of scale must be balanced by economies of scope – that is, economies enabling the production of a variety of products as opposed to the mass production of single products.

This is not to say that economies of scale are now irrelevant to competitive performance. Rather, the balance between workforce rationalization, the intensification of inherited working practices and the pursuit of new flexible patterns of work organization is dependent upon the scale, scope and speed of the decline and decomposition of demand for an enterprise's core, standardized products and the associated speed of product renewal. The precise nature of this balance hinges upon a series of strategic choices linking novel and established marketing and production priorities within an overall strategic change agenda.

There is then a crucial link between the nature of the market and organization and job design. In mass markets for standardized goods, the ability to satisfy demand profitably rests on economies of scale and productivity depends upon the elaborate division of labour as the subdivision of tasks not only increases output per unit of input but also increases total output (Sabel, 1982: 34–5). However, if there is no market for the increased output a firm will not expand production to take advantage of a more productive division of labour – even though, by so doing, it could reduce the price of its products. The important strategic decision concerns the balance between the stable and unstable components of demand. To the extent that demand is stable, Fordist principles of specialization are pursued, but these give rise to the problem of inflexibility if the nature of demand becomes less stable and predictable. It was Alfred Sloan's major criticism of Ford himself that the master of Fordism failed to master changes in consumer demand (Sloan, 1986). As demand becomes less stable, more differentiated and more dynamic (i.e. fast changing) it becomes important to build into an organization the capacity for flexibility of response.

Fordism was predicated upon the one-dimensional strategic imperative of economies of scale. Henry Ford's Model T ('any colour as long as it is black') provides its ideal type of product. After Sloan, economies of scope entered the equation but scale still predominated.

Sloan recognized the need to elaborate upon Ford's basic product in response to changing consumer demand. The problem was to resolve the conflict between the need for standardization to cut manufacturing costs and the model diversity required by the increasing range of consumer demand (Womack *et al.*, 1990: 41). He did this by standardizing many parts across General Motors' entire product range, and producing these parts for many years with dedicated production tools. At the same time, he built change into the system by annually altering the external appearance of each car, introducing an endless series of design features to titivate consumer interest. This approach found its apotheosis during the legendary Harley Earl period of almost baroque external styling changes to a product that remained remarkably unchanging in its engineering specification under the shell (Bayley, 1983).

The 'demassification' of the market in the 1980s changed the nature of the design game and brought scope to the fore of management thinking in a far more radical way. Social theorist Alvin Toffler (1980: 248) observes that 'the mass market has split into ever-multiplying, ever-changing sets of mini-markets that demand a continually expanding range of options, models, types, sizes, colors, and customization'. Companies were faced with the need for fundamental change, a point on which marketing gurus agreed.

> The eighties will be remembered in marketing history as the decade of transition. Every established norm in advertising and promotion is being transformed by the new economy and the new technology. We are living through a shift from selling virtually everyone the same thing a generation ago to fulfilling the individual needs and tastes of better-educated consumers by supplying them with customized products and services. (Rapp and Collins, 1987: vii)

The disintegration of Fordism has been stimulated by the decomposition of mass demand for standardized goods coupled with high rates of product innovation, and enabled by the advent of flexible capital equipment under the impetus of the new Japanese competition. Only those companies and nations (Piore and Sabel, 1984) that adopt industrial policies meshing niche marketing across associated product families, and the novel productive capabilities of programmable technologies operated by committed flexible upskilled workforces, can achieve a durable competitive advantage.

## After Japan

For us the key aspect of the emerging HRM agenda is its implications for managers who are ultimately responsible for its implementation. In Ford Motor Company we see management attempting to undo the legacy of a management system that has been phenomenally successful in the past to facilitate the development of new human resource initiatives. This involves managers in a fundamental analysis of their own human resource assumptions, how they should relate to employees and, equally if not more important, how they should relate to each other. At the same time management has had to learn how to balance what it sees as new strategic imperatives to change behaviour with the safeguarding and reinforcement of those traditional management practices, themselves the fruit of past learning, that are still useful. A delicate balancing act indeed! It is important to remind ourselves that in a time of turbulence and change there is something to be said for continuities. Much of the literature on HRM tends to emphasize discontinuity. Firms that have survived over the long term must have been doing something right. The managerial task is to sort the viable in the existing system from those elements that are redundant.

Too strong distinctions between supposedly distinct variants of personnel practice suggest an either/or choice for management; for example, between the production and the HRM models. In practice, different approaches will tend to co-exist, at least during those transition periods when firms move from one model of personnel management to another, as our Ford example illustrates, and even having negotiated such a transition period, elements of previous models might prove worthy of retention. As our Ford example also illustrates, the key personnel problem is to adapt approaches established in a very different competitive environment to the demands of an environment of fast change and unpredictability where principles embedded in previous approaches such as the Fordist paradigm of management no longer apply.

To understand the present we have to be sensitive to the constraints rooted in companies' histories. The majority of firms find themselves faced with a complex transition period in which to negotiate and experiment with the exact balance between continuity and change. They cannot afford the luxury of throwing away the rule-book and starting over. Only firms setting up on greenfield sites start with a *tabula rasa* (Guest, 1989) but even in this apparently privileged situation company tradition can make such developments far more problematic than they initially appear, as Ford itself learned in its attempts to establish a hi-tech electronics components plant in Dundee (Starkey and McKinlay, 1989). The starting points for the present are employee relations and management styles established in very different times, unsuitable for the 'new times' we are now faced with (Murray, 1988). A change agenda can take up to a generation to work through a company as the 'old guard', the previous vanguard, ages and finally retires.

For Ford the major strategic challenge of the 1980s was Japan. Ford of Europe – or, more precisely, some of its top management – awoke to the threat of Japanese competition in 1979. Like many other firms, commentators, analysts and academics, Ford set about examining the roots of Japanese competitive advantage. For much of the 1980s the company was concerned with deciding what constituted the core of the Japanese threat. Ford of Europe's major change initiative of the early 1980s was called 'After Japan'. Further change initiatives in the company throughout the 1980s focused upon Japan and what it has to teach us. In a sense, Ford's experience of the 1980s can be understood as a dialogue, sometimes explicit, other times implicit, with Japan.

The study of Japanese management practices suggests that the link between corporate strategy and HRM comprises four major elements. These are: human resource management practices – their content and rationale; strategic vision – how HRM impacts upon corporate strategy; corporate governance – the representation of stakeholder interests in strategic decision-making; and learning – the critical reflection upon experience and the ongoing search for self-development. We examine each of these in turn.

## Human Resource Management in Japanese Firms

The HRM explanation of Japanese success emphasizes the social organization of production based on such factors as teamwork, skill flexibility, good communication between management and employees so as to tap workers' tacit knowledge, positive organizational culture and long-term employment. At its root is the argument that organizations are social entities that depend, for optimal performance, on trust, subtlety and intimacy, aspects that Ouchi (1981) argues form the basis of Japanese management.

Ouchi (1981) compares Japanese organizations with their Western counterparts. The latter are characterized by short-term employment, individual decision-making, individual responsibility, rapid evaluation and promotion, explicit, formalized control and specialized career paths; while Japanese organizations have lifetime employment, consensual decision-making, collective responsibility, slow evaluation and promotion, implicit, informal control and non-specialized career paths. Western employment practices lead to segmented concern: individuals and groups concerned for their own good and not that of the organization as a whole, so that individualistic and political forms of behaviour result. Japanese management demonstrates holistic concern for the good of the whole.

According to Dr W. Edward Deming, himself a notable influence in teaching the Japanese how to manufacture quality products, the stress on purpose at work and worker self-respect as sources of competitiveness, and a rethinking of the production management system are at the roots of Japanese advances. The conventional Western management approach, he argues, deprives workers of their right to do good work and be proud of themselves. This, according to Deming, 'may be the single most important contribution of management to poor quality and loss of market' (Deming, 1982: 166). A major critique of the conventional Western approach to work organization based on scientific management has it that people seek identity and meaning in work, and that work arrangements in which people have no input in decision making undermine trust, teamwork, and the opportunities that work can and should offer to develop creative, problem-solving, and cooperative capabilities. The alternative posed by Japan and proponents of HRM is to create 'the learning firm [which] is in accord with the pursuit of meaning in work' (Best, 1990: 161).

Influential Japanese managers describe their competitive advantage over the West in HRM terms. Konosuke Matsushita, founder of Matsushita Electric Industrial Company, has this to say:

> We will win and you will lose. You cannot do anything about it because your failure is an internal disease. Your companies are based on Taylor's principles. Worse, your heads are Taylorized too. You firmly believe that sound management means executives on the one side and workers on the other, on the one side men who think and on the other side men who can only work. For you, management is the art of smoothly transferring the executives' ideas to the workers' hands.

> We have passed the Taylor stage. We are aware that business has become terribly complex. Survival is very uncertain in an environment filled with risk, the unexpected and competition . . . We know that the intelligence of a few technocrats – even very bright ones – has become totally inadequate to face these challenges. Only the intellects of all employees can permit a company to live with the ups and downs and the requirements of the new environment. (Best, 1990: 1)

Akio Morita, chairman of Sony, welcomes new recruits to the company with the following greeting:

> Now you have become a Sony employee. You will spend the most brilliant time of your life here. Nobody can live twice. This is the only life you can have, so I want you to become happy at Sony. If you don't feel happy, you better go out and change your job. But if you decide to stay with us, you must devote yourself to make your life happy and also to make your colleagues happy. People work together here for all of us in mutual benefit, mutual interest. (Mintzberg and Quinn, 1991: 847)

One can also consider the Japanese approach from the perspective of optimal forms of managerial control and in terms of 'economies of atmosphere' (Williamson, 1975: 37–9). Bureaucracies develop to facilitate managerial control but they create their own problems. Hierarchies seem inexorably to create their own bureaucratic 'vicious circles' (Crozier, 1964). Managers strive to extend and impose rules. Those 'subject' to these rules resist and strive to subvert them. Centralization and impersonality create conflict, communication distortion and breakdown no matter how elaborate and all-encompassing the rule-book.

> The battle between superiors and subordinates involves a basic strategy by which subordinates resist rules which encroach upon their discretion, whilst pressing for rules which will limit the discretion of their superiors over them. (Pugh et al., 1983: 128)

Bureaucracy breeds inertia as both superiors and subordinates cling to rules that become increasingly inappropriate to the extent that the firm's environment changes. The success of Japanese enterprise suggests that management style can break the log-jam of bureaucracy. This argument is most clearly articulated in Ouchi's (1981) comparison of bureaucratic and clan forms of management. Clan management is the term used to characterize the Japanese approach. Williamson and

Ouchi (1981) address this issue in terms of forms of contracting within organizations. They argue that there are two major options which they designate as 'hard' and 'soft' contracting. Under hard contracting, the parties pursue tightly defined (closed) contracts to maximize their own interests. Soft contracting presumes much closer identity of interest between parties and the formal contract is much less complete (more open). Bureaucracy is characterized by hard contracting, the clan-management style is associated with soft contracting. Whereas the former relies heavily on legal and economic sanctions, the latter relies much more on social controls and relationships of trust. 'As compared with hard contracting, soft contracting appeals more to the spirit than to the letter of the agreement' (Williamson and Ouchi, 1981: 361).

There are obvious parallels between soft contracting and the management practices espoused by Peters and Waterman in their study of excellent companies. Soft contracting is particularly appropriate in conditions of environmental uncertainty where hard contracts cannot be drawn up in the detail needed to accommodate all the uncertainties of an unpredictable future. Successful management needs to address the economics of atmosphere. Studies of clan management demonstrate that between alternative forms of internal organization, the clan appears to realize greater advantage in circumstances in which uncertainty is great. The clan would appear to be most appropriate, therefore, in service industries, high technology industries, and others characterized by extreme performance ambiguity. The Japanese, however, seem able to use the clan management approach in a variety of other industries, including automobile companies. Increased levels of uncertainty are afflicting a growing number of industries, making hierarchical and bureaucratic forms less appropriate (Clark and Starkey, 1988).

Much of the debate about Japan has tended to focus on relative productivity and efficiency in manufacture, and on quality. More recently product development has emerged as a key issue (Clark and Fujimoto, 1991). John Oldfield, Ford of Europe Vice-President for product programmes, has recently set out the challenge in this area in stark terms: 'Unless we can manage more product programmes faster, at lower cost and with lower investment, we will not be competitive' (Done, 1992). At issue here is the strategic flexibility to respond to dynamic consumer markets (Starkey, Wright and Thompson, 1991). Firms are differentiating their products both by offering extended product ranges – in automobiles, Toyota's Lexus, Nissan Infiniti and Ford's Jaguar, for example – and, perhaps more significantly, by the constant updating of their existing model range through accelerated product development. Product differentiation through speedy product development rather than the proliferation of numerous product derivatives at any one point in time is the emerging strategic agenda. Japanese firms' speed of product development clearly distinguishes them from Western firms in a variety of industries. Production flexibility is sustained by the skilled use of new manufacturing technologies and a product development process based on simultaneous engineering with product design and manufacturing working in tandem rather than the sequential functional specialization of the West, and the integration of suppliers into just-in-time relationships to facilitate the prompt response to fluctuation in demand. HRM, as we shall see, has a major role to play in improving the product development process.

## Strategic Vision

Pucik and Hatvany (1983) argue that what distinguishes Japanese management is its ability to combine cultural, organizational, and strategic imperatives in an integrated management system. Japanese HRM practices impact upon business strategy in a variety of ways. The socialization into a company culture characterized by its own unique sense of purpose helps develop competitive spirit. Long-term commitment of core employees to the company and the company's commitment to them generates a long-term perspective. Management systems motivate employees throughout the company to commit themselves to long-term growth-orientated strategies based on continuous improvement and innovation.

It is generally accepted that the Japanese firm is organic and entrepreneurial rather than mechanistic and bureaucratic, less planned therefore less rigid and more mission-driven than the Western firm (Ohmae, 1983). Hamel and Prahalad (1989) claim that a fundamental difference between Western and Japanese companies is attributable to their different sense of mission. Western strategic thinking, they argue, is dominated by notions of strategic fit between resources and opportunities. Typically, competitor analysis focuses on the existing resources (human, technical and financial) of present competitors but Hamel and Prahalad argue that assessing the *current* tactical advantages of known competitors will not help you understand the threat of potential competitors. The emphasis on strategic fit, the typical Western strategic frame of reference, is on trimming ambitions to match available resources. The opposite to strategic fit is 'strategic intent', leveraging resources in pursuit of seemingly unrealistic long-term goals, a strategy pursued by successful Japanese firms. The focus on the long-term mission (Canon's 'Beat Xerox', Komatsu's 'Encircle Caterpillar', Honda's 'Success against all the odds') can lead to spectacular long-term developments in firms that are not immediately identifiable as threats.

The emphasis on strategic fit can only lead to incremental short-term gains. Strategic fit is geared to the search for advantages that are inherently sustainable, while strategic intent emphasizes the need to accelerate organizational learning to outpace competitors in building new advantages, and the proactive quest for new rules that can devalue the incumbent's advantages. Strategic intent is clear about ends but flexible as to means. It differs from a purely incremental approach in its long-term goal of shaping the environment rather than adapting to it, and is based on the obsession with winning at all levels of the organization in the battle for global markets. Winning becomes the organization's *raison d'être*. Management focuses the organization's attention on the essential task of beating the competition. Crucially, strategic intent lengthens the organization's attention span, while providing consistency to short-term action, and provides a common set of objectives throughout the organization, not different goals for each business unit, as in portfolio planning.

The key strategic goal is not to find a niche within an existing industry structure as in the Western approach. Hamel and Prahalad see this as competitive suicide because it is based on conformity to the existing industry roles which are defined by industry leaders. With strategic intent the key goal is to redefine the nature of competition, to redefine industry structure. The only goal that is worthy of commitment is 'to unseat the best or remain the best'. HRM is a key factor in this endeavour because the organization's capacity to improve existing skills and learn new ones is the most defensible competitive advantage of all. *The* challenge of the 1990s, according to Hamel and Prahalad, will be to enfranchise employees to invent the means to accomplish ambitious ends. Developing a shared vision is an integral part of articulating a shared culture. HR tasks associated with the development of strategic vision include empowering people through information, building teamwork and developing a shared set of values to inculcate a shared sense of purpose.

Hamel and Prahalad (1989: 72–3) are dismissive of the reductionism of Western strategic thinking, arguing that it is worrying to think that 'the essence of Western strategic thought can be reduced to eight rules for excellence, 7 S's, 5 competitive forces, 4 product life-cycle stages, three generic strategies, and innumerable two-by-two matrices'. This limits the number of strategic options management is willing to consider and creates a preference for selling businesses rather than developing them. It also yields predictable strategies that make you very vulnerable to competition. They conclude that the strategist's primary goal should be not to find a niche within an existing industry space (i.e. playing by existing rules), but to create a new space off the map that is uniquely suited to the company's own strengths. Strategic vision, they argue, depends on the ability of top management to harness the efforts of multiple teams towards ambitious strategic goals, not on the isolated activity of entrepreneurial individuals and small teams pursuing their own ends. This recalls the comment of one researcher that senior managers at Honda are 'romantics who go in quest of the ideal' (Nonaka, 1991: 103).

## Corporate Governance

The term 'corporate governance' encompasses the entire set of incentives, safeguards and dispute-resolution processes that orders the activities of various corporate stakeholders. According to Rappaport (1990: 103), 'Governance is the final frontier of reform in the public company . . . What most public companies lack, and what institutions must work to create, is a governance system that provides an effective monitoring of and checks on managerial authority'.

The concept of stakeholder is fundamental here (Freeman, 1984). The term stakeholder refers to any group or individual who has a legitimate expectation of a firm. Stakeholders include stockholders, employees, customers, suppliers, creditors, managers, local community, special interest groups such as environmentalists, the general public, government and any other groups who have entered into relationships with the firm. The implication of thinking of the organization as a complex array of stakeholders, each with their own legitimate expectations, is that managers must ask themselves searching questions about the nature of these expectations.

In firms such as Ford one can construe major changes in management approach as, in part, a redefinition of the corporation's responsibility to its employees and other stakeholders. Here Japanese management practices have played an important role in changing accepted managerial wisdom in the West. Japanese management seems more oriented to the maximization of the interests of employees than shareholders and it has been suggested that this has helped Japanese firms develop a long-term approach to strategy, free of the short-term market for corporate control constraints that operate in the West. Stakeholder analysis suggests that the Japanese firm attributes more importance to employee welfare than the Western firm.

Life-time employment of core workers in Japan is a vivid expression of the employer's sense of responsibility. Akio Morita's welcome to new employees sounds strange to Western ears in its emphasis on long-term commitment to the company but, according to Morita, it is life-time employment that presents the acid test of managerial responsibility for employee welfare. It is a nettle the Japanese have grasped. According to Morita, people in the West are always talking about human rights, but when the recession hits them they don't hesitate to cut down on their work force. The Japanese believe that if you have a family you cannot just eliminate certain members of that family because profits are down. Nor is it motivating to be informed that, according to the portfolio planning techniques used by your company, you are a 'cash cow' or a 'dog', ripe only for harvesting or divestment.

In the West the demand for more responsible behaviour from employees in the form of increased efficiency and quality is often perceived as a threat by the employee to his/her own welfare. This presents a major problem in developing a sense of mutual responsibility between management and workforce. In the words of one Western manager from Xerox, a leading company in responding to the lessons of the Japanese style of management:

> We need to get over the hurdle that means that efficiency, quality and competence results in loss of jobs. You need to have a sense of security to take risks with new jobs and new skills.

A key factor in the Japanese system is the relationships of trust between long-term stakeholders rather than the potential for short-term financial gain. Japanese companies prefer long-term trust relationships with other companies based on implicit, bilaterally self-enforcing contracts to ownership of these companies. It is a system of corporate governance that has largely obviated the necessity for a large market for corporate control in Japan itself, has limited the activity of Japanese companies in foreign markets – in the US, for example, Japanese corporations were involved in 132 mergers and acquisitions transactions in 1988 at a total cost of US$12.6 billion compared with the 389 transactions by British firms for a total of US$31.7 billion – and has kept Japanese companies immune from foreign bidders (Kester, 1991). The term 'Japan Inc' (Eli, 1990) encapsulates some of the issues in this area. It denotes the phenomenon of a highly efficient interaction of economics and politics, administration and society, based on the joint efforts of Japanese industrial groupings, the *kigyo keiretsu*, which is unique to Japan.

Here one needs to qualify Hamel and Prahalad's one-dimensional focus on winning as the essence of strategic intent. Strategy is certainly about competition but it is also, and perhaps increasingly, about cooperation. Corporate responsibility to society is of increasing strategic importance. Visionary organizations whose missions capitalize on emerging social trends have been among the success stories of the 1970s and 1980s. Body Shop, with its new vision of the cosmetic industry as socially responsible, is a case in point. Apple, with its vision of democratizing the computer industry by bringing computer power to the people, also springs to mind. At the turn of the century Henry Ford's vision of democratizing the automobile industry led to mass production and the spectacular early success of the company he founded. Other visions focus on internal transformation. The 'Aspirations Statement' of Levi-Strauss, for example, begins: 'We all want a company that our people are proud of and committed to, where all employees have an opportunity to contribute, learn, grow and advance based on merit, not politics or background.' Mission statements increasingly refer to a broad range of stakeholders. This represents a broadening of firms' responsibility agendas, particularly in the area of internal stakeholders, driven by a reanalysis and redefinition of their core values.

## Learning

A central question posed by Ouchi (1981) is: what can we learn from Japan? The *can* is important. Learning has three facets:

*content* – what there is to learn
*ability* – the capability of the learner to assimilate lessons
*will* – how willing individuals, groups and organizations are to rethink their current behaviours as they assimilate new learning

One of the major lessons Japanese firms have to teach us is how to learn.

Michael Cusumano points out in his pioneering history of the Japanese automobile industry (1985) that it is a story of Western lapses and Japanese innovations, innovations based upon a sophisticated capacity for continuously improving the knowledge that performs the basis of strategic decision-making and action. Japanese firms initially learned from the West and, having learned how to emulate Western best practice, continued the learning process to see how they could extend, refine and, where necessary, change Western practices.

Critically, Japanese managers such as Toyota's Taiichi Ohno did not accept US practices as the *only* viable way to produce automobiles and did not believe that US firms had reached the limits possible for capital and worker productivity, quality or inventory turnover (Cusumano, 1988). In contrast, by the early 1960s American managers had come to view automobile manufacturing as a stable, 'mature' industry with predetermined limits to productivity and quality, unit costs and minimum efficient scales of production. The original 'American paradigm', based on principles of mass production and economies of scale, and increasingly espoused by European managers, was thus characterized by large production runs, push-type production scheduling, extreme worker specialization, and quality control through inspection. This paradigm provided the model for the UK industry. The Ryder Report of 1975 used it as its benchmark to criticize the declining UK auto companies and as the basis for an attempted rationalization of the UK's fragmented industry.

Indeed this approach to manufacturing was extremely successful at high-volume production of a limited range of models. In Japan, limited demand and the fragmented nature of the home market led Toyota and then other Japanese producers to become equally then more efficient at far lower volumes through incremental (but, over time, major) improvements in a variety of areas, such as higher worker output and utilization rates for machinery, faster inventory turnover and ever higher quality. 'Just-in-time' systems entailed the ongoing eradication of defective parts and equipment breakdowns. Also, 'Japanese workers producing in smaller lots found they paid greater attention to what they were doing – as opposed to American workers making thousands of components of one type, with large piles of buffer stocks to draw on if they made mistakes' (Cusumano, 1988: 22). What the Japanese discovered was the virtue of 'lean production', whose core principles include teamwork, communication, the efficient use of resources, the elimination of waste, and continuous improvement (Womack et al., 1990). Lean production welds the activities of everyone in the organization from top management to line workers and suppliers into an integrated whole that can respond with unprecedented speed to changing market demand.

The decline of much of Western manufacturing can be attributed to a failure to appreciate that one needs to go on learning. One manager with experience of working in both the West and Japan captures a key difference in the following observation:

> The contrast between Western and Japanese cultures hits you between the eyes at teamwork presentations when teams present their project-work. The Westerners expect praise and to be told 'That's a wonderful job. Thank you very much'. But the Japanese teams would be most disappointed to receive such adulation. They would ask 'Tell me how to get better'. In Fuji Xerox, the best teams are severely criticized and asked what their plans are for improvement. It goes back to the Samurai principles and to their religious philosophy. This tells them that a person does not reach the equivalent of heaven unless he has tried all his life to improve himself and has helped others to do the same. (Giles and Starkey, 1988)

A key lesson of the work of Argyris (1991) is that company success depends upon learning but that the well-educated, high-powered, apparently highly committed managers in the Western firm are usually not very good at learning and are very defensive when it comes to critically examining their own behaviour. Their whole career development emphasis has been on acting as 'productive loners', often in competition with their peers. Learning is threatening because the very act of accepting that you need to learn is seen as an admission of failure and a cause for guilt. Yet the self-renewal of organization requires the dissolution of the existing organizational order and the only means for accomplishing this is learning (Nonaka, 1988).

Nonaka (1991) characterizes the best Japanese companies as 'knowledge-creating': 'To create new knowledge means quite literally to re-create the company and everyone in it in a nonstop process of personal and organizational self-renewal' (Nonaka, 1991: 97). This requires not the processing of 'hard' 'objective' 'facts'. Rather it involves tapping knowledge that individuals are only vaguely aware they possess, tacit knowledge, which is then widely disseminated and tested to judge its general usefulness. The best that top management can do is to clear away any obstacles and prepare the way for self-organizing groups or teams. According to Jaikumar (1986), in the factory of the future the new role of management will be to develop project teams whose intellectual capabilities produce competitive advantage. What has to be managed is intellectual capital and not just equipment.

Honda's success in the US was based upon learning rather than streamlined strategic planning (Pascale, 1988). Success was achieved by senior managers humble enough to learn from their subordinates. Middle and upper management saw their primary task as guiding and orchestrating this input from below rather than steering the organization from above along a predetermined strategic course. Strategic management was essentially about 'strategic accommodation' and 'adaptive persistence', the sensitive adjustment to unfolding events. Pascale sees this kind of approach to be at the roots of Japanese success with all employees contributing incrementally to such things as the improvement of quality. He argues that in Japanese firms it is rare for one leader (or a strategic planning group) to produce an overarching strategy that guides a firm unerringly from the top. Far more frequently inputs are from below and information and ideas move from the bottom to the top and back again in 'continuous dialogue'. In this way strategy evolves as the organization adapts to and shapes its environment.

Pascale (1990) contrasts the learning capacity of Honda and General Motors (GM). In GM the finance function dominates the entire organization. In Honda decision-making is far more dispersed and responsive to the views of different functional groups. In General Motors the status quo dominates, and newcomers are socialized into conformity with it. Honda encourages constructive dissent and challenge. Privilege and status at GM are dependent upon position in the elaborate bureaucracy. In Honda rewards follow initiative and achievement. The Honda management process stimulates learning, GM's inhibits it. Honda has thrived, GM is struggling against what some analysts perceive as terminal sclerosis and a white-collar bureaucracy that has proved particularly resistant to change. Former GM CEO Roger Smith described this as the 'frozen middle'. In Japanese organizations middle management has a crucial role to play in what Nonaka (1991) calls 'compressive management'.

> The essential logic of compressive management is that top management creates a vision or dream, and middle management creates and implements concrete concepts to solve and transcend the contradictions arising from gaps between what exists at the moment and what management hopes to create. . . . Mr Tadashi Kume, president of Honda, expresses the role of middle management as follows: 'I create dreams . . . John at Honda Ohio is not able to see the company's overall direction. We at corporate headquarters see the world differently . . . It is middle management that is charged with integrating the two viewpoints emanating from top and bottom management. There can be no progress without such integration'. (Nonaka, 1991: 129)

## Quality and Two Management Legacies

We can discern two traditions of thinking about management coming together in the HRM approach (see figure 1.1).

These are the dominant tradition, based upon scientific management and Fordism, with its emphasis on science, economics, rules and structure, and the dissident human relations tradition with its emphasis on social needs and the search for value, in a non-economic sense. In the West the dissident tradition finds its latest expression in the highly influential 'excellence' movement (Peters and Waterman, 1982). Japan drew together what it considered the best aspects of the two traditions in the post-World War Two period, strongly influenced, ironically, by Western gurus such as Deming, Juran and Drucker, as well as the production philosophy of Henry Ford.

Drucker (1990) himself argues that in the new emphasis on quality 'after Japan' we are beginning to see emerging a new science of management that resolves the differences of the two traditions. Drucker's argument is that (1) the introduction of statistical quality control (SQC), based on the work of Deming and Juran, is radically changing thinking about manufacturing management through its impacts on the social organization of the factory, and (2) that the

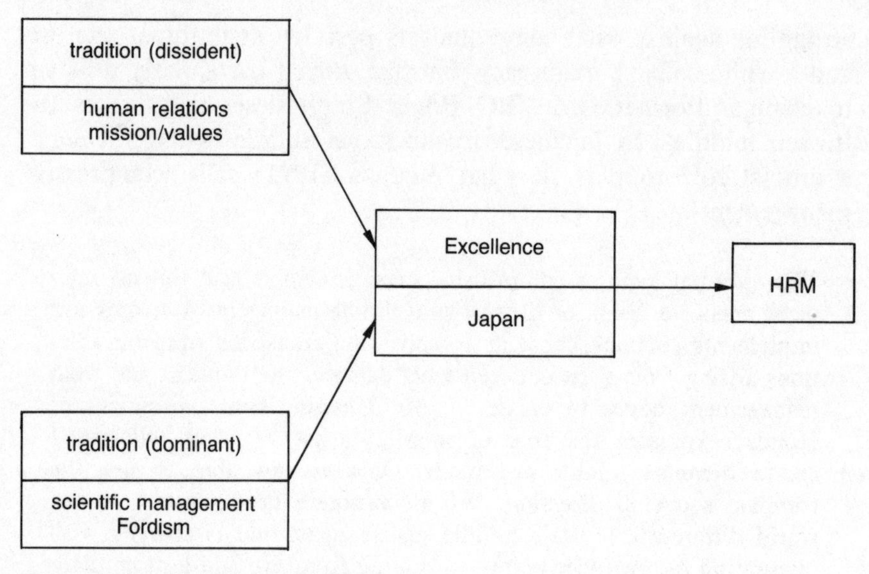


**Figure 1.1** The origins of HRM

West has to follow Japan in this respect. By aligning information with accountability SQC resolves the apparently irresolvable conflict between the 'scientific management' and the 'human relations' approaches. Both of these approaches were aimed at improving quality and productivity but, according to Drucker, it is only with the advent of SQC that the management of manufacture becomes truly scientific, and the dream of Taylor, and worker pride and knowledge (the key factors in the human relations approach), can be fully capitalized upon:

> without SQC's rigorous methodologies neither scientific management nor the assembly line could actually deliver built-in process control. With all their successes, both scientific management and the assembly line had to fall back on massive inspection, to fix problems rather than eliminate them.
>
> The human-relations approach sees the knowledge and pride of line workers as the greatest resource for controlling and improving quality and productivity. . . . But without the kind of information SQC provides, you cannot readily distinguish productive activity from busy-ness. It is hard to tell whether a proposed modification will truly improve the process. (Drucker, 1990: 96)

SQC provides the knowledge technology to design both quality and productivity into the manufacturing process by giving responsibility for the process and control of it to the only people who can assure quality – the machine operators. A major by-product of the new emphasis on quality is the establishment of a common language for both management and employees, with mutually acceptable objective definitions of terms, to discuss and negotiate the strategic problems facing the company. The language of quality, therefore, provides an important source of and impetus to consensus.

## Organization and Strategy

Although recent management writing, particularly that of Peters and Waterman, has emphasized that structure is not the only organizational variable that is important in strategic analysis, structure, in particular in its implications for the overall management process, is still of great importance, and particularly in the context of the multinational corporation (MNC). A central managerial issue that the MNC must resolve is the tension between central control and local autonomy. The single most important organizational question for the MNC is a governance issue – the degree of decentralization of decision-making that is most appropriate to its strategic concerns.

There have historically been three answers to this question according to the 'state of the art' study of the issue, Bartlett and Ghoshal's *Managing Across Borders* (1989). They describe these as *multinational* companies (the typical European structure and management approach developed before World War II), *international* companies (the approach developed by American MNCs after World War II) and *global* companies (the Japanese response of the 1970s and 1980s). (Bartlett and Ghoshal's use of the term 'multinational' is rather confusing until you remember that they use it to describe one particular strategic response while others use it as a generic term to describe the full range of companies competing internationally regardless of their structure and management approach.)

The key strategic strength of the *multinational* in Bartlett and Ghoshal's typology is its ability to build a strong local presence through sensitivity and responsiveness to national differences in demand. Many key assets, responsibilities and decisions are decentralized in this approach. Each national subsidiary is given a high degree of independence for strategic and operational decisions.

Management regards overseas operations as a portfolio of independent businesses.

The *international* organization adopts a different approach. Its main strength is its ability to exploit parent company knowledge and capabilities through its worldwide diffusion with limited local adaptation. The centre acts as the source of new product and process knowledge. Management regards overseas operations as appendages to a central domestic operation. Many assets, resources, responsibilities and decisions are decentralized but decision-making has to be ratified by, and is therefore still controlled by, the centre. A key source of competitive advantage is technology transfer (product or process) from the centre to subsidiaries.

The *global* company differs from the other two forms in degree of central control. Its main strength is the ability to build cost advantages through centralized global-scale operations. Most strategic assets, resources, responsibilities and decisions are centralized with tight central control of decisions, resources and information. Management treats overseas operations as merely delivery pipelines to a unified global market. Hence, in the United Kingdom, for example, the Japanese are criticized for investing only in 'screwdriver' assembly plants with strategic decision-making and product development done in Japan.

Each of these forms of organization has its own strengths. Each thrives in particular market conditions, the *multinational* form in markets that demand local sensitivity and responsiveness to a variety of demand at the local level, the *international* when the key source of competitive advantage is the transfer of knowledge with broad applications, the *global* when the key industry issue is global efficiency.

Ford historically provides classic examples of two of these forms. Under Henry Ford it dominated the world market for low-priced automobiles by exporting from its US Highland Park plant, at the time the most efficient production facility in the world. This was the classic global strategy replicated by the Japanese 50 years later (Barlett and Ghoshal, 1989: 46). With the increasing globalization of its business a certain degree of local responsiveness became necessary, but core competencies were retained in Detroit, its US headquarters.

In this phase of its development Ford fits the multinational organization model well in its particular complex of managerial culture and structure.

> These [US] companies [such as Ford] had built a reputation for professional management that implied a willingness to delegate responsibility, while retaining overall control through sophisticated management systems and the specialist corporate staffs. The systems provided channels for a regular flow of information, to be interpreted by the central staffs. Holding the managerial reins, top management could control the free-running team of independent subsidiaries and guide the direction in which they headed. . . . Despite corporate management's increased understanding of its overseas markets, it often seemed to view foreign operations as appendages whose principal purpose was to leverage the capabilities and resources developed in the home market. (Bartlett and Ghoshal, 1989: 50)

This 'appendage' mentality was reflected in the fact that between 1949 and 1961 Ford of America reacquired ownership of all its European interests, including the purchase of the share capital of Ford of Britain.

Ford's restructuring of its global empire into regional divisions was a watershed in multinational development. Before 1945 Ford was little more than a 'collection of truncated replicas' of the parent corporation (Auerbach, 1989: 266). Ford and IBM pioneered the development of the multinational as a planned global organization in which national subsidiaries were allocated specific roles within the corporation's European and worldwide strategies. The formation of Ford of Europe in 1967 was the first step in the creation of an integrated network of complementary specialist plants on a continental basis (Stopford and Turner, 1985: 24). But in 1967 Ford of Europe was itself a loose confederation of national manufacturing companies in Britain and Germany and sales companies throughout the continent. Over the next decade Ford of Europe became an increasingly integrated regional division of the global corporation: the continent rather than the nation state became the geographic unit of production (Beynon, 1984: 322–3).

The development of shared products was a critical learning experience for Ford of Europe. Of particular importance were the Capri, Fiesta and Escort product development programmes in slowly building pan-European manufacturing and marketing strategies and structures. These development programmes were crucial mechanisms for the final triumph of Detroit management processes in marketing and product planning (Bayley, 1983: 11–12). By 1976 Ford's pursuit of plant specialization and economies of scale had reaped a 10 to 15 per cent manufacturing efficiency advantage above the European average.

In theory, Ford of Europe is simply an organization coordinating the activities of independent national companies. In practice, however, Ford of Europe, rather than the national companies, has become the locus of all strategic decision-making and financial planning by 1979. Despite their full range of directors and executives, national companies such as Ford UK and Ford Werke exist primarily to satisfy particular legal requirements and act as the public face of Ford of Europe. All functional managements report directly to the appropriate Ford of Europe Vice President regardless of their national location. The essence of Ford of Europe's control system is the separation of activities into cost and revenue centres. National sales companies are revenue centres while every operating unit is a cost centre. This management information system consolidates cost, revenue and profit only at the European level. 'Ford UK', one European executive explained, 'is a legal fiction'. The locus of strategic decision-making is Ford of Europe and the parent company, not the constituent national companies.

Ford of Europe is by far the largest of the corporation's four autonomous regional companies reporting to Detroit – Europe, Asia Pacific, Latin America and Mid-East and Africa. There is only limited and indirect contact between these self-contained regional firms. What then is currently the relationship between Ford of Europe and global management in Detroit? As we shall see later this is a crucial question. Effectively, Detroit maintains its presence at the very peak of the European company but does not intervene in operational matters. The relationship between Detroit and the European headquarters at Warley, near London, is principally financial, rather than on a strict command and control basis. In reply to hostile questioning from a House of Commons Select Committee in 1975, Terence Beckett, Chairman of Ford UK, stressed that the loose coordinating role of Ford of Europe over its national companies was typical of the corporation as a whole. Ford Motor Company, insisted Beckett, was not hierarchical 'in an army sense or a Church sense'. Rather, 'the initiative comes from the bottom, the middle and the top. It is an interaction and an exchange' (Beckett, 1975: 238). And Ford of Europe management does indeed enjoy a high degree of discretion within its field of operations. Detroit prefers to set financial and market targets for the European company rather than detailed operational parameters. Ford of Europe is expected to generate 25 per cent of the corporation's earnings, achieve a 12 per cent market share in Europe as a whole and compete in every major market segment. In a strategic rather than operational sense the relationship is, as we hope to show, more complex.

Ford of Europe prides itself that it has a truly multinational management team, drawn from the national companies and their American parent. Executives frequently combine European and national company responsibilities with staffs in both Warley and Cologne. Although only a tiny proportion of Ford of Europe's staff are American they are concentrated at the very peak of the organization. Unlike GM, whose overseas operations were a corporate backwater with little cross-fertilization with Detroit headquarters until the early 1980s, in Ford an international posting was an essential prerequisite to a successful career from the mid-1950s. All the principal players in Ford's American turnaround in the 1980s – Philip Caldwell, Don Petersen and Red Poling – had either served in Ford of Europe (Caldwell and Poling) or had responsibility for Europe (Petersen as Vice-President of International Automotive Operations in the US). But beneath the fluid and almost wholly American apex of Ford of Europe there is a thin layer of permanent Vice Presidents who exercise power far beyond that suggested by their organizational rank (Alex Trotman, 1988: 4). This is especially true of manufacturing, the only area in which the functional apex has been dominated by European nationals.

## The Transnational Imperative

Changing conditions of global competition demand a new form of organization. The key strategic issues now encompass both global efficiency and responsiveness to the increasing variety of local conditions. Bartlett and Ghoshal (1989) describe the new organization necessary for this fast-changing context as *transnational*. The successful transnational, if and when it is developed – there is some uncertainty to whether any firm as yet has achieved this status – will demonstrate global competitiveness, multinational flexibility *and* worldwide learning. Its assets, resources, responsibilities and decisions will be dispersed *and* interdependent, subsidiaries given specific roles according to their special competencies, and there will be *joint development and worldwide sharing* of learning.

The key management tasks in the transnational include the

legitimization and balancing of diverse perspectives, the development of multiple and flexible coordinating processes, the building of individual commitment in pursuit of a shared vision and the joint development and worldwide sharing of knowledge. Multinational flexibility requires differentiated contributions by national units to the centrally integrated worldwide operations; specialized subsidiary roles built on core strengths but flexible and interdependent in terms of the total global needs of the business. The transnational provides global integration, local differentiation where necessary and worldwide innovation in the sense that innovation anywhere in this new form of corporation is quickly diffused throughout the organization.

To enable it to do this it needs a range of novel features. Each national unit is a source of ideas, skills and capabilities that can be harnessed for the benefit of the total organization. National units achieve global scale by making them the company's world source for a particular product, component, or activity. The centre adopts a new, highly-complex managing role which coordinates relationships between units but does so in a highly-flexible way in which the key is to focus less on managing activities directly and more upon creating an organizational context which is conducive to the coordination and the resolution of differences (Grant, 1991).

Creating the right organizational context involves 'establishing clear corporate objectives, developing managers with broadly-based perspectives and relationships, and fostering supportive organizational norms and values' (Bartlett and Ghoshal, 1989: 388). The key strategic issue becomes, in Sony's terminology, 'global localization'. What the transnational requires is a form of 'denationalization', a sense of global identity and responsibility that is not dominated by a national parent.

The international organization model in Bartlett and Ghoshal's typology is too loosely coupled in its relations between the centre and its subsidiaries. The latter have too much autonomy: there is no synergy between them and no coherent sense of identity or interdependence. Centrifugal forces tend to pull this form apart. The decision of Philips' North American subsidiary to outsource video cassette recorders manufactured by Japanese rivals rather than adopt the company's own V2000 is an extreme example of these forces. Not surprisingly it was Matsushita's VHS system that became the industry standard. At the other extreme, the global organization is too dominated by the centre. Local management has little sense of autonomy and little motivation to be creative. Its relationship is one of dependence. Here the dominance of home country nationals in senior positions poses an increasing problem. As a result, local national managers tend to feel isolated and excluded from positions of real influence and power. Bartlett and Ghoshal (1989: 184) capture the frustrations of the local manager, an American working for Matsushita, in the following quotation.

> It is ironic that the very factors that have made this company's management of its production workers abroad so successful [participation in decision-making, job security and advancement opportunities, and an egalitarian attitude] all seem to be missing from their treatment of management. I am becoming very doubtful that I can look forward to a satisfying career here.

The international form does not suffer to the same extent from this problem but there is a sense of over-dominance by the centre and the over-representation of home country nationals in key managerial positions that raises the question of the subsidiary's role in the grander scheme of things. Is there real mutuality in the relationship between parent and subsidiary or, in the final analysis, will the good of the parent be paramount? This is an important issue which, as we shall see, impacts upon strategic and HRM initiatives.

The present performance of the firm is, in hidden, subtle but important ways, hostage to its administrative heritage. We return constantly to this issue because we believe it is one of the most important facing the large, multinational organization. First, we need to gain a deeper knowledge of the emerging corporate strategy/human resource management agenda as experienced by one of its pioneers, Ford Motor Company in the United States.

# 2

# Corporate Strategy and Human Resource Management in Ford: the US Experience

Ford Motor Company in the 1980s provides a paradigmatic example of a major rethinking of the link between corporate strategy and human resource management (HRM). We choose to concentrate on Ford for four reasons: (a) because of the magnitude of the changes it is working through and what this teaches us generally about issues in the strategy/HRM areas; (b) because of Ford's seminal importance as pioneer of the dominant production approach to management (Fordism); (c) because it has been among the most proactive of Western companies in learning from Japan – in our experience only Xerox rivals it in this respect (Giles and Starkey, 1988); and (d) because the changes it initiated during the 1980s reflect a critical re-evaluation of the production approach and a significant move in the direction of HRM for strategic reasons. In the complexity of this process – the evolution of knowledge in the dynamic, complex context of the multi-national company in the throes of major strategic change – Ford's experience is of a broad relevance beyond its own immediate context.

## The Old Ford Culture

To understand the magnitude of the change process in Ford one has to understand its history. The Ford Motor Company was once synonymous with the creation of a particular management style, Fordism, based on bureaucratic organization, hierarchical decision-making with strict functional specialization and tightly defined job design (scientific management), and specialized machinery to mass produce a standard product for mass markets.

Historically, Alfred Sloan's work at General Motors provided the 'necessary complement' to Henry Ford's (Womack et al., 1990: 39). He added to Ford's factory practices new marketing and professional management techniques, particularly in the area of finance.

> It isn't giving Sloan too much credit to say that his basic management ideas solved the last pressing problems inhibiting the spread of mass production. New professions of financial managers and marketing specialists were created to complement the engineering professions, so that every functional area of the firm now had its dedicated experts. The division of professional labor was complete. (Womack et al., 1990: 41)

Managerial professionalism came to Ford late and only after the death of its founder. Henry Ford distrusted everyone but himself so he was not ready to share the reins of power with anybody else. It was Henry Ford II who was left to bring order to the chaos his grandfather left. To this end he recruited Robert McNamara and the other 'Whiz Kids' who were to have such a profound effect on the company in the 1950s and 1960s. McNamara came to Ford after the Second World War. He summed up his time at Ford in the following words: 'My real contribution to Ford was to turn a family company into an omniscient operating system . . . a modern American corporation'. He added, 'I would go out of my way to discourage my son from working in that system.' What he and his group of Whiz Kids – the brightest graduates of the best business schools – introduced into Ford was a management discipline based upon the power of numbers, a discipline the lack of which, under its founder Henry Ford, had brought the company close to disaster. 'Under McNamara, for the first time for more than twenty-five years, the company always knew where it was, how much it was spending and how much it was making, and it could project both costs and earnings' (Halberstam, 1987: 210). The one thing that McNamara did not understand was cars. Ironically it was the emphasis on numbers, the 'bottom line' and the rigid management control system that developed that brought the company again to the brink of disaster in the early 1980s.

McNamara's contribution to Ford was to bring discipline to the accounting system. He found Ford deep in disorder, the worst-run large company in America, rife with waste. Having become president of the company in 1960 he left soon after for even higher things, to become Secretary of State for Defence. His legacy was a company dominated by the Finance function. In the past, manufacturing had been all-powerful. Gradually with the arrival of McNamara and the other 'Whiz Kids' power moved from the factories to Detroit headquarters. The product engineers were also brought to heel:

> in most conflicts between the product people and their counterparts in finance, the advantage lay with the finance people. For the product men were arguing tastes and instinct, and the finance people were arguing certitudes. . . . To [Henry Ford II] a young man unsure of himself, taking over the family firm . . . wary of the excesses of the past and edgy about the future, there was comfort in the clinical new skills of these men. They were his support system, his guarantee that no one would slip something past him.
>
> Out of that need grew the immense power of the finance people. A powerful, confident, modern bureaucracy was being installed at the Ford Motor Company, sure of its skills, sure of its goals. It knew how to take care of itself, to help its own, and above all to replenish itself. For there was no easy way to replenish real car men, no graduate school readily turning out designers who were both creative and professional or manufacturing men who could run a happy, efficient factory. People of instinct and creativity, really talented ones, came along only rarely. The great business schools could not produce genius or intuition, but they could and did turn out every year a large number of able, ambitious young men and women who were good at management, who knew numbers and systems, and who knew first and foremost how to minimize costs and maximize profits. (Halberstam, 1987: 213)

At Ford the Finance function has dominated. Its power is captured in the following quotation:

> One of the many stringent tests which all Ford cars have to pass is to sustain a crash at 30mph into a concrete barrier with less than five inches of steering column penetration. This means that the steering column must not move more than five inches towards a driver. In management terms in Ford, the nearest thing to that concrete barrier is probably the finance staff – and many projects are fated to crumple entirely on impact. (Hackett, 1976: 9.1)

Finance is 'the functional glue that holds the organization together' and as such is synonymous with managerial control and discipline.

Its critics argue that Finance has taken the managerial imperative of control too far.

> Finance is a very disciplined organization. Finance is all about total attention to detail and total overkill. . . . they're empowered to ask dumb questions and to inhibit things. Over-control. I don't think it's a lack of confidence in the quality of management, just an obsession with control. The funny thing was, if anything ever went wrong it wasn't the Finance community's fault.

But Finance, the discipline and the control system it has spawned also have their defenders, particularly among the elite of the company, many of whom have come to the top via Finance.

A typical career at Ford before the changes of the 1980s has been described as follows.

> I joined the Ford Motor Company in 1966, after four years in the US Air Force and graduate studies in Industrial/Organizational Psychology. At age 25, I was thrilled with the opportunity to launch a career in this highly respected, and then stable, organization. Like nearly everyone else, I came to work early and stayed late. But after 90 days I received a sub-par performance evaluation. I responded stoically, but also had visions of losing this opportunity for which I'd worked long and hard to prepare.
>
> I sought guidance from several sympathetic veteran colleagues in the hope of gaining perspective and riding out the storm. They explained that arriving early and staying late was something that the organization valued and, therefore, something I should continue to do. They also told me to continue my work in mastering the written material about my job and the Company, but that there were some important things that I should know that were not written down. A partial list of their advice went something like this:
>
> - Don't disagree with the boss
> - Don't rock the boat
> - Look busy, even if you're not
> - Don't smile, let alone laugh too much
> - Be obsessive about getting your numbers right; estimates won't do
> - CYA [Cover your ass]
> - If a colleague gets into trouble with the boss – don't help; be grateful it's not you
> - Observe the dress code

> They provided me a set of 'unwritten rules' for survival and, possibly, for getting ahead. Not until 15 years later did this advice begin to make sense to me when the subject of 'corporate culture' began to show up in the literature (Deal and Kennedy, Kilmann *et al.*). I have since gotten from Ford colleagues many similar accounts of their early days with the Company, primarily in the pre-1980 era.

A confluence of market and internal factors in the 1980s forced Ford to rethink its organization, its approach to personnel management and its management culture. The changes Ford initiated in the US brought the company back from the very brink of disaster at the end of the 1970s.

The beginning of the 1980s found the company bereft of attractive product and moving ever more deeply into loss. Strategic renewal in Ford was predicated upon a redefining of the link between corporate strategy and HRM. The organizational model for Ford's rethinking of its approach to personnel management was, in part, Japanese-inspired. The company had its close links with Mazda, in which it owns a 25 per cent stake, to serve as a source of competitive benchmarking. This benchmarking formed the basis of its long-term strategy, as did the analysis of what it considered truly outstanding US companies.

Don Petersen (1991), who became Ford Chairman and CEO in 1985, describes the company's situation when he became company president and chief operating officer in 1980. In a triumph of understatement he observes, 'Ford was operating in difficult times back then'. He carries on to describe the magnitude of the difficulties.

> In 1980 alone, it lost more than $1.5 billion – then the second highest one-year loss in US corporate history. To make matters worse, our market share was slipping steadily, and customers were increasingly disenchanted with our cars. We were relying on the same basic theme we had used throughout the 1970s, and we hadn't introduced anything dramatic in years. . . . Ford was rated lowest among the Big Three automakers in the quality and styling of its cars, and it was also pretty obvious by this time that the Japanese automakers had gained a substantial edge over us in the quality of their cars and the efficiency of their factories. (Petersen, 1991: 5–6)

Petersen attributes Japanese success to a sense of common purpose, involvement and teamwork among employees. He refers to the study trips made to Japan by senior Ford executives.

> Before those visits, many of the people at Ford believed that the Japanese were succeeding because they used highly sophisticated machinery. Others thought their industry was orchestrated by Japan's government. The value of our visits, however, lay in Ford people's discovery that the real secret was how the people worked together – how the Japanese companies organized their people into teams, trained their workers with the skills they needed, and gave them the power to do their jobs properly. . . . they had managed to hold on to a fundamental simplicity of human enterprise while we built layers of bureaucracy. This knowledge was essential. (Petersen, 1991: 20)

For Petersen the greatest importance of these trips to Japan was that they convinced Ford management that changes had to be made. Quality became the focus of Petersen's thinking and he turned to Dr W. Edwards Deming for lessons on how to improve it, something Deming had taught the Japanese themselves in the 1950s. Petersen attributes to Deming's statistical process control techniques the return to the assembly line of a sense of discipline, self-esteem and pride in workmanship and the acceptance in the company of the need for continuous improvement. Deming was also instrumental in challenging Ford to rethink its basic philosophy and values.

> At subsequent meetings, Dr Deming began to talk about what he called the next priorities: primarily, the need to eliminate fear from the workplace and give workers the opportunity to do a better job. It all sounded so logical, because it seems to me that Dr Deming's philosophy is rooted in basic concepts of human behavior, such as trusting your fellow man and living by the Golden Rule. Everything he says starts from the importance of the human being and moves on from there. Sometimes I think a lot of us get sidetracked because we believe that everything has to turn on a set of sophisticated or complex notions, but a seemingly simple humanistic philosophy is the well-spring of any transformation. (Petersen, 1991: 9–10)

It was root and branch transformation that Ford set out to achieve.

## Envisaging/Envisioning the Future

The growing sense that the company could not continue in the way it had always done in the post-McNamara era, incrementally improving on the way it had done things in the past, led to a fundamental re-examination of the Ford mission and culture. Petersen and others felt unable to put into simple and straightforward words a set of ideas that employees could understand and aspire to. They also felt it imperative to do this to give the company a clear sense of its future direction.

> An organization's vision is worthless unless employees understand it and are willing to help management carry it out. . . . You have to create a sense of urgency that will dramatize what you're up against and convince everyone that important changes must be made in order to improve. (Petersen, 1991: 18)

A top management team comprising the top three operating people in the company – Petersen himself, Tom Page and Harold ('Red') Poling – set about examining the key concepts they wanted the company to express with a view to putting these on paper. Meetings were conducted with a variety of groups throughout the company. Breakthrough occurred when it was suggested at one of these meetings that Ford's values could be expressed with three P's to make them easy to remember – people, products and profits. According to Petersen, the most important feature of this list of elements was that it put people first.

This point seems to mark a radical transition in Ford's management philosophy and culture. One only has to read Beynon's (1984) *Working for Ford* to appreciate that in general the old Ford approach saw employees as a *means* to an end – profit – rather than an *end* in themselves. This was certainly the way in which employees experienced working for the company. One Ford story describes the dialogue between a Ford recruiter and a potential employee:

> 'What does Ford make?' asked the interviewer.
> 'Cars,' replied the eager interviewee.
> 'No,' the Ford interviewer replied, 'Ford makes profits.'

Petersen himself acknowledges that the old Ford system 'thought of the worker as a single purpose machine tool' (Mintzberg and Quinn, 1991: 482). The new emphasis on people marked a new point of departure.

Having focused on the importance of values and, more importantly, the importance of people as a core value, the group went on to develop a broad statement of its mission, values and guiding principles (figure 2.1).

**Mission**

**Ford Motor Company** is a world-wide leader in automotive and automotive-related products and services as well as in newer industries such as aerospace, communications and financial services. Our mission is to improve continually our products and services to meet our customers' needs, allowing us to prosper as a business and to provide a reasonable return for our stockholders, the owners of our business.

**Values**

How we accomplish our mission is as important as the mission itself. Fundamental to success for the Company are these basic values:

**People** – Our people are the source of our strength. They provide our corporate intelligence and determine our reputation and vitality. Involvement and teamwork are our core human values.

**Products** – Our products are the end result of our efforts, and they should be the best in serving customers world-wide. As our products are viewed, so are we viewed.

**Profits** – Profits are the ultimate measure of how efficiently we provide customers with the best products for their needs. Profits are required to survive and grow.

**Guiding Principles**

**Quality comes first** – To achieve customer satisfaction, the quality of our products and services must be our number one priority.

**Customers are the focus of everything we do** – Our work must be done with our customers in mind, providing better products and services than our competition.

**Continuous improvement is essential to our success** – We must strive for excellence in everything we do: in our products, in their safety and value – and in our services, our human relations, our competitiveness, and our profitability.

**Employee involvement is our way of life** – We are a team. We must treat each other with trust and respect.

**Dealers and suppliers are our partners** – The company must maintain mutually beneficial relationships with dealers, suppliers, and our other business associates.

**Integrity is never compromised** – The conduct of our Company world-wide must be pursued in a manner that is socially responsible and commands respect for its integrity and for its positive contributions to society. Our doors are open to men and women alike without discrimination and without regard to ethnic origin or personal beliefs.

**Figure 2.1** Ford Motor Company: Mission, Values and Guiding Principles

Ford's mission is to be a worldwide leader in automotive and related products and services and in newer industries such as financial services. (The company has since withdrawn from the aerospace business.) As we have seen, its basic values are described as people, products and profits. The guiding principles form a code of conduct that encapsulates policy towards employees, customers, dealers and suppliers. These guiding principles include commitment to the following: quality in all aspects of the business, enhanced customer focus, continuous improvement, and employee involvement and teamwork at all levels. Ford strategy is underpinned by its strategic vision of being a low-cost producer of the highest quality products and services which provide the best customer value, best in class in all segments of its product markets. The human resource re-evaluation is reinforced by the emphases on employee involvement (a 'way of life'), trust, respect, teamwork and social responsibility.

To ensure unity throughout the organization behind the new direction the new leadership team of Petersen and Poling took the opportunity to speak to everyone at Ford (April 1985) through the medium of a ten minute videotape just two months after they took over the Company's top two positions. They used the statement of Mission, Values and Guiding Principles, released in November 1984, as a framework for their remarks. The following are excerpts from the transcript:

> *Petersen*: As we were preparing to take over our present positions, we had many discussions about the future of the Company . . . and about the strengths it would need to succeed in a rapidly changing world. We had already spent several years getting back to what we call the basics of our business. Indeed, those efforts were the force behind our historic turnaround from the grim realities of the early nineteen eighties to the successes of the last couple of years.
>
> But Red [Poling] and I saw a need even more basic – even more fundamental. It seemed to us that Ford, as a Company, needed to look inward, to find and develop its most *essential* strengths, in order to be ready for the challenges ahead. All of us had been taking the things Ford stood for pretty much for granted. There was nothing wrong with that – because our system *worked*. We did a lot of things right. We had history and tradition and years of success behind us.
>
> But times are changing, and the nature of our business is changing and people are changing. We're changing, and we're learning a lot from these changes – good changes like ours start with Participative Management and Employee Involvement, for example . . . but there is so much more that we must do! So Red and I decided to take a fresh, introspective look at our Company and its value system.
>
> *Poling*: We concluded it was time to redefine our purpose and direction, and establish a set of priorities for the Company appropriate to *these* times. We believed it was time to articulate what Ford Motor

Company *is* . . . and what it must *become*. We believe it is time for everyone in the Company – including Don and me – to live and work by principles that will help Ford realize its ultimate potential.

*Petersen*: We want this statement to be – to Ford and all its employees around the world – a basic platform on which we all stand together. We want everyone to recognize that these Guiding Principles are much more than just words or slogans. I see the Guiding Principles as a code of conduct, if you will. They tell us how to do our jobs . . . how to behave towards one another and toward our customers, dealers, and suppliers . . . these principles remind us of what's expected of us . . . and what we should demand of ourselves. I believe, moreover, that what we in management *do* to live by those principles will speak far more loudly in their support than anything we *say*.

People at Ford are looking for more and deeper rewards from their jobs or careers than just pay. And the people to whom we sell our products shop for far more than just the lowest prices. So how can we satisfy them? How can we compete successfully for talent inside and for customers outside in the face of these changes?

*Poling*: Pete, I think that's what the Guiding Principles are all about. They are the rules that shape and govern all our future actions, as individuals and as a Company wherever we interact with people. They tell us *how*. For example, there was a time when many found satisfaction in guarding their own turf. Under the Guiding Principles, those days are over. Interpersonal skills and team effort are now a key part of the performance review process. All of us – including me – will be judged on success in this area.

I also think it's worthwhile to mention what the Guiding Principles are *not*. They are *not* a substitute for personal or departmental or corporate responsibility or accountability. They don't let anyone – me included – or any function, or any activity, off the hook. Our Company is still about decision-making, implementation, and results. It's also important to remember that the Guiding Principles do not supplant authority. Even in the fully participative environment we hope to achieve, the buck must stop where the responsibility has been delegated. There will continue to be levels of responsibility and accountability. Building the basis for decision-making has to be a team process in which everyone participates and to which everyone contributes. The final *decision responsibility* must rest with the principal team player – the captain, the coach, the boss, the top manager. The rest of the team has the responsibility to contribute to the decision process, and to *support* the decision, once it is made, in a positive way. We need teamwork in the process leading to decision, and we need it even more in the process of implementation. So, under the Guiding

Principles, each level of management has the right to *expect* the confidence, respect, and support of subordinate ranks. But at the same time, they also have the *obligation* to *earn* it. How will they do that? By demonstrating consistency, dependability, and predictability in all of their actions. They are the very same qualities the *Company* must demonstrate towards its customers, suppliers, dealers, and stockholders.

*Petersen*: The Guiding Principles are a sort of vision of the future. Using them, all of us, working together, can ensure the future growth and prosperity of Ford Motor Company.

## Employee Involvement/Participative Management

The major organizational challenge that Ford management set itself was to support its strategic agenda by developing a cooperative employee relations environment to improve its capacity for strategic change. This actually began in the 1970s with discussions between the company and the United Automobile Workers (UAW) about the advisability of developing greater employee participation in 1973 (Banas, 1988). Employee involvement as a systematic, viable joint union–management initiative, had its principal origins in the 1979 negotiations between the company and the UAW. During these negotiations, the company and the union discussed the potential benefits of increased involvement of employees in matters affecting their work. Employee involvement, it was agreed, held great promise for making work a more satisfying experience and for improving work outcomes. It was seen as a way of enhancing employee creativity, of improving quality and efficiency and reducing absenteeism. In October 1979 a 'Letter of Understanding' was signed committing union and company to the process of employee involvement. The move was towards cooperative employee relations policy and practice in a firm and industry that had been synonymous with industrial strife. The starting point was a recognition by employees, unions and management alike that their common interests are best served when there are agreed common goals and mutual benefits (Banas and Sauers, 1988).

In October 1979 Philip Caldwell, then president, later chairman, made the following statement to top Ford executives:

Our strategy for the years ahead will come to nothing unless we ask for greater participation of our workforce. Without motivated and concerned workers, we're not going to lower our costs as much as we need to – and we aren't going to get the product quality we need. (Banas, 1988: 391)

In November 1979 Caldwell issued a 'Policy Letter on Employee Involvement'. The essence of company policy was expressed in the opening paragraph:

> It is the policy of the Company to encourage and enable all employees to become involved in and contribute to the success of the Company. A work climate should be created and maintained in which employees, at all levels, can achieve individual goals and work satisfaction by directing their talents and energies toward clearly defined Company Goals.

In the US the troubles of this time were seen as firmly rooted not just in problems of the business cycle and in the new competition but in a lack of trust between management and labour, a lack of clear corporate values and sharply defined goals, and in a turbulent history of adversarial labour–management relations. Employee involvement (EI) thus began with a growing conviction that employees wanted more out of work than extrinsic rewards and that management and unions working together could create a work environment in which employees could achieve job satisfaction by directing their ingenuity and creativity toward improving their work and overall work environment. EI assumes that employees want to develop their full capabilities and participate in the success of the company. It is based on the recognition by employees, unions, and management that their common interests can best be served when there are common goals and mutual benefits.

> Reduced to its essentials, EI is the process by which employees are provided with the opportunities to contribute their minds, as well as their muscles, and hopefully their hearts, to the attaining of individual and Company goals. Through a variety of techniques – such as problem solving groups, new product launch teams, ad hoc quality and scrap involvement teams – opportunities have been created, for hourly employees to contribute their ideas, their analyses, and their solutions to job-related problems. Since 1979, virtually every hourly employee, either directly or indirectly, has been affected by this process. Today EI is functioning in virtually all major Ford facilities. (Banas and Sauers, 1989: 3)

It was felt that EI provided the best way to enhance employee creativity, thus contributing to improvements in the workplace in support of the strategic goals of achieving highest levels of efficiency, the traditional Ford panacea for success, and also the highest-quality products that the newly demanding consumer expected as of right.

The initial focus of EI was on problem-solving groups akin to quality circles. Subsequently involvement was extended to include participation in other processes usually reserved for management, such as planning, goal setting, communication and decision making. The objective was to make participation the preferred way of management throughout the company. To support the development of EI an extensive program of training in skills appropriate to a participative approach was given to both employees and management in such areas as team-building and organization diagnosis (the gathering of information about work relationships and the work environment). This reflected the premise that key elements of an implementation strategy had to include union/management support, a common language, knowledge and understanding, implementation guidelines, local ownership, adequate resources and funding, and education and training. Important extensions of the EI approach included the setting up of interface groups to solve common problems cutting across organizational divides.

The emphasis, uniquely for Ford, was on qualitative rather than quantitative factors. There was to be no formal, quantitative measurement of the groups' performance. This was a remarkable management concession, given the existing culture of a company famous/notorious for its attention to the bottom-line. During the heavy cost-cutting exercise of the early 1980s, when the US company fought to turn around large corporate losses, the financial and human resources required to sustain EI were considered 'sacred' and were, therefore, not affected. EI was a key element of the new statement of corporate Mission, Values, and Guiding Principles. ('Involvement and teamwork are our core human values'.) In the words of Donald Petersen, then president of Ford Motor Company, 'it took employee involvement to chart a new standard for labour and management relations. . . . I believe that we are just beginning to grasp the potential that lies ahead. . . . I want Ford to be recognized as a 'people' Company – and I want our performance to be measured by our human enterprise as well as our economic enterprise' (cited by Banas, 1988: 402).

The other side of the coin of EI is Participative Management

(PM). Employee involvement was embraced at the top level of the company, and policy managers were expected to act accordingly. PM is premised on the belief that employee involvement is unattainable without developing the skills that managers need to provide employees and fellow managers with opportunities to participate. PM is essential to the process of eliciting employee involvement. Employees cannot have upward influence unless management creates and maintains a participative climate in which to do so. The processes offering opportunities for participation include consultation (to maximize information and commitment), collaboration (based on a norm of consensus) and delegation (the manager assigns responsibility for an agreed outcome to an individual or group). A major goal of the change initiative, therefore, was managerial behaviour. The company had accepted Deming's assessment of their quality problems as primarily rooted in management practices and not, as management had previously believed, worker failure to conform to management dictates. A major aim was to tap into the potential (competencies and commitment) of the workforce at all levels. EI efforts were initially aimed at educating and training hourly employees. PM focused on the education and training of managers and supervisors.

Participative management came onto the managerial agenda as a response to the question 'How do we [managers] respond to the EI-trained workers?' Participative management was championed in Ford's diversified products operation (DPO). This is the internal supplier for a range of components ranging from glass to wipers and electronics. The dilemma facing DPO was stark. There was tremendous pressure to improve the quality of its products and services, to bring them up to Japanese standards of quality and cost, or to face the danger of closure. DPO embraced EI and set about analyzing its management requirements. To this end a task force was set up to study well-run American companies. From a list of 40 'truly outstanding' six firms were selected – IBM, TRW, 3M, General Electric, Dana and Hewlett–Packard. Ford concluded that these companies had ten things in common.

1. Each firm circulated a statement of corporate goals and values, and its executives spent 50 to 80 percent of their time outside their offices, trying to communicate those ideas to their employees.
2. All six emphasized the importance of people and respect for every individual. They agreed that the skills and quality of their people were their only competitive advantage. Products or technology can be purchased, but usually don't help the company for long.

3 They substituted trust for strict rules and controls. When the task force met with Hewlett-Packard's CEO, John Young, one of the first things he said was 'We trust our people.'
4 Every firm made a big fuss about being customer-driven. IBM told the task force that there were very few ways an IBM employee could get fired, but one of them was keeping a customer waiting or letting a phone ring more than twice in a customer service center.
5 All six used teamwork, particularly multidepartmental teams, to develop cutting edge products and services.
6 They tried to eliminate levels of management and to drive down authority. At one Dana plant, there were only three layers – the hourly workers, their bosses, and the plant manager.
7 The companies emphasized free, open, face-to-face communications. Hewlett–Packard called this 'management by wandering about'.
8 Managers relied on peers – and occasionally on subordinates – to help evaluate other managers. Team players were promoted over individualists.
9 All six offered sophisticated training for managers as well as hourly employees.
10 Managers at the corporations made a habit of asking their people, 'What do you think?' (Petersen, 1991: 50–1)

Participative management (PM) is defined as 'the techniques and skills that managers use to provide employees with opportunities to participate actively in key managerial processes (planning, goal setting, problem solving, and decision making) affecting job-related matters' (Banas, 1988: 406). The other aspect of PM which, as we shall see, became increasingly significant, is the way it is linked to the solution to a key managerial problem – the integration of managerial effort across rigid functional barriers which members of the company speak of in terms of organizational 'chimneys'. The success of Ford's strategic shift away from the mass production of utility vehicles towards a product spectrum targeted at specific market segments hinges on the integration of design, manufacture, sales and marketing. Japanese companies, like large prosperous high technology companies in the West, are seen as owing much of their success both to their human resource management *and* to the degree to which they are able to manage their inter-managerial relationships in a way that facilitates responsiveness to increasingly turbulent market conditions. Responsiveness based on *managerial* flexibility is something which a traditionally organized, tightly controlled, bureaucratic, hierarchical company finds extremely difficult (Piore, 1986: 158).

Participative management was championed in the US by Petersen, whose attitude is well encapsulated in the following statement from a meeting with plant managers: 'If I could only get everyone in this Company, particularly those in leadership positions, to ask their people much more frequently "What do you think?", then we would reap the benefit of all the accumulated knowledge, experience, dedication and creativity of our people.' According to Petersen, PM is 'simply a style of operating in which you give your peers and subordinates an opportunity to say what they think, and you include their ideas in the overall decision-making process' (Petersen, 1991: 52). This gives you better information for decision-making and means that those who are involved own the decisions. The contrast between this approach and the unwritten rules of the 1960s referred to earlier illustrates the difference in the Ford culture, pre- and post-1980, as it impacts upon the individual member. PM/EI rests on a powerful assumption that 'imagination, ingenuity and creativity are widely distributed throughout the entire work force, as are dedication and the desire to contribute' (Ford Employee Involvement Policy letter), and that management systems, procedures and practices are to take this assumption into account.

## Product Development

In 1979 Don Petersen startled Jack Telnack, a leading Ford designer, with his questions concerning designs for 1980s new product.

> 'Is that really the best you can do?' Petersen asked.
> 'No, it's not,' Telnack answered.
> 'Would you really want to drive that car yourself? . . .'
> 'No,' . . .
> 'Then show me what you can do'. (Halberstam, 1987: 647)

The old Ford system had emphasized discipline, cost-control and efficiency as the essence of strategy. Innovation in product design was consequently devalued. In the increasingly demanding world of the 1970s this became a major strategic weakness.

The new emphasis on product development in Ford in the 1980s highlights the importance of design as a strategic weapon, pioneered in Ford of Europe and diffused to the US through designers like Telnack with European experience (Lorenz, 1986). Design and quality came together for Ford in a new strategic vision of the company as design leader. Ford's turnaround in the US was design-led with the new Taurus/Sable range. The company hit rock-bottom in 1980, the year it initiated the Taurus and Sable program (Halberstam, 1987: 647). With participation and involvement came the opportunity to experiment and design innovative products. Creativity was no longer stifled by bureaucracy. Crisis was critical in the launching of a new 'bet your company' product strategy:

> the combination of hard times and severe competition had finally forced Ford to do what it should have been doing all along, use its immense reservoir of talent to build the best cars imaginable instead of conservatively sitting on the sidelines, figuring out how to take the minimum amount of risk in a business where true success came only with risk. (Halberstam, 1987: 650)

The key strategic issue became innovation rather than efficiency. The old Ford and the new Ford came together in its new strategic vision of being a low-cost producer of the highest quality products and services which provide the best customer value.

The context was not encouraging. A scene in Ford's corporate design centre illustrates the problems of the early 1980s:

> A few consumers had been asked in to get their reactions to Ford's prototype cars for the future. The cars were very similar to GM's and almost identical to Ford's own boxy-looking 1980 models currently rusting on dealers' lots. One member of the audience stood up and said, 'I know, these are all phony. The real car is behind the curtain back there, isn't it?' The Ford people didn't know what to say because there were no other cars. Further discussion with his corporate designers convinced Petersen that they were equally uninspired by the future models. At this point the new management decided to turn the designers loose to develop ideas, without trying to second-guess their bosses or merely copying what the competition was doing. (Mintzberg and Quinn, 1991: 486)

At the time Ford was in the process of planning for the replacement of its midsize car range. This is the crucial segment of the automobile market where volume sales and maximum value-added meet, so it is fundamental to profitability. Ford was faced with a choice between a radical, expensive 'clean sheet' design or a low investment 'muddle-through, parts bin car' based on 'cannibalizing' ideas and parts from the Tempo and Topaz models due to be introduced in 1983. Despite the losses it was facing the company opted for the former and a $3.25 billion investment in a radical new design. This was the birth of the Taurus/Sable range and the search for the grail of world class leadership in this key market segment.

The Taurus marked a new approach based on simultaneous rather than sequential car design and development. Here participative management as inter-functional collaboration across organizational divides (the functional 'chimneys') had a major role to play (Clark and Fujimoto, 1991). Here again the lessons of Japan were crucial and Ford led the way. The Taurus program was based on a specially constituted Team Taurus in which representatives of planning, design, engineering, manufacturing and marketing conjointly held responsibility for the program outcomes. According to Lew Veraldi, head of the Taurus program,

> The auto industry is constructed with 'chimneys' – engineering, marketing, suppliers. The prevailing attitude has been, 'Don't touch my field.' Design would pass its ideas to manufacturing, then manufacturing would claim that the design didn't work. You have to get everything together working toward a common objective. If you don't have teamwork, then the work isn't devoted to the good of the product. (Zimmerman, 1991: 138)

Veraldi describes the importance of teamwork to the Taurus project as follows:

> Involving all groups in the process although seemingly more complicated, actually lowered costs because each group was not optimizing at its own level. It was much easier to get people to talk about and come up with constructive changes when they couldn't pass off responsibility by saying, 'that's really a manufacturing problem not a design one.' There were no specific incentives set up for this project other than pride of workmanship. We found out that most people want to do a job right when they get a chance. When they are given that chance they have as much of an 'equity' in the project as any designer does. We motivated people by making sure they had an equity in the product – and then we listened to them carefully. At every stage of the process we had inputs from customers and users. Customers and users were considered to be those in the later stages of the design and introduction process – as well as actual consumers in the marketplace. (Mintzberg and Quinn, 1991: 493)

The Taurus team set about systematically examining what they had to do to make a product that was 'best in class'. The car program management group dropped Ford's traditional 'Detroit-knows-best' and 'Not Invented Here' attitudes, methodically set out to identify what were the world's best-designed and engineered automotive features, and tried to incorporate as many as possible into the Taurus. Starting in 1982, they selected cars, subsystems, and components from around the world with superior features and reverse engineered them to learn how they were designed, manufactured and assembled. The new relationship with suppliers set out in the company Mission Statement ('Dealers and suppliers are our partners') was geared to developing long-term contracts with a reduced number of suppliers based on mutual trust with the goal of developing pioneering new 'best-in-class' components.

In the design process itself Ford broke with tradition. It conducted its most intensive market research exercise with a view to breaking with the mind-set that had brought it to crisis. The extensive inputs from consumers had a major impact on the build complexity of the car. The Taurus Team was able to reduce the marketing entities for the Taurus (and the Mercury Division's version of the car, Sable) to the lowest number ever offered in this segment. Marketing entities comprise the models, series and order specification groups production has to be organized around. The Taurus/Sabel range ended up with 37 compared to its predecessor's 188. This design for manufacture increased average build repeatability to 13,000 compared to Toyota's 7,000 in this segment. The range had 1,700 fewer parts than its predecessor.

In the plants, new levels of quality were achieved through employee involvement. In the words of Lew Veraldi again:

> I saw a dedication I had never seen before . . . the workers stayed until 8:00 P.M. to show how they were building the parts. At each station the workers had small charts on easels or taped to desks – they were all different – and they would say, 'This is how we are going to manufacture this part at this station – and this is how we're going to make it perfect.' They all had their own way of showing you how they were doing statistical process control; the methods were common, but their individual applications were all different since the plant manager had given them the latitude to run their own businesses in the way they thought best. (Mintzberg and Quinn, 1991: 494)

Responsibility for quality assurance was invested in the assembly line. Only 1 per cent of cars required repair after the end of the assembly process compared with a previous 10–15 per cent.

The outcome of all this was the new Taurus/Sable range of aerodynamically styled cars aimed at the crucial family market, particularly the 'baby-boomer' professionals with discretionary income to invest. The cars offered Japanese quality and European styling. The team development approach based on simultaneous engineering saved in excess of $250 million on product development and reduced model turnaround from six to four years. Participative management and employee involvement were recognized as crucial to innovatory product development.

## Conclusion

The key strategic question that came to the fore at Ford, both in the US and Europe, in the late 1970s was 'How good are we as a world manufacturer?' The answer, after Japan, was 'Not good enough'. Ford's response in the US was a commitment to radical change. Pascale (1990: 119–21) concludes his study of a range of American companies with the words, 'Ford stands alone in appearing to have truly transformed itself.' From a loss of $3.3 billion between 1980 and 1982, Ford moved to profits in 1986 that surpassed General Motors for the first time since 1924. In 1987, Ford broke all previous industry records for profitability. Pascale asks how Ford did it. 'Was the success the result of improbable coincidences, or can it be replicated? . . . at first blush, Ford did no more than apply a set of techniques that have been around for some time . . . what distinguishes Ford is not *what* they did, but *how* they did it' (Pascale, 1990: 120). Pascale notes a common point of agreement among participants in Ford's transformation: they shared a deep sense of *crisis*. Pascale deals with the role of the crisis in focusing managerial attention. He highlights the importance of leadership factors, the complementarity of Petersen and Poling, Petersen the visionary champion on the new Mission and of EI/PM, Poling dealing with the restructuring and rationalization, the cost efficiency/benchmarking side of the business. (Pascale actually treats participative management and employee involvement in only a few of its aspects despite his assertion that Employee Involvement was the most powerful variable altering the face of Ford.)

A Ford internal analysis concludes that 'the real accomplishment was seizing on the opportunities for change as they presented themselves' (Banas and Sauers, 1989). In this same internal Ford publication, the authors suggest that there were several key factors accelerating the successful change process; the crisis, the leadership of a succession of company chairmen (first Caldwell, then Petersen, and now Poling), and Ford's commitment to a different human resources strategy – participative management and employee involvement.

Chester Barnard (1938) taught us that a primary role of senior management is the fostering of shared values in the organization. The Ford example illustrates how major strategic change necessitates a fundamental re-examination of the organization's value system. At Ford the re-examination of values came before the framing of the mission and the guiding principles and, indeed, was a necessary precursor to the later initiatives. Strategic change focused on the need for better quality products to compete with Japanese automobile firms. The key to unlocking the potential to manufacture to this quality was the redefinition of the value of people to top management. To tap the potential of employees in the organization major management changes were introduced along with employee involvement and participative management.

Employee involvement was introduced to develop the processes by which employees at all levels have the opportunities to participate actively in the key managerial processes affecting job matters. It emphasized consultation to maximize information and commitment, collaboration based on a norm of consensus decision-making, and delegation of managerial responsibilities. Employee involvement and participative management at Ford can be construed as an attempt to introduce a new image of collective responsibility for decision-making and implementation into the organization. It is the combination of mission and values that can create the common identity necessary to unite the large number of people who constitute a large organization (Senge, 1990).

Lee Iacocca's autobiography (1986) is an eloquent reminder of the reality of organizational politics and their dysfunctional consequences. In describing the political battleground that was Ford in the mid-70s he emphasizes management grounded in autocracy and greed (self-seeking behaviour at the expense of others' and the overall good). The problem of coordination and integration of the organizational sub-units that have resulted from functional specialization has long been a major concern of organizational analysis (Lawrence and Lorsch, 1967, 1969; Davis and Lawrence, 1977). In Ford the propensity of different functional groups to become introverted and selfish in their dealings with other units is captured in the image of 'organizational chimneys' – an organization structured for vertical relationships within functions that work against horizontal linkages between functions. Participative management has as one of its main goals the changing of managerial attitudes and the dismantling of what is now perceived as dysfunctional hierarchy. Its aims are to simplify managerial control, devolve authority and break down the barriers between managerial groups which have their basis in hierarchy, functional specialization, organizational culture and managers' cognitions.

After Japan, and Employee Involvement/Participative Management, human resources became a key strategic issue for Ford. The shaping, in Pascale's phrase, of a 'set of ground rules for effective collaboration' becomes a key management issue. All of the company's strategic issues such as quality improvement, customer satisfaction, innovation and cost reduction have one common denominator. They all explicitly depend on the capacities, competencies, and commitment of Ford employees. The key strategic issue, now and into the future, is how to create and sustain a flexible work force with the capacities, competencies, and commitment (including the technical and managerial leadership) that will give the company a competitive edge in a turbulent, uncertain world marketplace (Johnson, 1988). Ford's Mission, Values and Guiding Principles includes a clear commitment to the owners of the business, employees, dealers and suppliers and broader social responsibility. In Ford one can construe major changes in management approach as, in part, a redefinition of the corporation's responsibility to its employees and to other stakeholders. One of the major lessons 'After Japan' and the other adaptation alluded to in this chapter is that organizations are strengthened if they demonstrate a broad sense of responsibility to a variety of stakeholders, both external and internal.

We now turn to Europe and the fate there of the HRM initiatives pioneered by Ford in the US.

# 3

# American Initiatives, European Responses: Employee Relations in Ford UK

One of the first Ford of Europe executives we spoke to warned us to be wary of taking the rhetoric of human resource management at face value.

> One thing you *must* remember is that the Ford Motor Company is introducing teamworking *not* as a form of humanity but because our hierarchical 'chimney' organization couldn't respond to the complexity of the new competitive situation.

In fact, this warning proved unnecessary: Ford managers were insistent that the corporation's new worker involvement strategy implied no slackening of control or diminution of managerial prerogative. If Ford was moving from an adversarial to a consensual form of labour relations then this was driven by the bottom line rather than a purely philosophical revolution in the Ford boardroom. This appreciation of the necessary relationship between flexibility, worker involvement and competitiveness proved to be a constant theme in all our discussions with Ford executives. In this chapter we examine Ford UK's industrial relations inheritance, Ford's initial understanding of the nature of the Japanese enterprise and the impact of the Employee Involvement strategy in Europe.

## Continuity and Change in Ford's Industrial Relations

Perhaps more than in any other area, Ford has come to symbolize a distinctive pattern of labour relations. The Fordist factory was based on the direct managerial control of deskilled labour within a minutely detailed division of labour. Competitiveness in the era of mass production hinged on progressive cost reduction. Radical product and process innovation was systematically sacrificed in favour of efficiency (Abernathy, 1983). Deskilling and direct control were the fundamental managerial imperatives. But ultimately Fordism proved to be self-defeating, unable to withstand either the internal pressures imposed by an alienated workforce or the novel competitive challenges issued by Japanese manufacturers.

One of the major barriers to change in Ford has been the legacy of the company's chequered industrial relations history. Ford's dubious inheritance of low trust labour relations is superimposed on the inherent conservatism of the British car industry, whose combination of competitive multi-unionism and sectional shopfloor bargaining tends to dissipate radical initiatives. A distinctive characteristic of Ford within the British industry has been the company's pursuit of coherent labour relations strategies, suitably amended to reflect changes in the economic, legal and political environment (Tolliday, 1991). In this section we shall argue that the current phase in Ford's industrial relations strategy represents a break with previous policies, tempered by important elements of continuity.

From its arrival in Manchester in 1911 Ford mounted a vigorous anti-union campaign which successfully excluded trade unions from their factories until the end of World War II. In these years, working conditions inside the Ford plants were primitive and supervisory discipline harsh and unyielding. Faced with an increasing number of disruptive, minor disputes Ford finally conceded union recognition. From 1945 to the late 1960s Ford attempted to maintain a collective bargaining regime which dealt exclusively with national trade union leaderships, ignoring shop stewards. Inevitably, unpredictable eddies of shopfloor turmoil developed beneath the relative calm of official collective bargaining. The slow disintegration of Ford's policy of union containment accelerated during the 1960s. Labour shortages and high turnover levels undermined the company's selective recruitment policy while the company's young, restless workforce posed immense disciplinary problems for supervisors accustomed to exercising arbitrary control (Beynon, 1987). On the shopfloor, each tightening of supervisory authority had the opposite effect. Far from subduing the workforce, stricter discipline was met by increasingly unpredictable forms of labour resistance, from vandalism through to near riot. The bitter industrial conflicts which shook the car industry between 1968 and 1972 finally undermined Ford's attempt to limit collective bargaining to senior union officials.

For Ford, the modernization of their labour relations system through the incorporation of shop stewards in collective bargaining was the adoption of a pragmatic industrial pluralism. Paul Roots (1984: 36–7), formerly director of Industrial Relations for Ford UK, explained that Ford's efforts to incorporate factory conveners into the formal bargaining process was to neutralize the shop stewards as an independent force.

> It reached a point where the conveners were such a powerful body that all they were doing was sitting back and criticizing the negotiators. So we thought 'if they are going to have all the power we will give them the responsibility as well'. So we put them in the negotiating room and now they can't duck it and blame the full-time officials.

The appointment of Bob Ramsey as Director of Industrial Relations in 1973 symbolized the company's belated rejection of 'the Ford industrial creed' of paternalism and direct control (Friedmann and Meredeen, 1980: 234–6). From the mid-1970s, winning employee endorsement of collective agreements was regarded as essential to the long-term stabilization of labour relations and enhanced productivity. However, the coherence of Ford's national strategic initiatives stood in sharp contrast to plant management's insistence on unilateral managerial control. The resulting running battles at plant level seriously hampered production continuity and threatened to become a critical competitive handicap. This experience forced Ford executives finally to recognize that structural reforms of internal bargaining institutions alone were insufficient to sustain a profound process of organizational change. The task for Ford's senior management was to devise structures and processes which would not only involve shopfloor representatives in maintaining collective agreements but also to qualitatively extend this principle to include informal responsibilities for productivity and innovation.

## After Japan

The primary impetus for change at Ford arose from the growing incursions of Japanese manufacturers into the corporation's core American and European markets. The new industrial competition from Japan altered the basic contours of competition by introducing new standards of product quality and design (Abernathy et al.,

1981). Ford's response has been to increase the variety of model derivatives, compress the response time between marketplace and production, and generate internally a heightened awareness of product design as a critical competitive factor. For Ford UK such competitive pressures were exacerbated by lacklustre productivity and quality performance, compared to Ford's Continental European plants (Bhaskar, 1979: 143–4, 399). If Ford UK's first strategic goal was to reduce the company's breakeven point by rationalization and increased efficiency then the second was to lay the organizational foundations necessary for competitive edge in the 'new industrial competition'. In short, Ford has confronted its productivity dilemma – how to reconcile increased efficiency with innovation – head on. It is this double awareness, of the productive *and* innovative advantage enjoyed by Japanese car producers, which has determined the pattern of organizational change in Ford during the 1980s.

The 1980s witnessed both change and continuity in the company's industrial relations strategy. Historically, major shifts in the strategy have been essentially reactive, policies of containment triggered by shopfloor unrest. Conversely, the current phase was activated by a self-consciously proactive management approach whose aim is to enable, rather than foreclose, the possibilities of organizational change. The greatest change was Ford's efforts to develop a co-operative industrial relations environment which will enable, perhaps even accelerate, strategic change and work reorganization. The uncertainty inherent in this open-ended reform process was tempered by Ford's determination to maintain managerial hegemony in the workplace through the retention of a tight disciplinary code.

Two major change strategies distinguished the 1980s. The first, 'After Japan', an internal study of Ford's productivity levels, was the direct response to the company's new awareness of the Japanese competitive edge. Its limited success in its human resource management aspects, in particular the failed effort to introduce quality circles into the Ford's United Kingdom factories, is attributed by senior management to union resistance and a mishandled implementation process. The second change initiative centred around Employee Involvement, a labour relations strategy with distinctive Japanese features, and Participative Management, both imported from the US. The impact and challenge of Participative Management will be examined in following chapters.

After Japan (AJ) was Ford of Europe's initial response to the Japanese advantage following a trip to Japan by Bill Hayden, Ford of

Europe's Vice-President of Manufacturing, from which he returned in a state of shock. 'What I saw scared the living daylights out of me,' is how he still describes this trip. Until Ford's entry into the small car market with the Fiesta launch in 1977 the company simply ignored the Japanese cost advantage. AJ represented a transformation of Ford's conception of the Japanese challenge as being based on cheap labour and a sheltered domestic market. Ford's investigation of Japanese car manufacture was triggered by Detroit's disbelief at Mazda's unbeatable tender to produce transaxles for Ford US. Initially, Hayden's report was received with only mild interest by the Ford world executive team. This executive indifference was confirmed by a report by Dearborn's Corporate Strategy office which concluded that Ford was just as efficient as its Japanese competitors. Before AJ Ford of Europe was satisfied that Ford Germany was the most efficient continental manufacturer while the UK company outpaced its British competitors. Hayden's chill warning of the Japanese efficiency advantage was heard first and with the greatest force, therefore, by Ford of Europe.

It is almost impossible to exaggerate the symbolic importance of AJ for Ford's European managers. Indeed, almost all the Ford of Europe executives we interviewed prefaced their remarks by dividing history into the periods 'before AJ' and 'after AJ'. Above all, AJ exploded the myth of Ford's European superiority. AJ's starting point was a detailed comparison of Ford and Japanese production, from scrap rates to the uptime achieved by specific machines. On 7 May 1980 Bill Hayden made a full-day presentation to Ford of Europe's senior managers. Hayden hammered home one simple message: Japanese manufacturers enjoyed significant efficiency advantages at all stages of the production process. Ford took three to four hours to change press shop dies compared to Toyota's five or six minutes; Ford made twenty day's stock on each die run, Toyota less than one day's stock per turn. Ford UK, Hayden demonstrated, was particularly disadvantaged in terms of operator efficiency: a simple operator repair in Japan became a logistical nightmare involving up to seven different trades and hours of delay in Ford UK.

Hayden rammed home his message by reminding his stunned audience that these efficiency differentials were a condemnation not just of Ford's failures but of their *successes*. The logic and method of the AJ exercise owed much to the product 'teardowns' Ford used to cost their rivals' vehicles in minute detail. Lindsey Halstead, the recently retired Chairman of Ford of Europe, described the strengths and weaknesses of the 'organizational teardown' Ford used to understand Japanese manufacturing efficiency:

> The AJ study began to focus on the cost differences . . . Even the way Ford of Europe did that study tended to be a bit functional – benchmarking plant by plant; benchmarking process by process. That's not a criticism – that's the way the Ford structure forces you to think.

The great limitation of AJ, continued Halstead, was that it 'looked at the world through Ford's eyes'. In other words, the AJ analysis of Japanese decision-making and manufacturing processes was constrained by 'Fordist blinkers'. But if this method established the scale of the Japanese efficiency and quality advantage it contributed little to understanding *why* such a gap existed.

The conclusion Ford of Europe's Manufacturing directorate derived from AJ was the need for efficiency improvement and lowering the company's breakeven point. The challenge of AJ was to accelerate 'towards greater efficiency *within* our established system: to take the Ford system to its limits'. In this sense, whatever the novelty of AJ's competitive benchmarking, its organizational implications were familiar enough to Ford's highly cost conscious management. 'AJ was about cost reduction – its how Ford has always responded to the unknown. . . . AJ was a typical Ford drive to streamline the organization.' Two contradictory elements were central to Ford UK's assimilation of the lessons from Japan. On the one hand, corporate executives were impressed by the sheer intensity of work in the Toyota factories they visited (GLC, 1985: 17). 'The few people we saw on the lines worked hard and quickly. They were mostly jogging with parts to workstations. What we saw represented an incredible utilization of manpower.' But, on the other hand, AJ implicitly recognized that the Japanese management style was diametrically opposed to the Western model, the key being management by consent rather than control, to mobilize worker knowledge behind company goals rather than to eliminate all vestiges of worker discretion. Armed with the endorsement of the American parent company, Ford of Europe introduced quality circles in 1979 with the threefold objective of improving manufacturing productivity; stimulating motivation and involvement on the shopfloor; and providing an informal forum for communication between management and labour. If the Japanese vision of AJ represented a gigantic leap in corporate imagination then implementation betrayed strong continuities with Ford's deeply entrenched one-dimensional understanding of organizational change as the unproblematic outcome of structural reform.

Initially, Ford envisaged the introduction of quality circles as the first step in the rapid 'Japanization' of the company; from training the workforce in problem-solving and inter-personal skills to 'just-in-time' and more stable relations with component suppliers. But the dead hand of direct control was inscribed in the very constitution of Ford UK's quality circles initiative. Each circle of 8 to 15 employees was to include a supervisor and quality inspector, reflecting management's deep-seated belief that quality control and production planning problems should be divorced from the shopfloor (Gill, 1985: 70).

In the UK the employee relations elements of AJ foundered on union resistance to quality circles. Ford managers acknowledge that the blanket union hostility was understandable and that implementing such profound changes in company labour relations required delicate diplomacy rather than ill-considered unilateral action (Guthrie, 1987). 'Participation', as one executive involved in this 'fiasco' put it, 'could not be introduced by imposition':

> the AJ initiative was classic non-participation. Bill [Hayden] comes back from Japan. We analyze everything the Japanese do that we don't: hey presto, quality circles – that's the answer. We march in to the unions and say we are now having quality circles and you're going to participate. They say . . . we think quality circles are divisive and we're not having it. . . . We screwed it. We were so clumsy in the ham-fisted way we tried to introduce participation by imposition. And that put quality back as a topic for a long time.

For the manufacturing unions, quality circles threatened to by-pass existing bargaining institutions by subsuming issues far beyond quality improvement. In one way or another, from national level bargaining to the informal accretions of 'custom and practice', every aspect of work and employment within Ford had slowly become *negotiable*. Put another way, the Ford unions regarded quality circles – and later involvement programmes – as a management ploy to restrict the scope of collective bargaining. In particular, supervisory-led quality circles threatened to supplant the intimate relationship between the shop steward and the workgroup and erode the dense web of informal 'custom and practice' agreements which regulated shopfloor life. This, in turn, would undermine the very concept of mutuality – that there is formal or informal agreement between management and workforce prior to any substantive change in work practices, payment or manning.

The chastening experience of this aspect of AJ served, though, as a learning experience, forcing Ford to abandon their grand vision of wholesale 'Japanization' and to adopt a more pragmatic, long-term approach to organizational change. The company's long history of adversarial, low-trust industrial relations necessitated a gradual, processual approach to modifying company culture rather than structural reorganization alone. In itself, this was a major advance in managerial understanding of the change process and one which informed subsequent company strategy. After AJ Ford pursued a twin track change strategy: on the one hand, pushing through rationalization and efficiency measures by traditional top-down methods; on the other, developing a more complex, longer-term approach based on building more consensual management-labour relations.

At the same time the company remained determined to safeguard its managerial prerogative. This was most apparent at factory level where supervisory authority was underwritten by strict rules which stated that should any workgroup refuse to accept supervisory direction pending fuller consultation then they were automatically suspended, risking knock-on lay-offs in adjacent work stations (Buckley and Enderwick, 1985: 114). In November 1980 Ford attempted to go beyond these established sanctions by introducing a 'New Disciplinary Code' in all British plants. Halewood was the focal point of resistance to Ford's new rules which stated that 'non-cooperative' workers could summarily be laid-off, suspended or dismissed. Nevertheless, the extent of unofficial action forced the company to withdraw the Code and to pursue a more cautious, consultative approach in the preparations for the major technical change which began in Dagenham in 1981 (Silva, 1988: 252–5). But, as the robotization of Dagenham revealed, Ford's acceptance of a teamworking manufacturing strategy was far from complete: the rhetoric of human resource management co-existed uneasily with traditional, hard-line managerial autocracy.

## Technical Change and Work Organization

Perhaps the greatest irony of Fordism was that, despite the superior efficiency of mass production compared to craft divisions of labour, it was never fully effective in its own terms. Far from appropriating all shopfloor knowledge, Fordist management proved incapable of entirely eliminating or, alternatively, tapping into their workforces' tacit understanding of production organization. The imperatives of centralized managerial control sharpened still further the cleavage between line workers and supervisors. The tensions inherent in Fordist work organization were fully exposed by the full employment and rising wages of the long post-war boom. The car factories of Western Europe and America became the storm centres of shopfloor protest which began in the 1960s. Worker alienation and industrial conflict were symptoms of the inherent contradictions of Fordism. Under the impact of the new competition the pressure to raise efficiency and quality while accelerating product innovation made production flexibility a vital strategic issue. The logic of the flexible technologies installed at Dagenham and increased model variation demanded a less rigid division of labour while the complex new capital equipment could not be adequately serviced by traditionally organized maintenance teams (Scarborough, 1984).

Dagenham was at the forefront of a wave of investment in process technologies which transformed the British car industry between 1980 and 1982. But the installation of around 120 robots at Dagenham differed from, for instance, British Leyland's robotization of Longbridge's Metro production in several important respects. The robot technology of Metro production was based on long-established patterns of work organization and characterized by rigidity, a high level of automation and, paradoxically, by unnecessary and under-utilized islands of excessive process flexibility (Willman and Winch, 1985: 53; Williams et al., 1987: 56–66). By contrast, the robotization of Dagenham was pragmatically designed to achieve the maximum flexibility consistent with maintaining scale economies. 'Flexibility', a Ford production engineer explained, 'is normally a cost problem. Why should we install something flexible if we never need it? You just complicate the process and waste money'. The objective was to move to a one-line system for mixed model production of 950 Sierras and 150 Fiestas per day while accommodating several variants of both models (Silva, 1988: 149–50; Jones, 1983: 24).

Car body components are deeply pressed sheets with highly contoured joint edges. Spot welding involves the manipulation of the weld electrode through a complex pattern of positions and attitudes. Only with a machine possessing the programmability and dexterity of an industrial robot can the process be automated. Careful product design, particularly enlarged body components, combined with automation to massively reduce the number of manual welds: from the 3508 manual welds formerly applied to the Cortina to 503 in the Sierra. If the balance of automation and manual intervention was primarily a trade-off between cost and flexibility then robotization's impact on industrial relations was an important secondary consideration. Robotization replaced the least skilled short-cycle jobs, where friction and defects were at their greatest (Marsden et al., 1985: 53).

The initial phase of robotization at Dagenham revealed much about Ford management's 'schizophrenic' policies toward labour relations. In 1980–2 Ford introduced specimen robots to prepare for the transition from Cortina to Sierra production. But although Ford was careful to familiarize the Dagenham workforce with the new robot technology there were no substantive negotiations with shop stewards about work organization. Formal negotiation was restricted to company level between managers and national union officials (McLoughlin and Clark, 1988: 87–8). By imposing job designs unilaterally, management failed to capitalize on the considerable interest and goodwill the workforce displayed towards the new technology. This failure was compounded during the installation of the robots in 1982. The construction of the new robotized production facility was completed during the summer shut-down. On their return, the workers discovered that their rest areas – personalized by calendars, kettles and posters – had been demolished, and their possessions discarded (Jary, 1985: 72, 76). For the shop stewards, this insensitivity compounded their exclusion from the bargaining process and effectively undermined the goodwill derived from the one-year familiarization process. There was, in short, no comparable investment in trust-building to parallel the capital investment in flexible technologies.

## Employee Involvement

The successor to AJ's failed attempt to introduce quality circles was the Employee Involvement (EI) initiative. EI was not Ford of Europe's response to the company's failure to implant quality circles (Bradley and Hill, 1983). Rather, EI originated in Detroit and was rapidly disseminated throughout Ford's global empire (Bamber and Lansbury, 1989; Lever-Tracy, 1990; Silva, 1988). However, although the American experience determined the fundamental characteristics of EI, national companies were given considerable leeway in the precise manner in which the involvement strategy was to be implemented. Ford of Europe conceptualized EI as a long-term trust-building exercise with time horizons of ten to fifteen years.

EI was launched as a joint initiative between Ford in America and the United Auto Workers (UAW) in 1979 with mutually agreed goals of improving work experience, increasing efficiency and quality, and reducing absenteeism. EI groups are voluntary, meet in company time and set their own agenda, though issues covered by contract negotiations are deemed to be taboo. In the USA, EI began with hourly paid workers and was only gradually extended to encompass salaried grades (Banas, 1988). Conversely, in Ford UK, the structures of EI were accepted only by salaried staff unions, and even then only temporarily. Shopfloor unions abstained from the EI programme, which they regarded as contrary to the established contractual job-control orientation of workplace trade unionism. Among staff grades the EI process made slow progress, had a highly uneven impact and proved subject to abrupt reversal. In central functions (notably Finance) which are essentially non-union environments, EI assumed other objectives, such as increasing Ford's ability to retain highly qualified finance staff. Before examining the fate of EI in Ford UK we shall pause to examine the genesis of the involvement strategy in the American company.

The joint development of EI by Ford and the UAW closely paralleled worker participation schemes at General Motors. Both Ford and GM regard worker participation programmes as a way to fundamentally reorient collective bargaining (Wood, 1988). Although contractual issues are explicitly excluded from participation forums these have undoubtedly been used by management as a way of relieving the pressure on both the central contract binding the corporation and the UAW, and the grievance procedure at plant level. During the 1960s and 1970s Ford's American industrial relations system slowly silted up with local issues. Ford US's bargaining process was regulated by a complex form of case law and precedent, a legalistic approach which, for management, squeezed responsiveness and dynamism from negotiations. The formal agreement between Ford and the UAW was supplemented by thick volumes of 'letters of understanding' and even more voluminous arbitrators' decisions. But whereas GM had been at the forefront of radical initiatives such as the Quality of Working Life in the 1970s, Ford's industrial relations functionaries remained wedded to a legalistic approach whose sole rationale was maintaining an over-burdened *status quo* (Kochan et al., 1986: 39; Katz, 1985: 75–9). Above all, Ford's industrial relations system was increasingly remote from the company's deep-seated production problems, particularly the fast-deteriorating build quality of its products. In 1978 Ford US actually recalled more cars than it produced (Banas and Sauers, 1989: 2).

The key to Ford's spectacular corporate turnaround in the 1980s was the cathartic experience of a crisis which threatened the company's very existence. Between 1980–2 Ford US experienced a bewildering range of overlapping crises simultaneously – financial collapse, imploding market share, and an archaic product range. Even the worst-case scenarios built into Ford's renowned financial forecasts understated the extent of the corporation's cash crisis (Shook, 1990: 16). This was a creative crisis in a double sense. First, these crises could not be resolved sequentially, slowly nor solely by traditional belt-tightening measures. Second, 1980–2 constituted a crisis of corporate imagination. The executive team was stripped of the historical certainties of Fordist management. With no concrete vision of a reconstituted, revitalized Ford Motor Company to guide them, Detroit management began from an essentially negative starting point: a rejection of the strategy, structure and management processes which had been refined since 1945. In effect, Detroit executives concluded that their central task was to challenge their own history by replicating their own experience of 'creative crisis' within every Ford plant in America. And EI, later supported by Participative Management, was the vehicle for issuing this profound challenge to every plant manager and shopfloor employee.

The deep recession which hit the American auto industry in 1979 coincided with the arrival within Ford and the UAW of union and corporate executives committed to the expansion of cooperative management–union programmes. UAW endorsement of EI legitimized the programme and it quickly blossomed into thousands of small-scale projects. As EI expanded it highlighted the excesses of Ford's system of direct control and, in turn, stimulated demands from line management for similar involvement in joint programmes. The result – Participative Management (PM) – consolidated what Pascale (1990) vividly describes as 'a set of tributary actions . . . flow[ing] into a river of change'. Pascale's imagery perfectly captures the uncontrolled, organic nature of change and implicitly contrasts the spontaneity of the EI process with the mechanical, structural orientation of classical Fordism. With some difficulty, Detroit restrained itself from attempting to manage and measure the EI process and instead assumed a leadership role in the corporate learning process.

In Ford UK the EI initiative failed to win the endorsement of the manufacturing unions (De Vos, 1981: 69). But this was not the sole reason for EI's limited impact on the shopfloor. Against a backdrop of closures and falling manpower levels, albeit achieved by voluntary redundancy, there was some uneasiness among Ford's European management about the credibility of pushing EI during rationalization. In particular, senior Manufacturing executives had deep misgivings about 'going on the EI stump' while announcing redundancies. In Europe, unlike Ford US, the pressure to reduce manufacturing headcount was seen as conflicting with the corporation's worker involvement strategy.

Plant-level management expressed similar reservations. One Dagenham manufacturing manager bluntly endorsed teamworking by explaining that the rationalization of the early 1980s was 'a period of opportunity: When you've got them by the balls, the head and the heart soon follow'. The reluctance to 'spout Americano' was not just individual obstinacy but symptomatic of the quite different experience of Ford's European executives. Unlike their Detroit counterparts they had never stared collapse in the face. On the contrary, Ford of Europe, and the British company in particular, had been a vital source of revenue and profit during the crisis years of 1980–2. Far from being assailed by the self-doubt which opened Detroit's boardroom to radical ideas about organization, AJ revealed a European management confident about the ability of established strategies and structures to deliver the efficiency gains necessary to maintain competitiveness. For very pragmatic reasons, therefore, Ford UK regarded EI as a long-term investment, rather than a short-term necessity. Paul Roots (1986: 8), former Ford UK Director of Industrial Relations, defended the company's cautious approach:

> Ford has always differed in important respects from other car firms, notably in its profitability, and the company has had less need of dramatic change than have some other firms. It is wary of making sudden moves that could undermine its progress, and seeks continued change as part of a considered programme of development.

For Ford UK, the prime virtue of slow change was that it permitted the retention of the organizational bases of the company's market strength and profitability, a virtue which far outweighed the inevitable tensions between the long-term goal of employee involvement and the short-term necessity of maintaining shopfloor discipline.

EI was endorsed by the white collar unions from 1985 to 1989. But even in largely non-unionized areas EI had mixed results. Ford tracked the impact of EI among white collar grades through a series of annual surveys and focus groups. These discovered widespread scepticism about the ability of EI to significantly change the Ford system. In 1985 internal consultants reported frustration and low morale among system technologists:

> they feel that they are left working in the dark, getting their information from the grapevine or surmisal, stuck too often with mindless coding jobs, promotionally 'invisible' and without any clear understanding of the jobs' context. They believe they are not heard. They believe they are not utilized. And they believe they are over-controlled and under-managed. They are aware that they have no direct connection with, or real awareness of, broader business issues.

The prevailing organizational climate was described as 'conditioned apathy' marked by demoralization and powerlessness. The organization was focused sharply on the task rather than on the people involved. Management style was perceived as totally task-orientated. Far from working in a climate which welcomed pragmatic innovation, the information technologists routinely deferred to unworkable management instructions despite strong professional reservations: 'they are afraid of calling a halt. It would have to be approved. And there's the danger of being accused of not *wanting* to make it work. So they struggle on believing the project unworkable.' A 1985 survey conducted in Finance revealed a deep pessimism about EI 'being allowed to succeed'. Just over a third of white collar respondents regarded EI as an expedient, a charade to massage morale rather than a historic departure from Ford's established management practice. Even those who welcomed EI doubted the commitment of Ford of Europe's senior management to the concepts and questioned what would happen 'when Reichenstein [American Vice-President of Finance and a champion of EI] goes back'.

A follow-up survey conducted three years later revealed that levels of job satisfaction, expectations that individual achievement would be recognized by supervisors, and business awareness had all doubled, from 30 to 40 per cent to 65 to 82 per cent. Nor was this due to a reduction in workload: in 1988 55 per cent of system technologists considered their workload excessive, an increase of 4 per cent from 1985. Nevertheless, inter-functional rivalries and a management style obsessed with control remained a pervasive concern. One supervisor commented that management were failing to capitalize on the commitment of their white collar staff: 'Our involvement is enormous and management still doesn't understand the possibilities and *opportunities*. They don't understand how inefficient we are.' Despite such impressive gains, however, EI had not become embedded in the culture of the organization. For 70 per cent of respondents EI remained marginal to their working life and remote from the demanding daily grind of 'our special world of tight deadlines and set objectives'. In an organization still dominated by vertically-structured management processes, control and inter-functional politics continued to weigh heavily on staff who regarded even their own immediate supervisors with cynical, detached amusement:

> There is a pedantic obsession with detail – constant corrections, tinkering and phrase-changing. And extreme pettiness – the type of arrows on organization charts to be dotted or solid. . . . the whole purpose seems to be to show their department as successful. Status reports still get checked for not being positive enough. Even a disaster has to be a positive disaster.

EI was perceived as an activity restricted to 'the EI people' rather than the first infusion of teamworking principles into the mainstream of the company. Equally, 'the EI people' were frustrated by the experience of working informally, across functions and with a non-hierarchical orientation in a decision-making business architecture that remained stubbornly formal, functionally determined and hierarchical. For the EI participants, the most obvious source of tension was where they had crossed vertically structured communication channels. The transformative mission of EI brought it into sharp conflict with a first-line management whose authority and promotion prospects were bound to upholding traditional Ford control systems. Supervisors perceived EI as an activity performed by groups over whom they had little control and were largely insulated from the conventional disciplines of the workplace. Hard-pressed supervisors also dismissed EI as a lightweight exercise which actually diminished their capacity to meet immediate targets: 'we have to fund the process with man-hours from our teams'. Finally, supervisors resented the disparity between their own unobtrusive efforts to maintain throughput and the high visibility gained by members of non-productive EI groups: 'All that EI has achieved is to boost the morale of the people involved, giving them increased visibility with senior managers to the detriment of their colleagues.' The withdrawal of union (MSF) sponsorship of EI at the national level in 1989 marked the end of Ford UK's attempt to directly emulate the EI experience of the American parent company. But the union's decision conveniently coincided with Ford management's conclusion that the experiment was producing diminishing returns as the formal EI process became ever more remote from the mainstream of company life. The death of EI was even seen as a positive step forward in the struggle for improved employee relations. As one European director put it, 'the barrier of the acronym has gone' – 'the evaporation of EI has been beneficial because EI had become an activity which in many parts of the company "had to be resisted". So EI went and what was left was the basic quality of the process itself.'

The infrastructure of EI, the facilitators and steering committees, were allowed to wind down. 'There will be no "son of EI".' But the strategic intent remains unchanged – remorseless improvement in efficiency and quality through worker involvement. The quality focus emerges as crucial even if the 'passion' for quality has yet to be diffused throughout the organization.

> One thing we are struggling with as an organization is that you can make fairly impressive improvements in the first several years and then you plateau. The States plateaued about two or three years ago and they are struggling to resume their momentum in reducing faults. We are starting to plateau now. . . . You can apply statistical process control and all the other techniques to measure quality performance. But unless you have the absolute burning desire then you just play the game. You play at the process sheets and the control charts and all the rest of the things without giving these techniques any deeper meaning for the people involved. You have to have a *passion* for quality and I don't think that is there.

The almost total failure of EI on the shopfloors of Ford UK reveals the importance both of a wholly committed executive team *and* of trade union endorsement to worker participation programmes. On both counts Ford UK was found wanting. As Eddie Haigh, of the Transport and General Workers' Union, told the Ford UK's inaugural EI conference in June 1989,

> The fact that there is no shopfloor worker, steward or officer here shows the level of mistrust that exists about the EI process. The missing ingredient which would have turned this from a success story into a fairy tale is the manual workers.

EI symbolized Ford's new conciliatory approach to labour relations. But EI's highly uneven impact on largely non-unionized staff areas demonstrates how easily the process was marginalized without the participation of the big battalions of the manufacturing unions.

## Flexibility and Collective Bargaining

If Ford UK made only limited gains in introducing flexibility through formal worker involvement programmes such as EI then it did achieve a significant breakthrough in conventional collective bargaining. Ford UK's industrial relations strategists regard the 1985 Pay and Working Practices Agreement as a breakthrough both in terms of work organization and in the informal diffusion of the principles of EI: 'it was revolutionary by our standards'. Ford UK's managements preparations for the 1985 bargaining round differed from previous practice in that plant management were involved in a dialogue with Ford of Europe advisers to define the negotiators' brief: 'We had a number of meetings where the line managers were invited to say what they needed from the negotiators to help reach their efficiency targets, to get cost effective, to achieve their quality aims.' For Ford of Europe's industrial relations strategists this novel bottom-up approach had the important benefit of binding plant management to deliver any efficiency, quality and flexibility gains made possible by the 1985 Agreement. The short-term aim for Ford UK was to use the 1985 Agreement to close the efficiency gap with its continental plants (Casson, 1987: 231–7). More than that, however, it reflected the cumulative lessons derived from AJ and the robotization of Dagenham. Both experiences highlighted Ford UK's unfavourable ratio of direct to indirect workers and the serious effect of discontinuous production on productivity. In contrast to

Japanese car plants, where inspection and routine ancillary tasks were performed inside the work cycle, these were performed by indirect workers in Ford UK. The key work organization elements of the 1985 Agreement were: individual versatility and collective flexibility. The Agreement dismantled Ford's own rigid bureaucratic categorization of semi-skilled work and the craft demarcations inherited from British trade unionism.

These principles were applied to both craft and production operatives. Maintenance workers were expected to gradually expand their skill base and work across the electrical–mechanical divide (Income Data Services, 1986: 21; Enderwick, 1985: 117). In semi-skilled work Ford challenged the deskilling logic of fifty years of mass production and direct control: 500 job titles were reduced to 50. The title of 'production operative' incorporated what had previously been 86 job titles. Line workers were no longer assigned solely to a specific task but expected to perform minor maintenance, use quality assurance techniques and repair minor product defects. In return for accepting such changes in work organization line workers and maintenance craftsmen received an 18.5 per cent pay rise, dependent upon enhanced efficiency and flexibility. Importantly, the flexibility allowances paid to semi-skilled employees were targeted at groups of workers on related tasks but only received if every worker satisfied the efficiency and flexibility criteria. In other words, co-operation between workers, rather than individual productivity, was made a condition of the bonus payment (Kaplinsky, 1988: 458).

Ford UK had been seeking such changes from 1979 but until 1985 had been as unwilling to pay for them as the unions had been to negotiate flexible work principles. Ford derived a triple efficiency gain from the 1985 Agreement: additional manpower flexibility, increased intensity of capital usage and greater continuity of production. Within two years Ford UK had reduced unit labour costs by an estimated 17 per cent and made budget improvements of 17 per cent, compared to the 4 per cent which was the previous norm. The final innovation introduced by Ford UK in the mid-1980s was a new approach to quality. 'Quality', in this sense, is an umbrella concept embracing several non-price factors such as design, reliability and service. To be quality-conscious is, therefore, to utilize consumer definitions of product acceptability rather than those of the production engineer. Moreover, responsibility for shortcomings in build quality was attributed to management rather than the workforce, to work planning rather than execution. In turn, this approach entailed a fundamental shift in the meaning of quality measurement – away from inspection, rectification and a constant search for improved product design, and manufacture premised on zero defects.

Unlike quality control, a cornerstone of low-trust factory regimes, quality assurance demanded the active engagement of production workers. Two years after the 1985 Agreement the number of Dagenham Paint, Trim and Assembly inspectors had been reduced from 340 to 60. But throughout robotization and the devolution of additional tasks and responsibilities to assembly line workers, Ford has retained tight control over the labour process. Through computerized measurement of efficiency and quality, particularly in capital intensive areas, Ford carefully monitors worker productivity (Pettigrew, 1985; Williams et al., 1987: 62–3). In sum, the changes in work organization enabled by the 1985 Agreement mark a shift in emphasis, a hesitant but significant, movement away from the Fordist paradigm of task fragmentation and the progressive extension of a minutely detailed division of labour. Flexibility has not displaced Fordism on the shopfloor, rather the two patterns of work organization co-exist. The self-sustaining momentum of deskilling and direct control – definitive characteristics of Fordist management strategy – has been interrupted by the emergence of flexibility and worker involvement in Ford's global response to their faltering competitiveness and fragmenting product markets.

## Conclusion

During its eighty-year existence Ford UK has passed through a number of distinct periods in terms of its labour relations strategy. The initial exclusion strategy gave way to one of containment during World War II which, in turn, was succeeded by incorporation in the mid-1970s. Each new strategic direction was triggered by the failure of its predecessor. In this respect, the worker involvement strategy which emerged from Detroit in the 1980s was an implicit admission of the ultimate failure of the incorporation strategy.

But EI represented much more than this. EI was an implicit admission that Fordist patterns of work organization, authority and labour relations were now a crippling competitive disadvantage. Before EI, Ford's industrial relations strategies had one common theme: the search for institutions which would neutralize the shopfloor as an effective source of opposition to management strategy.

EI looked beyond institutions and envisaged the workforce not as inherently hostile or, at best, sullenly quiescent, but as a vital source of untapped knowledge and potentiality. 'The great novelty of EI,' one HRM specialist told us, was that 'for the first time the company attempted to capitalize on the human resource. Before the 1980s Ford had tried to capitalize on the impersonal dimensions of organization – systems, structure and control'.

EI placed the human resource squarely on the strategic agenda for the first time. The 1980s witnessed a qualified but significant reversal of the deskilling rationale which had formed the bedrock of company policy since its foundation. Ford of Europe's gradual transition to lean production supported by HRM practices may only be in its early stages, but the future trajectory of management strategy is clear: worker involvement, flexibility and teamworking will become ever more important to maintaining Ford's competitiveness in British and continental markets. At issue is how to develop a management process on the basis of learning from the experience of the 1980s. In Ford UK, EI stalled not just because of the opposition of the manufacturing unions but also because it was not *essential* to the company's very survival. EI moved HRM issues onto the corporate agenda of Ford UK but it did not displace efficiency and cost reduction as the prime management objectives. The time was not yet ripe, neither for employees nor, as we shall see in the next chapter, management.

# 4

# Managing for Ford: the Challenge of the Past

One of Ford's internal HRM consultants recalled that he had worked for three organizations during his career: the Jesuits, the Navy and the Ford Motor Company. 'And of the three the Ford Motor Company was the most authoritarian, the most regimented, and driven by fear'. In this chapter we detail what it meant to manage for Ford before and after the changes unleashed in the 1980s. The Ford experience challenges the unquestioned assumption behind so much contemporary management theory which suggests that reducing hierarchies automatically releases an organization's latent entrepreneurialism. Real change is far more complex and demanding than this.

In Ford, as in so many other organizations, low-trust was as endemic in managerial grades as in labour relations. In other words, relations within and between managerial groups were highly antagonistic and politicized, a contest controlled by the arcane rules of finance specialists. Organizational change did not occur as an overnight transformation of these relationships as a result of the moves towards employee involvement and participative management, but was inextricably linked to a *necessarily* slow unravelling of Ford's prevailing conservative management culture. We stress the complexity and limits of the change process among Ford's managers as an antidote to the quick fix solutions so fashionable in Western business schools. Unravelling the past is now seen in the company as 'the task of a generation'. However, the enormity of the change experience for the company's managers, despite its limitations, cannot be exaggerated. One senior European executive reflected, 'I've been making profits and cars for Ford Motor Company for over thirty years. And now I've to accept that almost everything I've learned is wrong!'

## Managing for Ford

Studies of work in the car industry have been fixated on the rigors of working on the assembly line. Managers feature rarely in seminal studies such as Huw Beynon's *Working For Ford* (1984), except as remote, shadowy figures who design the factory to maximize their control over an alienated, resentful workforce. However, the organization and job design philosophy that led to the alienated labour of the mass production factory was paralleled by an equally hierarchical division of managerial labour.

The global reach of Fordism only emerged after 1945 with the marriage of the assembly line to the multidivisional structure developed by Alfred Sloan of General Motors. For James Womack and his colleagues (1990: 41), the world's leading authorities on the international motor industry, Sloan effectively 'solved the last remaining problem inhibiting the spread of mass production'.

> New professions of financial managers and marketing specialists were created to complement the engineering professions, so that every functional area of the firm now had its dedicated experts. The division of professional labour was complete.

Ford's approach to management organization was the mirror image of the assembly line – specialized, hierarchical, and tightly controlled. So deeply was the pursuit of control embedded in Ford's corporate psyche that one manager likened it to a smoker's addiction to nicotine: 'We are as we are. The company is like a smoker who knows if it's harmful but who's been a smoker for twenty years. We know what is needed for long-term competitiveness but it's very difficult to break old habits.' Ford managers, just like the men on the assembly line, also operate in a harsh, confrontational environment. Historically this has been especially true of Manufacturing management, where the individual was under no illusion of what was expected of him: 'we played the role – we knew what was expected of us. You knew what you had to do to get on. You had to be tough and if you worked in manufacturing you had to be a bit tougher still'.

The autocracy of the assembly line was simply the cutting edge of an omnipresent corporate culture. If technical expertise was an essential characteristic of the Ford manager then this was not enough to secure promotion. Looking back one manager reflected, 'There is none of the *violence* that used to exist: it was the Rambo rather than the Einstein who was invariably given the job'. Current managers occasionally expressed this dramatic cultural shift through a series of almost wistful recollections of, for instance, the middle manager so terrified by the prospect of making a presentation to a meeting chaired by a Manufacturing executive that he deliberately broke his reading glasses. To his disappointment the meeting was postponed until later. To avoid the reconvened meeting, the anxious manager snapped his dentures. Even more graphically, one manufacturing manager recalled,

> I've been here twenty years and I remember the days when most managers walked in fear of their bosses. Back in the early seventies I would have buttons (on the phone) and I'd ring through to the other guy's office, a long ring, and he'd pull his trousers on if he was in the toilet, and he'd run in and say, 'Yes (Mr X), what do you want?' And there was fear, real fear in the structure. . . . In those days it was the biggest bull elephant who led the pack. *That* was the style of the company.

Such organizational 'myths' capture the experience of the old Ford culture. The Ford Motor Company of the 1960s and 1970s was managed through layer upon layer of autocracy, by confrontation and ultimatum rather than leadership and negotiation. Ford's famous 'Blue Book' defined the tasks and authority of every employee in the factory, manual *and* managerial. Its precision, even then, was seen as a mixed blessing: 'the clarity of the structure was terrific – the rigidity of it was terrible'. The Ford culture was universal:

> It's an absolute truth that you can take me or any other guy who has worked in Ford Motor Company for ten or more years and drop us in a Ford factory in Outer Mongolia and we'll feel immediately at home. And that's not just because the structure and systems are the same: it's a philosophy, a culture, of how your management talk to each other, down to the way they dress.

Ford has always operated a 'pressure system' on middle management: efficiency, discipline and selection through sheer intensity of workload. Promotion was based on the individual's ability to handle pressure, to deal with impossible workloads. To bend under pressure, to admit to being overloaded was a sign of weakness in a system which placed a heavy premium on managerial *machismo* and blind bureaucratic compliance during the ascent of the managerial hierarchy. 'Everyone in here is a workaholic and those who aren't make damn sure they look as if they are'. Virtually unchecked elite individualism and the deadweight of Ford's bureaucratic decision-making processes combined to produce a ferocious task culture.

> Certain types of projects were done very quickly under the authoritarian system because everybody jumped to attention and was very committed. Fear does generate commitment. There were people who used to be working until 9, 10, 11 and 12 o'clock at night because they must not miss a deadline for producing finance figures. . . . In those days you didn't question whether the figures were really that urgent – you didn't want to display that sort of weakness. It was a very macho culture. If you needed to work until 2 or 3 in the morning you just did it without question. That culture did produce astonishing performances from management and support staff. . . . The task absolutely dominated their thought processes. We've lost that sort of commitment: the fanatical commitment that the old macho, autocratic structure bred into people.

Individual accountability within a task-oriented bureaucracy – 'the Ford credo' – isolated the Ford manager. Functional loyalty did not extend to a tolerance of personal frailties. 'It's hard to imagine,' admitted a data processing manager amid the hubbub of a busy office, 'but it used to be a lonely life for a manager in this company. You knew you would only survive if you made your numbers, if you were the best: you were always looking over your shoulder'. Ignorance, uncertainty and error were all taboo for the Ford manager: 'the three toughest words in Ford were – "I don't know".' Nor was this isolation offset by the dense network of allegiance which bound each functional hierarchy together. Such loyalties may have been expressed in personal terms but they were not the reciprocal ties of friendship and collegiality. They were determined by the imperative of defending functional power and prestige. Strong functional loyalties were deeply engrained in the Ford culture and shaped the relationship within and between functional management groups. This was especially true of the Finance function. Finance specialists unselfconsciously referred to themselves as belonging to a Finance 'community'.

Ford has always been a highly politicized organization, from the absolutist rule of Henry Ford I to the war of attrition between Lee Iacocca and Henry Ford II, when the Detroit boardroom seethed with battles for succession and control in the 1970s. But the boardroom was not the only political arena in Ford. Robert MacNamara attempted to create a bureaucracy purged of politics in which egos and sectional interests were subordinated to statistics. But the ambition to create an ascetic organization simply changed the rules of political engagement and placed Finance – the 'beancounters' – in the roles of final arbiter, kingmaker and honest broker within Ford. Finance's defining role was to maximize profit at least cost, a role which gave it power in every nook and cranny of the organization. More than anything else, Finance was *the* integrative function within Ford, 'the glue which holds the organization together'. Both respected and feared – in the words of one non-Finance manager, 'calling that collection of piranhas a community is one of life's great ironies' – Finance epitomized both the strengths and weaknesses of the company's rigorous analytical approach. *Every* decision had to be justified in financial terms, an unbending principle which generated constant tension between Finance and operational functions.

## Feudal Politics

The Ford manager's every decision was conditioned by his reading of the political balance of forces at a given moment.

> One group of directors or V[ice] P[resident]s wouldn't attend a meeting where certain individuals were present. Those kind of feudal politics were a fact of life in Ford. Self-preservation meant that you had to develop as wide a knowledge of the personal and functional animosities as any technical skill. To succeed – to survive – you had to develop antennae very quickly indeed.

And the conflicts were not just between Finance and other functions. Beneath the apparent objectivity of negotiations conducted in quantitative terms between Manufacturing and Marketing functions, for instance, the hidden agenda was sectional advantage rather than corporate objectives. Marketing's demand for maximum product diversity and short lead times conflicted with manufacturing's concern for stable, predictable production schedules. One computer systems manager, an intermediary caught in the cross-fire of this functional feud, described the relationship between sales and manufacturing:

> Historically sales and manufacturing have always fought a never-ending war of attrition. That has been the nature of the relationship. There's a big wall and they just lob bombs over it – back and forth. Sales have taken the view that until we give them to you they're *my*

> orders from *my* dealers and you're not going to have them. Manufacturing took the view that once you've given us the orders, its *ours* and *we* decide when *we* process it.

Such managerial tribalism was accepted as an essential element of the Ford planning system.

> The tradition in Ford has been for functional heads to come to planning meetings with their own plans to defend. It was an adversarial system. And in an organization like Ford where Finance had been top-dog for so long, figures weren't used to improve the quality of decision-making but as weapons to gain a sectional advantage irrespective of what the overall cost was. That's why Ford managers are good at negotiating with the Unions – they're used to horse-trading as part of the *management* process.

In Ford's task-driven, fiercely competitive culture the organization's functionally-based politics were universally acknowledged and informed managerial behaviour.

Importantly, organizational politics was not universally condemned by Ford's middle managers. Before the initiatives of the 1980s the political dimension of Ford's decision-making process was rarely questioned and never challenged. An inevitable consequence of the company's functional hierarchy, it was simply accepted as normal behaviour. But inter-functional rivalries were a source of deadlock rather than dynamism within the planning system. Perhaps the greatest cost penalty of this introverted decision-making process was time, a penalty which by the 1980s resulted in Western manufacturers – Ford was, of course, not the only culprit, or victim, of this way of managing – unable to match the product dynamism or quality of their Japanese competitors.

> That's why you had such stiff quality control, because it was the policeman catching the thieves. Production was know as the thieves, and they'd try to push through the numbers at any cost, to beat the quality control. It was pretty funny the strokes people used to pull to get the numbers. But it was totally internal: a game within the company with no thought to the customer.

Quality control was synonymous with search and punish in a system which increasingly and inevitably was losing touch with the people it thought it was serving.

## Participative Management after 'After Japan'

As in the US, the 1980s saw Ford of Europe initiating efforts to streamline its managerial hierarchy, fundamentally change the organization's managerial culture and make radical new demands of its managers. The After Japan study initiated these changes. Participative Management arriving in Europe from the US extended them.

Historically Ford represented the archetypal 'machine bureaucracy', the classic institutional form of big business in the twentieth century. Perfectly attuned to the demands of environmental stability, it becomes a major barrier to change in more dynamic market settings (Mintzberg, 1983). The dominant image of contemporary management imagination is of the 'excellent' organization, of managers becoming the leaders of a liberating Odyssey leaving behind the alienating experience of the 'scientifically managed' corporation. Competitiveness, empowerment and humanity are presented as the necessary components of the renewing corporation. In the machine bureaucracy information flowed up – never across – and decisions down the hierarchy. The starting point for much of what Rosabeth Moss Kanter (1989) calls 'the new managerial work' is a challenge to the impersonal, uniform, 'scientific' rules which lie at the heart of bureaucracy. Post-bureaucratic management begins from an inversion of the logic of the 'machine', emphasizing organic relationships, informality over rules, personal responsibility over impersonal systems, and collective creativity through teamwork rather than an individualistic task culture (Joiner, 1986). The management of culture replaces the administration of structure as the central role of strategic management.

If the chief executive is the prime symbol of the post-bureaucratic corporation then, according to its most vocal proponents, it is the duty – indeed, moral obligation – of each and every manager to embody and nurture the emergent culture. It is at this point that the breathless optimism of much recent management writing breaks down (Fulop, 1991). The vision of the middle manager as entrepreneur and leader primed to unleash the latent creativity of the corporation by empowering employees requires a colossal act of faith. It is precisely middle managers who have the most to *lose* through decentralization and empowerment. Diminished hierarchies mean an erosion of the old bases of managerial authority. In this scenario, the middle manager has to develop alternative sources of power and authority based on his or her ability as motivator and facilitator; while balancing the demands of existing functional responsibilities and those of collaborative project teams. As Kanter (1989: 89–90) perceptively comments, these may well be competing priorities which make novel and exacting demands on the individual manager.

> In the collaborative forums [that are emerging], managers are more personally exposed. It is trust that makes partnership work. Since collaborative ventures often bring together groups with different methods, cultures, symbols, even languages, good deal making depends on empathy – the ability to step into other people's shoes and appreciate their goals. This applies not only to intricate global ventures but also to the efforts of engineering and manufacturing to work together more effectively. Effective cooperative effort rests on more than a simple exchange of information; people must be adept at anticipating the responses of other groups. 'Before I get too excited about our department's design ideas,' an engineering manager told me, 'I'm learning to ask myself, "What's the marketing position on this? What will manufacturing say?" That sometimes forces me to make changes before I even talk to them.'

Ford's contribution to post-bureaucratic management is its Participative Management (PM) initiative. PM was, as we have seen, developed in Ford US in response to the clamour of middle managers caught in the rising tide of workforce expectations stimulated by EI. It was a tacit acknowledgement that Ford's front line managers felt exposed under the EI regime, uncertain of their authority and unversed in the inter-personal skills being deployed by the EI problem-solving groups. PM became the other side of EI, the essential complement to Ford's drive towards worker involvement. In other words, the bottom-up demand for PM was an attempt by middle managers to understand and gain some leverage within the process of organizational change. PM has two main themes. First, to simplify management control systems, devolve authority and increase operational responsibility by developing self-contained project teams. By broadening managerial spans of control Ford US was attempting to narrow the distance between strategic and operational priorities. Second, PM confronted the deep mistrust characteristic of Fordist management, as evident in the management process as on the shopfloor. In the classic Fordist regime collaboration between functionally-defined management groups was regarded at best as a necessary evil and a highly political process in which the protection of vested interest was of paramount importance. PM was, in short, an assault on the managerial culture of Fordism – individualist, cynical, task oriented, politicized and deeply mistrustful. In structural terms it presents a fundamental challenge to a management system constructed on the basis of 'organizational chimneys'.

The changed expectations of managers in Ford of Europe began not with PM but with After Japan. If AJ failed to 'Japanize' Ford of Europe's labour relations then it did initiate a major rethinking of the company's management system and culture. No group of Ford managers returned from study trips to Japan more chastened than those from Finance. Ford's initial appraisal of their emerging Japanese competition focused on manufacturing but this was quickly followed by cost comparisons with the infrastructure of the Japanese corporation. Subsequent to AJ Finance initiated a study of its own operations that went beyond the narrow cost comparisons of AJ. This second wave examined Japanese business practices in their own terms, rather than refracted through parameters determined by Ford's existing structures and practices. Ford's financial controllers concluded that, in comparison with their own organization, the Japanese control process is simple; that control is shared throughout functional areas rather than monopolized by Finance; and that the entire Japanese enterprise is organized for cost reduction (Strebel, 1987: 120–8).

But it was not simply the organization of the Finance function that differed between Japanese and Western companies. Rather, the dispersed nature of financial control in Japanese companies represented a qualitatively different balance between trust and control – supported by a different organizational culture – than in the concentrated functional specialisms in Ford. The target set for Ford of Europe in 1980 was to reduce its Finance headcount by 30 per cent within three years. As Bud Marx, then Ford of Europe's Finance Vice President, acknowledged, not only did this target mean stripping out layer upon layer of procedural controls. It also entailed a radical change in the nature of Finance's role within the organization. But, Marx warned,

> greater delegation of authority . . . necessitates increased trust throughout the financial control system. Achieving the right balance between 'trust' and 'control', however, will require some trial and error and will need a backup system of tough audits. (Strebel, 1987: 120)

The central aim of AJ was, as we saw in our examination of labour relations, cost reduction *not* a revolution in corporate culture. Nevertheless, the note of caution sounded by Bud Marx suggests that Finance was aware that a relaxation of their established controls would result not just in cost reduction but also in the erosion of their organizational power base. Given the uncertainties of this transition, Finance had both to relinquish traditional controls *and* maintain its vigilance over the change process. Each time a particular procedure was challenged by line managers it implicitly raised more general and fundamental questions about control and the role of Finance specialists in Ford. But the *cultural* impact of this loosening of mundane financial control procedures was only fully appreciated afterwards. AJ, one European HRM executive reflected, was after all 'an exercise in organizational destruction which proved to be enormously creative in a cultural sense. But this was an unintended consequence of AJ'.

Importantly, although four top-level steering committees were established, the AJ process was driven by operational management rather than financial controllers. It was not a case of Finance specifying which controls they considered superfluous but of line managers having *their* choices ratified. For Bill Hayden, the prime mover behind AJ, it was precisely this bottom-up approach which distinguished AJ from traditional cost-cutting exercises within Ford: 'we did address cost and quality issues in a traditional way but there was one important difference: it was not cost-cutting led by the people at the top. It was cost-cutting by plant managers, by section heads – it went all the way down.' Cost control mechanisms were dramatically reduced. For instance, checking frequencies were reduced by up to 60 per cent, monthly reports by 25 per cent and in major investment and product programmes only indicative rather than comprehensive costs were considered necessary at the initial strategy and concept stages.

> AJ was a significant event. AJ meant a major upheaval, a complete reconstruction of the Finance community. Prior to AJ we had armies of people checking what other people had done. . . . It was a nonsense system, a nonsense process. We now believe our management are responsible, why employ armies of people at all levels simply to check and recheck what responsible people have done. AJ finally recognized that. Large chunks of the finance community disappeared overnight. . . . Along with that was hacked away a lot of administrative

> overheads we had accumulated in the numbers of forms which detailed every step for even the smallest decision or transaction.

But, as Bud Marx insisted in 1980–1, strict financial controls remained in place. Not all of the remaining fixed points are warmly regarded by operational management. As one Manufacturing manager caustically observed,

> We've still got lots of procedures which get in the way of the business. We've got sacred cows like headcount or capital budget which we worship. Before AJ we had to worship these things monthly; at least it's been reduced to annual worship.

In Finance the AJ target was a 30 per cent headcount reduction within three years from 1980. In fact, Finance personnel within Ford's European companies dropped from 5,186 in 1980 to 4,270 in 1983, a fall of 17 per cent. Almost 70 per cent of the reduction was achieved during the first year with a variety of voluntary redundancy packages targetted at staff with limited or no promotion prospects. Although there were no compulsory redundancies, headcount reduction was not an entirely painless exercise: finance staff who rejected voluntary severance packages were eased sideways into less demanding jobs. Such 'AJ casualties' endured a considerable loss of power and status, and became 'emperors without empires'. Within Finance the headcount reductions were uneven, varying between the 30 to 40 per cent achieved in Purchasing Cost Analysis and Financial Analysis and the 9 per cent reported by Systems Group. The most significant reductions, in other words, were among 'checkers checking checkers'.

AJ's failed attempt to introduce quality circles into Ford UK was perceived by the shopfloor unions as symptomatic of an aggressive, opportunistic management intolerant of trade unionism. AJ was perceived quite differently by line managers: stripping out controls on middle managers symbolized increased trust within the organization. One of the clearest examples of the low trust and extremely time-consuming bureaucratic controls eliminated by AJ were the monthly reports compiled by section managers which costed every member of staff's activity to the nearest half hour against an individual task. In turn, these reports were cross-checked and managers asked to account for any discrepancies between projections and actual time budgets. 'Before AJ the manager had to be a good administrator of pseudo information flows. There were so many rules and regulations that you spent half your time administering routines rather than managing.' Paradoxically, this fetish for control actually undermined the authority of the individual Ford manager. Managers were no less a cog in Ford's bureaucratic machine than assembly line workers: 'Managers used to be just like specialist workers on the assembly line. Just like line-workers there were operators of a procedure. The same principles applied'. Traditionally, managerial authority was invested in the structure rather than individual managers.

> AJ was a real turning point as far as the management process was concerned. It started to give managers authority. Previously we had responsibility but no authority. AJ was the turning point when that started to change. AJ took us off a historic plateau and started to give authority to line managers.

Although the reduction in the management headcount, the decentralization of decision-making and the introduction of Participative Management were nominally separate processes, in practice they overlapped to a considerable degree. It is impossible to determine the relative impact of numerical, structural and processual change on managerial behaviour and expectations.

> The hierarchy is still there but there have been major changes. The headcount reduction thinned out the management hierarchy and that – plus the participation initiatives – has increased peoples' roles, encouraged them to take initiatives without necessarily taking direction from the top. Your actual authority within the company is determined by what you can carry rather than what is assigned to you by the formal organization chart.

For the individual manager perhaps the most visible aspect of these changes was their exposure to a much greater level of what would previously have been considered commercially sensitive information. From AJ onwards Ford of Europe's top management have stressed the need for strategic information to percolate down to middle management level. Decentralization and commercial awareness have dramatically changed Ford managers' perceptions of themselves and their role within the company.

> Ford managers are now much less system administrators than businessmen of some kind. Managers in all functions and at all levels are expected to have a much wider appreciation of the business and its inter-dependent nature. The ideal Ford manager is more dynamic, reacting to change, to problem-solving, rather than grinding the Ford system, facilitating other people to do their job better rather than operating the routine of the system.

## Entrepreneurship, Risk and Trust

The process of decentralization and the stripping of layers of control from an organization is not an entirely unmixed blessing for those on the receiving end. As one Systems manager memorably put it, decentralization 'just means the sharks are a bit closer to you'. Eradicating much of the routine and reducing hierarchical structures have lessened the insulation middle management had against being measured directly against business rather than administrative objectives. If the thinning out of Ford management has opened up new space for 'entrepreneurial' behaviour, then it has also demanded that individual managers acquire the confidence that organizational change has progressed sufficiently far for them to risk personal failure. Again and again line managers stressed the personal risks involved in attempting even limited changes within the traditional Ford structure, which was *designed* to resist innovation: managers 'knew the bureaucracy would review the hell out of any initiative anyway'. The immensity of such a change in an organization such as Ford should not be under-estimated: CYA ('cover your ass') had become a reflex action for experienced Ford managers. For one long-serving Ford manager the following anecdote encapsulated the CYA mentality.

> Once upon a time there was a senior guy who was called to see the Chairman, but couldn't find out what the topic was. So he thought, 'Oh my God: have I got something hanging out? What's gone wrong?' So he got his key people and he said, 'I want you to review the state of the business and put together some binders for me. Where have we got problems, where have we got *potential* problems?' So he gets all these people working flat out to provide him with back up. The day arrives and he enters the Chairman's office. The Chairman sits him down, smiles and congratulates him on thirty years service with the company.

> To anybody who's been with Ford for a long time that story illustrates two things. First, if the Chairman wants to see you it's got to be bad news. Second, you've got to cover your butt by having as much back-up as possible. You've got to guess the most off-the-wall questions he might just ask so you can come up with the answer. That's the Whiz Kid tradition: the bright bushy tailed finance guy who knows the answers to questions before you've even dreamt them up.

Overcoming the endemic low trust of Fordist management is an essential precondition for organizational learning and for the effectiveness of the cross-functional project teams that are beginning to emerge (see the next chapter). And in an important sense, the political skills so essential for the survival of the classical Fordist manager remain a vital element of managing for the Ford of the 1990s. There is, however, one crucial difference: the astute Ford manager now chooses appropriate moments to display – not disguise – his networking abilities and willingness to share knowledge across functional boundaries.

> You can't legislate for the new problems that arise. You just have to keep practising, find out where it hurts, resolve that problem and try again. Experiment, not a concept Ford managers would traditionally have found comfortable, but that's what our best managers are getting used to doing. Traditionally, you progressed up the hierarchy by using the structure as a platform for subterfuge, building networks to advance your career and sometimes to thwart others. Now, the best people are realizing that the only way to maximize their careers is to be *seen* to be good at building networks for the good of the business rather than personal advantage.

But there has been no clean break with the past within Ford. The transition from low to high trust within and between managerial groups remains highly uneven and fragile. Time pressure is the great enemy of participative management. Under pressure there is the danger of 'reversion to type'.

> EI/PM says everything is up for discussion. But when you get to the crunch point, when you're up to your ass in alligators all that stuff goes out the window: it's back to the old autocratic approach. The company reverts to type.

One manager was dismissive of those who maintained they had *always* had a participative management style. Such managers, he insisted, 'really don't understand the dynamics of the organization. Participation was a high-risk personal tactic. It was a gamble that left one exposed to future attacks by other managers who now had information from your function'.

Experience of the newly emergent efforts at project management exemplify both the distance travelled and the residual power classical Fordism retains within the organization. Typically, delegates to cross-functional project teams have only limited authority. Delegates have to refer important project decisions back to their host function for approval: power remains rooted in the hierarchical structure rather than the emerging cross-functional network of project teams: 'functional responsibilities are still where the business is really done'. The hesitancy of progress towards a flat, network organization is directly attributable to the continued potency of inter-functional politics and the legacy of the traditional management culture.

> The process [of introducing cross-functional project teams] is slow and extremely fragile. People are easily discouraged by lack of reciprocity in other areas. If the corporation is to get away from the warring tribes of functions then it has to install *empowered* project teams all over the business. Its difficult if one group of managers puts down its sword and shield and is then attacked by a function which has decided to remain a warring tribe.

The old Ford hierarchy was 'mechanistic' in the sense that it was made to be tinkered with, to adjust over time. This was a structure designed to be reactive to a slow-changing environment. Fordist hierarchies and processes were, quite literally, 'designed for a different world'. The greater fluidity of project management embedded within fixed structures has strained Ford's traditional command and reward systems. Managers and staff with dual responsibilities – to both functions and projects – effectively have two lines of accountability, and 'when you have two bosses or a number of bosses the system starts creaking'. The personnel planning specialists ruefully admit that their traditional two-dimensional organizational charts are incapable of representing an organization in which the horizontal communication of transitory project teams is becoming as important as vertical command and control hierarchy.

When I joined the company, it was full of empty boxes and you could put anybody with any intelligence at all in any one of the boxes, give him a statement of functions, the relevant procedure manuals, his authorities, and he could read through these and do the job. The whole company was structured that way. There were a large number of people involved in writing policy manuals to make sure it was all kept up to date. Things are changing so fast that this could no longer be kept up to date. Its difficult enough to keep the organization chart up to date now. All our personnel policies and procedures are designed for a rigid, hierarchical company.

The personnel planning system is under pressure because we're doing what we ought to be doing, which is destructuring the company.

## The Lure of Nostalgia

Post-AJ the nature of quantitative information has been qualitatively changed. Before AJ all plant-level statistics were transformed from useful information about, for example, headcount and absenteeism, to the dollar values necessary for Finance's centralizing and highly esoteric purposes. Since the early 1980s this logic has been reversed. Operational utility is the prime objective of plant-level statistics. Using physical values to identify scrap levels at different locations in the plant is part of the wider philosophy of empowering operational managers 'rather than channelling *all* contentious decisions upwards'.

As a result of the process of change set in motion by AJ, financial analysts retained control over budgets and yields but devolved authority for approving investment up to $100,000. This delegation of investment decisions was accompanied by a shift away from Ford's inherited faith in the absolutes of rational planning and an acceptance that responding quickly to increasingly uncertain markets necessarily involves intuition and risk. 'As a consequence of PM,' a manufacturing plant manager suggested, 'decision-making in Ford has become more relative whereas before it was black and white. As managers we now accept that there are grey areas, that there are differing interpretations . . . and no single "correct" answer'. Reflecting on precisely the same experience, a Finance manager remarked, not without a hint of nostalgia,

financial decisions aren't quite as tidy as they were say ten years ago. All the 't's' aren't crossed and 'i's' dotted. We used to analyse everything to death. We'd bludgeon every investment proposal until it stopped moving. It's more judgemental now – we don't check obviously correct proposals a thousand times for minor defects. The old system used to focus on the defects at the expense of the project as a whole; that's reversed now.

Yet the past still has its attractions. Perhaps somewhat perversely our respondents not only understood but actually empathized with the direct, demanding style which had been the hallmark of Ford's senior managers. It was the sheer force of personality which enabled these managerial 'bull-elephants' to break through the gridlock of Ford's time-consuming bureaucracy. There were dissenting voices among the European executives we interviewed who were less enthusiastic about the shift from intense structural and procedural controls. Behind their doubts lay a deep fear that dismantling basic procedures refined over forty years risked a general breakdown in order. It might be gradual, a slow erosion of attention to detail, but, however trivial and slight the individual lapses might seem, the fear was that their cumulative result could prove cataclysmic.

Ford's great strength was that we understood that every problem had a solution so long as it was well defined and criteria were set. We were locked into that system and it was no bad thing. We got things done, we made cars, we made money. We may not have had 'ownership' of the strategy but we damn well made sure we did what we were told, did it accurately, did it quickly and did it profitably.

For such sceptical executives, the changing role of the Finance function, particularly its diminishing role in policing Ford's decision-making processes, is not without costs. For Bill Hayden, influential Vice-President of Manufacturing from 1975 to 1989, analytical rigor was the great strength of the system established by MacNamara after 1945:

It's very easy in Ford Motor Company to blame 'The System'. You'll always find that it's 'The System' that stops you doing anything. Now I've never yet found the office marked 'Mr System' or I'd have marched in there and crucified him! But that's what they will tell you – its the financial control *system* which gets in the way. I grew up in Finance: joined it in 1962 and I helped develop it, to perfect it, to defend it. And I agree that Finance have strong power and influence within Ford Motor Company, but financial control is important. . . .

> The 'System' has forced me to think rigidly about alternatives, it's forced me to answer all kinds of stupid questions, and it's taken far longer to get things done. That's the negative; the positives are that people don't do things off the cuff. There's no back of the envelope calculations in Ford Motor Company. It does force you to think through alternatives; it does force you to be logical. In meetings I'd say, 'is that a fact or an opinion?' Ford Motor Company is an arena in which there are very few times that you express an opinion as a fact without the system itself correcting you. And that's a good self-discipline.

## Conclusion

After Japan was a watershed in Ford's corporate strategy, its conception of work organization and its approach to routine management. Whereas AJ had only limited direct success in recasting industrial relations, for Ford managers it signalled the need to radically alter the company's culture. AJ's cost comparisons challenged not just Ford's European manufacturing efficiency. It also served notice that the bureaucratic control mechanisms of mass production were a deadweight in terms of cost and time. The role of the powerful Finance function within Ford was called into serious question for the first time since 1945. The reduction in Finance personnel and the decentralization of decision-making were the structural results of AJ.

Equally important, however, was the Participative Management initiative. In the US PM was introduced in response to the success of the EI worker involvement programme. By contrast, in Ford of Europe PM served primarily in the short-term as a top-down process to facilitate corporate restructuring. In the longer term it fed into new initiatives designed to facilitate cross-functional communication that we examine in the next two chapters. In this sense, PM has developed a momentum of its own far beyond any initial agenda.

Rationalization and the increased administrative efficiency necessary after After Japan would have been impossible without the introduction of a more participative approach to management. Indeed a Finance specialist – 'I'm one of the guys in grey suits with sharp pencils' – suggested that initiatives such as PM were designed to compensate for the loss of traditional procedural controls over managerial behaviour: 'AJ didn't just take out costs it also took out a certain amount of our structural controls and a certain amount of our [Finance] capabilities. All our "people" initiatives have been surrogates for our old controls.' This view was echoed by a Manufacturing manager:

> PM is really making a virtue out of necessity – with fewer people in the organization we had to relax our little box mentality. Lateral communication might be the long-term strategic goal but it also had the short-term benefit of helping us paper over the cracks in the organization as we shed manpower, *managerial* manpower.

It would be simplistic, therefore, to attribute the changes in Ford's management style solely to PM. Structural change, particularly Finance's new role, had thrust new responsibilities onto middle management. Equally, however, no manager remains completely untouched by the emerging imperative of cross-functional teamworking.

Perhaps the most striking aspect of these changes, though, is that despite their diversity and unevenness, despite the lack of shared benchmarks to register the degree of change, despite the absence of a common definition of what PM means in abstract terms, there is a convergence in management thinking upon the emerging strategic necessity for more participation in management – whatever that might mean.

> If there is only supposed to be one definition . . . then we have clearly failed to achieve that. But I'm not sure that was ever the intention. I think Participative Management is almost like Motherhood. It has personal moments depending on the relationship you have with your mother. I feel that in some people it produces a warm, pleasant, relaxed feeling. For others, it brings nothing but frustration and heartache.

At the same time the majority of managers are careful to stress the limits of PM as much as its progress.

> It is certainly not unfashionable to adopt a PM attitude. Twenty years ago it would have been suicide, now it's survival. Twenty years ago if you had asked your staff what they thought the company doctor would have been sent for. That doesn't happen anymore. PM is accepted but there is a lot of lip-service. . . . [A common perception] is that it doesn't apply to us, it might be OK for unimportant things, . . . but not for Ford's quality drive or investment decisions.

Despite enthusiastic acceptance by some Ford managers as a necessary antidote to the old system, at a general level PM remains an *attitude* rather than a code of conduct. There is widespread scepticism among middle managers about executives whose long-established management style had been ruthless 'now banging the "participative drum".' Senior operational management, especially at plant level – 'the sharp end of the business' – were perceived to have clung tenaciously to their received autocratic management style. Despite the necessity of the structural and attitudinal changes accomplished since AJ, some managers still harbour doubts about their permanence when confronted by recession.

> Ford Motor Company is a very savage beast when wounded financially and its eyes will just cloud over and it will cast around for petty economies. And the change process could be a casualty. Finance would be the axe-man in this scenario. They would have no qualms about it. They're like the regular army: they're told to take that kill or eliminate those fixed costs and not to stop to count the bodies.

But, all the same, change has occurred and is occurring. What Ford managers are experiencing is a slow revolution in managerial skills. In the words of one of the company's human resource executives, 'change is so slow that you have to look back to realize that it has occurred. It's imperceptible on a day to day basis'. There is a shared sense that, at the very least, the range of possible management styles had been extended during the 1980s, even if these were seldom fully integrated in all situations.

> Our management has now developed a tremendous ability to change its style, to put on different hats in different meetings. Literally, the same group of managers will agree on quality initiatives of all kinds in a brainstorming session and then five minutes later reconvene as functional directors and say, 'We can't afford that, we're not having that, and that's impossible'. Same group of people, different sort of meeting.

Even among the sceptical there is an appreciation that, despite the pace of change, and even if change has been as much rhetorical as real, the new rhetoric and the slowly changing mind-sets are starting to have a considerable cumulative impact.

> The lip service to EI/PM *has* generated new expectations of how managers *should* behave to each other and their staff. . . . The EI/PM development is happening and it won't be stopped – not necessarily because senior management wish it – but because they've set the ball rolling. There's a chain reaction now that won't easily be stopped.

# 5

# Undoing the Past: Participative Management and Product Development

It is in product development, the activity, and Product Development, the function, that participative management has been most developed in Ford of Europe. Product Development 'took the lead in organizational experimenting' in Ford of Europe with its sights firmly set on the Japanese edge in this crucial strategic area. 'Experimenting' is the key term here. Moves towards participative management in product development were not the result of any formal EI/PM process. In this and the following chapter we examine the nature of product development and how Ford has attempted to come to terms with the legacy of its traditional approach. In particular we examine the reasons why this approach became unsustainable in the light of the new Japanese competition and how human resource management imperatives – such as teamwork, communication and, in particular, the integration of effort towards shared goals across organizational divides – emerged as crucial strategic concerns.

Product development includes product planning, car engineering and design. It covers all the activities between the identification of new product concepts through market research, the planning of products – in Ford's case with a strong input from Finance – to the completed design for production. In Ford of Europe product development is an integrated activity with equal inputs from the British and German sides of the company. The Product Development function is actually physically split into two groups, one in the UK and the other in Germany. A basic Ford philosophy of product development is simplicity of design to foster low cost of ownership in terms of price, quality, reliability and service. The company aims to produce the best car in each of its product sectors (which span every major product sector in Europe). With the acquisition of Jaguar, Ford of Europe has also entered into the luxury car market.

Ford of Europe product development is relatively independent of the control of its American parent. The original Fiesta development programme of the 1970s was the project which finally put the seal on this independence. Before Fiesta, Dearborn staff had prepared alternative designs for European products. The superiority of the Europeans in designing a small car, a new project for the company, and Henry Ford II's personal interest in this project guaranteed autonomy. However, the executive committee in Dearborn remains the ultimate arbiter in decision-making concerning the investment parameters for new products. It is this group that must approve final development and tooling.

It was Henry Ford II, therefore, who oversaw the decentralization of product development. Henry Ford I had demanded total control of the product and all manufacturing decisions under him emanated from Detroit. But decentralization caused its own problems, namely a growing product overlap in the smaller car range between Europe and the US. The issue of global standardization of products in each size class became a high strategic priority (Womack et al., 1990). If attainable this would produce enormous savings in development costs and manufacturing economies. The first attempt at Ford to coordinate product development across the Atlantic divide was the Escort, which had a world design team. Yet the final outcome of this 'world car' project was only 5 parts in common between Europe and the United States. The idea underlying the world car concept, however, remains as potent as the achievement is elusive. Ford of Europe is currently the 'centre of responsibility' charged with the development of the replacement for the Ford Sierra for Europe and the Tempo/Topaz for the North American market.

## Product Development: Key Issues

The process of engineering an object as complex as today's motor-car demands enormous effort from large numbers of people with a broad range of skills. Mass-production companies have typically tried to solve the complexity problem by finely dividing labour among many engineers of highly specialized expertise (Womack et al., 1990: 63ff). Fordism led to progressive specialization not only of production functions but of knowledge work in product design and development – product engineers specialized in engines, bodies, suspension, electrical systems, even door-handle technology. These 'knowledge workers' replaced the skilled machine-shop owners and the old-fashioned factory foremen of the earlier craft era.

> Those worker-managers had done it all – contracted with the assembler, designed the part, developed a machine to make it, and, in many cases, supervised the operation of the machine in the workshop. The fundamental mission of these new specialists, by contrast, was to design tasks, parts, and tools that could be handled by the unskilled workers who made up the bulk of the new motor-vehicle industry work force. (Womack et al., 1990: 32–3)

Traditional product development in Ford is described by Don Frey (1991), who was vice president of product development at Ford in the 1960s and a key player in the development of the very successful Mustang. Frey is highly critical of what was in his time at Ford the 'normal' approach to product development. The process was controlled by 'a centralized industrial research organization, typically far-removed from both operations and market' (Frey, 1991: 47). 'Bean-counter designs' dominated; quality suffered in the trade-off with cost. He illustrates this point in a description of a new car development.

> The quality problems were overwhelming. Someone had to 'dry the car up' – which meant stop it from leaking oil all over the place. I was that someone.
> We attacked the power steering pump, which one of the old hands said was 'a piece of junk.' When I asked how it got that way, he said the 'bean counters' had taken a dime of cost out of assembly each year. I said 'fix it' – and we did. I wondered (in my naivete) how financial planners could have anything to say about the matter in the first place. A bean counter's idea of cost control, I surmised, was to take an inch off the tail pipe every year. (Frey, 1991: 48)

Too many decisions were taken on the grounds of price alone (for example, on component supply), to the detriment of quality. Financial controllers made financial projections but had no feel for the product and no idea about how to make the company grow through building market share by introducing exciting new product. And Finance was not the only function to blame. Research and Development (R&D) people refused to leave the 'lab' and were 'snobbish' about the sales force. So divorced were the design engineers that 'they wouldn't know a customer if they tripped over one'. Senior executives were preoccupied with political power games.

Frey describes what he had to learn in pursuit of good products:

> First was to 'feel' my way through products, or rely on the intuitions that came from working from the ground up, not from the market data down. I had to learn the difference between the uncertain costs of experimentation and the certain disaster of standing pat. I had to learn to break down barriers in our corporate environment so that R&D people would explore customer needs, designers would learn to count on manufacturing, financial people would not kill projects just when they were about to pay off – and all of the above would not think their top management capricious. . . . the lesson that a CEO could have virtually no feel for a product – that, in consequence, a wonderful new proposal could get nowhere without a high-level champion – was not lost to me. . . . Nothing puts a greater drag on innovation than the inertia in your own organization, especially difficult manufacturing reforms or the politics surrounding the security of people's jobs. (Frey, 1991: 46–52)

Frey is particularly critical of linear thinking about product innovation which assumes that product development should take place in a staged process: a breakthrough is made in R&D, which is then passed on to be 'reduced' to practice through engineering, manufacture and sales, in that order. A linear process of this kind, he argues, is inherently inefficient because it takes too much time and is prone to failure. It also invites resistance because it tries to work across strong functional barriers, thus threatening to disrupt the power politics of the organization. (It is not surprising that Henry Ford II's view of Frey was that he 'may or may not be a genius but he is a pain in the ass!')

The history of the Fiesta, launched in 1976, illustrates the traditional approach to product development in Ford. The decision to build the Fiesta involved the building of a new plant in Spain and the targeting of an entirely new market for small cars in which the company had not previously competed. The traditional Dearborn philosophy had been that small was unattractive. Small cars meant small profits. Despite this, Henry Ford II accepted the views of Ford of Europe Product Planning and planning started for Ford's first small car.

Development of the Fiesta followed the traditional Fordist approach. Seidler (1976) describes the tensions between the product development system and this innovatory product. That the Fiesta was so successful demonstrated

> how man, with all his weaknesses, but also with his imagination, his initiative, his enthusiasm, and his individualism, somehow manages to triumph over the constraints and the obligations imposed upon him by one of the most tightly structured organisations in the industrial world. (Seidler, 1976)

The overriding product planning philosophy of the traditional approach is encapsulated in a quote attributed to a new product planning chief: 'we're the champions in popular cars . . . Value for money. The maximum of amenities at the keenest possible price. That's our credo' (Seidler, 1976: 19). The key strategic focus was cost control. This required 'total discipline'. Product development was structured in the typical Ford top-down manner. Development was a sequential activity involving Product Development fulfilling its role in the process and handing over to Manufacturing. Different groups of specialists took responsibility for each stage in the process, then handed on the responsibility.

Supervising each of the stages were the architects of the overall discipline of the process, the cost analysis experts, whose task was to judge both the quality of a component, the most efficient way of producing it and what it would cost. They negotiated the cost–quality trade-off, usually, critics of the system argued, in favour of cost. One of their key roles was competitive benchmarking. They did this by stripping down the cars produced by Ford's competitors and estimating to the last quarter of a cent (Ford's accounting unit is the dollar) the cost of component parts. They then used these figures as the benchmark for setting the targets for Ford's own components. These were the 'high priests' of the old approach:

> [They] knew all the rules by heart and all the parameters in the tablets of the law: the quality standards, the rigorous criteria for durability, the targets for weight and cost. They were the ones to choose between the various components brought in for their appraisal; condemning this one because it weighed too much, awarding that one the prize for durability, arriving finally at an order of merit for all the comparable components under two headings, weight and cost.
>
> These, after all, were the great enemies, the two culprits on which they had to pass judgment: excessive weight and abnormal cost. And these were the men . . . who finally told the experimental

> engineers: . . . 'Here are your specific objectives within the framework of the overall target. . . . This is what we think about the parts that make up the cars of the competition, their weight and their cost of production. You be the referees, you find the better ways'. (Seidler, 1976: 64–6)

Here again we see the legacy of Fordism. Quantification rules to the extent that Product Planning came to be seen as the elite of the company. Out of such analysis came the Red Books, volumes specifying objectives for each component of the car in terms of cost and weight and the investment needed to achieve them. The Red Book provided the base-line for forecasting variable costs and program investment. In this process financial imperatives dominated – reducing the total cost of the investment while increasing the return on capital employed. The Finance function had one clear mission – to support management decision-making with the objective of maximizing profit at least cost. Its influence was omnipresent and a constant source of tension between functional areas. New ideas were treated with 'a scepticism elevated into a system, a Cartesian philosophy anglo-saxon style' (Seidler, 1976: 23) and seldom survived the piercing analysis of the financial equivalent of the test crash at 30 m.p.h. The 'normal' outcome was that innovation crumpled on impact.

Looking back on this approach one older Ford manager commented upon the 'incredible rigidity of this highly compartmentalized design process: even minor changes to single components could take several years: it took just as long to change a door lock as it does to change half a car'. Engineers became incredibly specialized. Another manager described the situation in the following terms:

> We had a very strong functional engineering tradition. You had guys at the bottom of the pile engineering individual components like door latches, or rear light fittings, or bumpers. So the whole thing was atomized rather like Henry Ford atomized the production process. So we atomized the engineering process. You'd get these component engineers who'd spent their whole life just engineering these bits, never involved in engineering a car, always just bits of a car.

A crucial emphasis in the system was a concern with control: the system developed 'a design and release manual which included every engineer in the building so that he knew who to blame. You knew who designed the door-lock and on which side of the car. That was the heyday of the hire-and-fire organization.' The system developed the search for the guilty into a science.

The product design and engineering process epitomized 'old fashioned Ford thinking which was that if you specialize you will get people who are so expert that you will design the best of everything individually. Therefore, when you put it all together you will have the best'. This approach assumed that best product development was amenable to rigidly codified design principles, doing things 'by the book', but the system actually managed-out essential features of leading edge product design: 'The manual was an incredible piece of work but a manual doesn't build cars.' There was, first of all, a major problem of over-specialization, compounded by the problem of coordinating the specialists. This bred huge potential for conflict in the relationship between design and manufacturing engineers, a relationship that has always been 'very aggressive and confrontational'. There was also the problem of 'handover' from function to function during an essentially sequential development process. One manufacturing manager described a major problem that had arisen through the failure to think about the implications of product design for management on the shopfloor.

> The Mark III Cortina had at the top of the C pillar – that's where the roof joins the body side – the biggest patch of solder there had ever been on a Ford car since the V8 pilot. It meant that we had part-solderers and lead-diskers in their dozens and the lead-diskers had to wear air-fed masks, hoods, total body protection from the lead. The manufacturing problems that resulted from that – apart from the solder problems, technical problems – the labour problems alone were such that manufacturing went back to product engineering and said, 'When you replace this car you either replace it with a car that has a zero solder pad or only a very small one', and that's the first time we were ever obliged to engineer a vehicle to take account of manufacturing problems.

## The Sierra

The legacy of Fordism in product development is a combination of specialization in engineering, rigorous financial planning and control and insidious checks on innovation. The story of the Sierra exemplifies Ford's product development problems in the early 1980s.

The pre-1980s Ford system of development had enabled the company to prepare product specification for their appropriate markets in a way that its competitors envied but it had not been noted for producing quantum leaps in product terms. The Sierra was intended to change this.

The Sierra represents an important attempt at strategic discontinuity for Ford. The decisions governing the development of the Sierra were based on a major reassessment of the company's competitive environment. Its predecessor, the Cortina-Taurus, had been the best-selling large car in Europe and the company's most successful car ever. However, European competitors such as General Motors and the then Austin Rover Group had improved their competence in producing value-for-money volume cars. 'After Japan' had demonstrated unequivocally that Japanese competition was now far superior in the manufacture of small and medium cars, but Japanese superiority was judged not to apply to the more attractive larger vehicle market segment where margins were higher.

Analysis of its sales since the introduction of the Fiesta indicated that the company's full product line strategy had not been successful at the pan-European level. Despite major successes in increasing its Southern Europe penetration with the Fiesta, the small car segment of its product range was not demonstrating significant profitability. And outside of the United Kingdom the company had no sustained record of success in the larger end of the market. This was a problem in particular in Germany, where Ford cars were commonly perceived as inferior to domestic manufacturers such as Daimler–Benz, BMW and Volkswagen–Audi, for whose products German consumers were ready to pay a significant premium for their higher quality and performance features. There was a major strategic need to improve competitive performance in Northern Europe in the larger car segment. Otherwise Ford of Europe's object of continuing to contribute 25 per cent to total corporate earnings would be jeopardized.

Ford of Europe concluded that a major change in strategy was needed to ensure its long-term future. Its new product strategy became to compete directly against Daimler–Benz, BMW, Audi and other performance and luxury car manufacturers, thus enabling Ford to charge premium prices. The conclusion was that Ford would remain market leader in its 'home' market of Great Britain and that it needed to become more competitive, particularly in West Germany, while improving its profitability in Southern Europe. The Sierra project was championed by Bob Lutz, then President of Ford of Europe.

Lutz was hired from BMW in the 1970s. The key people involved in Lutz's recruitment were Philip Caldwell, then Executive Vice-President, International Automotive Operations, and Harold 'Red' Poling, then President of Ford of Europe, who had concluded from their European tour that Ford of Europe's long-term future lay in moving up-market and away from a strategy based primarily on volume and cost efficiency. Similarly, Lutz's vision was that Ford could move up-market from its Japanese and European volume car competitors. He described the logic behind the Sierra strategy as follows:

> the Japanese have taken over the no-nonsense, no-frills, high-value for money, reliable transportation part of the market. My goal is to be a mass producer of the type of cars BMW and Mercedes have a reputation for making. We are moving up in technology and credibility so we get the same price elasticity as they have. (quoted Lorenz, 1986: 91)

With the Sierra one sees a radical step forward in Ford's design philosophy. Successful design seeks to creatively blend the major elements of the design mix, namely performance, quality, durability, appearance and cost (Kotler, 1984). Reviewing his time with General Motors Sloan observes that car designers tended to be advocates of change, putting forward ideas that were often 'startling' to production and engineering executives. It is a credo of design, following Loewy's arguments in the designer's 'Bible', *Industrial Design*, that: 'Between two products equal in price, function and quality, the better looking will outsell the other' (quoted by Butman, 1991: 150). Firms like BMW, Audi and Saab, which served as models for the Sierra development, had all responded to crisis in the past with radical design. With the Sierra, Ford went for design leadership in an approach, championed by Lutz and Uwe Bahnsen, Vice-President of Design, that emphasized aerodynamic styling – an approach pioneered, but far less dramatically, in the 1980 Escort – against the opposition of a conservative marketing department. After this decision the Sierra proceeded through the normal product development process.

In retrospect the Sierra project had several flaws. Ford believed its dominance of its core British market to be beyond challenge. It ignored established motor industry wisdom that a market leader radically alters a successful product only at the risk of offending consumer taste. Indeed, during consumer clinics for the Sierra consumer reactions were strongly negative. Ford concluded that the market would need time to adapt to the new design and looked on this as a 'normal cost' of innovation. The Sierra over-emphasized one design feature – aerodynamics – at the expense of other important features. Under its exterior the product was far from technologically radical. In particular it used rear-wheel as opposed to front-wheel drive, a decision which some now see as short-sighted.

The rationale for the latter decision is disputed. Some claim that it merely reflected the consensus opinion in the company. BMW, for example, used the same drive configuration. Others argue that engineering was in favour of the front-wheel drive technology. It is even suggested that the key element in the final decision was the fortunes of the American parent which was, at this time, struggling for its very survival and needing all the money it could extract from Europe to ensure that survival. Front-wheel drive would have required a major investment in manufacturing process technology, even a new plant. As a result, critics of the decision argue, the Sierra design was compromised from the very first. Without the benefit of front-wheel drive the vehicle was deprived of a major potential source of weight saving. As a result, the designers and engineers shifted their focus to aerodynamic styling to reduce the air-drag coefficient and it was decided that the radical innovation in shape was essential.

The final shape of the car, its 'jelly mould design', has also been criticized and the car described as 'a coke-bottle shaped Cortina'. It was seen by Ford's competitors as major mistake, compounded by the dropping of the important Cortina 'brand' name, launch problems, and the fact that it was mechanically old-fashioned – 'they had destroyed the car's character, negated its heritage, confused its bloodlines'. In addition, 'it seemed like an overly modern body on an antiquated skeleton' (Butman, 1991: 40). It gained the dubious image of 'radical and dangerous' rather than 'new and exciting'. It lost market share to the new GM Cavalier, demonstrating that in the new, increasingly competitive environment of the 1980s even Ford was vulnerable in what it considered its impregnable UK market.

But flawed though it was the Sierra has had its champions. Christopher Lorenz (1986), Business Editor of the *Financial Times*, welcomed the Sierra as evidence of design at Ford of Europe in the 1980s coming of age and 'breaking the Detroit mould'. The Fiesta is perhaps more significant in the latter respect, but Lorenz correctly regards the Sierra as evidence of Ford of Europe's transformation from design dullard into leader, a company prepared to experiment even if it cut against the grain of company culture. The new design philosophy introduced in Europe with the Escort and the Sierra proved itself of seminal importance in the development of the very successful aerodynamically styled cars that helped to turn Ford around in the United States. The Sierra marks a crucial break from Ford's traditional strategy of providing 'worthy but boring' products on a narrow sales platform of 'value for money'. The company for the first time in generations embraced risk as the most appropriate strategy for redefining its image in the marketplace.

The Sierra might not have been the 'object lesson in the management of product development' (Lorenz, 1986: 91) but it certainly brought to the fore a new strategic agenda for the company. It was the Sierra that was responsible for fundamentally altering consumer tastes in established design. Overall it is probably best to consider the Sierra, like the major changes in organization and management that Ford of Europe undertook during the same period, as a major transition stage in the company's history. Situating it in the history of product development and of Ford management generally it is possible to see the Sierra in two different lights. In one sense, the Sierra design process marked a qualified break with the strictly controlled 'Fordist' model. The issue of over-specialization, for example, was addressed. Modular engineering allocated responsibility for a cluster of components to a team of 8–10 engineers rather than individual specialists. In this one can see the Sierra as a tentative move away from the Fordist heritage. But from another perspective one can also see it as the final failure, despite its qualified commercial success, of that heritage. One senior manager was of the opinion that during the development of the Sierra the old Ford system was stretched to breaking point: 'we strained the system beyond its ability to cope'. In the words of a senior manager in Product Development, 'That car was a product of the organization. The concept was radical but the product development was conservative!' Certainly after the Sierra, Ford of Europe could never be quite the same again. Cost and innovation had again clashed and compromised the outcome of the product development process. But now, at least, innovation was firmly on the strategic agenda.

## Product Development After Japan

Japan had major effects upon Ford's thinking about manufacturing management. It was equally if not more influential on Ford's thinking about product development. Studies of Japanese product development highlight three major sources of competitive advantage: speed (the speed with which new product development takes place); flexibility (with which companies adapt their development process to changes in the external environment); and productivity (overall product development productivity) (Womack et al., 1990; Clark and Fujimoto, 1991). The average Japanese firm has almost double the product development productivity of the average Western firm and can develop similar products on average a year faster. In a dynamic competitive environment speed of model-change is a significant competitive advantage. Japanese firms introduce far more new products, maintain a much shorter model life and expand their product lines more rapidly than Western firms, averaging less than five years between model changes, compared to American firms which average eight and European firms more than a decade (Clark and Fujimoto, 1991: 68–9; 91). As one Ford manager put it 'while we're doing business with each other the Japanese are getting new products to market'. Their products are also generally of high quality, and the Japanese firms use resources 'saved' in product development to invest in new technologies. Western companies, with their inefficient product-development processes, have found that they do not have the money or spare engineering capacity to expand their product range and renew their products as frequently.

The Japanese product development process is based on incrementalism and iteration, what Abernathy (1984) calls 'learning by doing', rather than the traditional Western approach of 'analysis–strategy–synthesis'. The path-breaking MIT study of the Future of the Automobile found four major differences in product development between Japan and the West contributing to Japanese competitive advantage. There is first of all clear *leadership* in the *shusa* system, where the project leader has the power to manage despite functional divides in the organization. Secondly there is a high level of *teamwork*, with a small team assigned to a development project for life, though individuals do retain ties to their functional department. Teamwork over the full life of the project enables teams to share and maximize knowledge generation. An emphasis on open *communication* means that differences are surfaced early in a project's life, in contrast to the West:

> many Western development efforts fail to resolve critical design trade-offs until very late in the project. One reason is the . . . team members

> show great reluctance to confront conflicts directly. They make vague commitments to a set of design decisions – agreeing, that is, to try to do something as long as no reason crops up not to. In Japan, by contrast, team members sign formal pledges to do exactly what everyone has agreed upon as a group. So conflicts about resources and priorities occur at the beginning rather than at the end of the process. Another reason is that a design process that is sequential, going from one department to the next at team headquarters, makes communications to solve problems very difficult in any case. (Womack et al., 1990: 115)

We know that the early detection of disharmony is a key feature of successful product development (Souder, 1988). Finally, Japanese product development uses the principle of *simultaneous development* rather than sequential – product and manufacturing engineers work in parallel on product and process technology. The example Womack et al. give is of the simultaneous development of the product and the dies needed to press out the body panels. Simultaneous development drastically reduces development time and eases initial manufacturing problems.

We can illustrate these factors in the development of the Honda City car. Honda's top management sensed the dwindling appeal of their best-selling lines – the Civic and Accord – to the youth market as an impending strategic crisis. The City was targeted towards this market segment and a young project team was given the responsibility for its development. Having signalled the change required and created the team to deal with it, top management devolved full autonomy to this team to develop the product. Top management determined the end goal of the project, 'to create a radically different concept of what a car should be like' and set very challenging design parameters – it had to be 'a resource-saving, energy-efficient, mass-oriented automobile'. Mr. Kawamoto, vice president in charge of development for Honda, described the management approach as follows:

> At times, management needs to do something drastic like setting the objective, giving the team full responsibility, and keeping its mouth shut. It's like putting the team members on the second floor, removing the ladder, and telling them to jump, or else. I believe creativity is born by pushing people against the wall and pressuring them almost to the extreme.

Because the development team is given the responsibility for its own organization and the autonomy to define the final product offering, this approach can be described as 'autonomous' as opposed to 'induced' in the sense that top management does not do the defining, but rather creates the conditions that facilitate innovation. Autonomy serves as a significant challenge.

The power to self-manage acts as an opportunity for the organization to break away from built-in rigidities of hierarchy and bureaucracy. Moreover, the new groups are composed of people from diverse functional specializations. Honda's City development team was composed of individuals from product development, production engineering and sales. Phase management of the product development process tends to be 'holistic and overlapping rather than analytical and sequential' (Imai et al., 1985: 349); that is, the project does not move through different phases in a logical, pre-determined sequential manner – from concept to feasibility study to definition, design and then production – rather it is an interactive process of a sort of experimentation, actually encouraging 'variety amplification' to maximize the generation of potentially useful information, particularly through increasing the sensitivity of everyone involved to changes in the market environment.

> Honda's City team adopted . . . a 'rugby' approach toward product development. Mr. Watanabe [the project leader] explained: 'I always tell my team members that our work cannot be done on the basis of a relay. In a relay someone says, "My job is done, now you take it from here." But that's not right. Everyone has to run the entire distance. Like in rugby, every member of the team runs together, tosses the ball left and right, and dashes toward the goal.' The important point to remember here is that critical problems occur most frequently at relay points within the sequential approach. The 'rugby' approach smooths out the process by involving everyone in the development project. Individual initiative is also a prerequisite, argued Mr. Kawamoto: 'If each and every one of us does his or her job well, then we basically won't need a structure'. (Imai et al., 1985: 353)

In the Japanese approach, therefore, ambiguity is tolerated, indeed, even encouraged, as are experimentation and learning; over-specification is avoided, information sharing is of the essence, decision-making responsibility is shared. A key part of the project management is to deal with the difference of opinion and the tensions and conflicts the approach gives rise to. Team responsibility is an important factor. The emphasis is on self-control through peer pressure. Japanese firms also encourage 'learning in breadth', or learning across functional lines, as the cornerstone of their human resource management approach. This helps counter functional specialization and encourages a generalist and strategic perspective throughout the company. Individuals from product development, for example, will receive 'practical training' in production, while public relations specialists will spend time on the production line as part of their socialization into the company (Womack et al., 1990). Long-term employment and an appraisal system that focuses as much on the group as the individual also help to inculcate the generalist strategic perspective. The MIT study also emphasizes the nature of career development in Japanese firms. Career paths are structured to reward team-players rather than individualistic geniuses with little regard for the common good (Womack et al., 1990: 63)

Nonaka (1988) also uses the development of the Honda City to illustrate what he calls the Japanese 'middle-up-down' approach to management. He distinguishes this from 'top-down' and 'bottom-up' management, which he describes as follows:

> Top-down management emphasizes the process of implementing and refining decisions made by top management as they are transmitted to the lower levels of the organization. Bottom-up management emphasizes the influence of information coming up from lower levels on management decision-making. (Nonaka, 1988: 9)

'Middle-up management', a characteristic of Japanese product development, is neither of these. 'It is a process that resolves the contradiction between the visionary but abstract concepts of top management and the experience-grounded concepts originating on the shopfloor by assigning a more central role to middle managers' (Nonaka, 1988: 9). Middle-up management has as a distinctive feature the acceleration of information creation which is of vital importance in innovation. The maximization of information becomes a key strategic issue when innovation is construed not so much as a process of gradually reducing uncertainty (processing information) in moving toward a prescribed goal but as a process through which uncertainty is intentionally *increased* when circumstances demand the generation of chaos from which new meaning can be created. From this perspective, innovation as a process is full of discovery, surprise, and redundancy. The challenge senior management at Honda set the project team was not to *process* information but to *create* it by forcing them to critically examine their most deeply-held assumptions.

> To do this successfully, project members had to confront ambiguity, contradiction and failure.
>
> The information-processing paradigm emphasizes the structure of the organization. The information creation paradigm, in contrast, stresses the process of creating meaningful information through personal interaction. The *quality* of information becomes more important than the quantity. Inductive, synthetic, and holistic methodologies become more useful than the deductive, analytic, and reductionistic ones used in information processing. (Nonaka, 1988: 12)

Top executives challenge their project teams with a broad programme mission. Project groups are led by 'heavyweight' programme managers with the power in the organization to champion products through from inception to completion. These managers are not mere 'coordinators' (Clark and Fujimoto, 1991). Team members actually put the good of the team and the project as their first priority rather than functional allegiance. Team process is crucial in transcending functional boundaries (Denison et al., 1991).

Middle management play a key role in this process.

> The Honda City case clearly shows the critical importance of Mr. Watanabe, the middle manager selected as project leader. His role had several key aspects: providing direct information links to top management; transforming top management's general vision into directions for the team's activities and for pursuing the creation of meaning; managing 'chaos' and keeping it within tolerable limits; and providing the context for integration across specialities. While Honda pays tribute to the energy and drive of the young researchers who generated the new product idea, top management clearly recognizes the strategic role of its middle management project leaders as well. (Nonaka, 1988: 13)

Japanese superiority in product development also reflects differences of organizational politics and culture, for example, in the status of different functional groups.

> [In the West] a kind of caste system has emerged in product development. Design engineers are focused on product features and performance, which have more prestige in the engineering world. Manufacturing people are mired in the grim and gritty details of production – in intermediate costs, in the ways components are actually put together. ('We've built one,' says design to manufacturing, 'now you build 10,000.')

> Nothing could be further from Japanese practice, where design specialists and manufacturing people work side by side, often in product teams, so that the designers will be more cost-conscious and oriented toward manufacturing simplicity. Japanese design engineers typically start out their careers in manufacturing plants, so they're intuitively thinking about the control processes that are needed to maintain consistently high quality. (Gomory, 1989: 102)

Status is as much a barrier to efficient communication as walls, doors or bureaucracy (Doyle, 1985: 379).

## Insight

During the 1980s Ford began to come to terms with the nature of competition in product development and learning both from Japan and from critical analysis of its own experience. It was in the Product Development function that participative management had its greatest effect upon the European consciousness. Matrix management was introduced to facilitate a participative climate conducive to problem-solving, with PM increasingly seen as the key to facilitating the management process necessary to support the new matrix approach. The context was a downturn in performance.

1984 was a dismal financial year for Ford of Europe. The core automotive business barely broke even despite the highest market share ever: 'we had a huge business turnover and no profit'. Fixed costs were too high and marketing expenses 'extraordinary' as the company fought to maintain market share. This was the trigger for a sweeping examination of the company's strategic vision and for self-examination by some senior management of its own behaviour. This self-examination led to

> a much wider organizational audit. But it went further than just the numbers. We, in the executive team, did a lot of soul-searching about our own conduct, the way we did our business, so it was as much a cultural audit as anything else.
>
> Some of the questions we asked were very basic. Is our prime objective cost control or increased quality? And hours of debate went on around that single issue. The point is that as a manager you can't expect a clear answer: the terms of the question are ambiguous and can conflict. The business answer is you balance cost and quality – it's a trade-off. You can't enforce the full Ford cost control disciplines

> while you pursue enhanced quality. The point is that these issues are the subject of free debate whereas seven or eight years ago they were not. Not only would they not have been debated, the issue would not have arisen: cost reduction took overriding priority.

At the strategic level the American experiment with participative management was diffused to Europe through senior executive conferences during late 1983 and 1984. One held in Montreux was particularly memorable.

> Suddenly the thing began and [senior managers] found themselves plunged into this completely magical world of participation and the consultants . . . I have to admire tremendously the job they did in three days . . . converted this bunch of hugely cynical and totally opposed group of people to a bunch who, with notable exceptions – I wouldn't pretend total conversion – but to a bunch of pretty enthusiastic energized people who suddenly discovered these processes that they'd never experienced before. Actually going into a sort of non-hierarchical group of people to discuss as an equal, to be actually advised to listen to what other people were saying and don't talk at the same time, to recognize that temperament can have an awful lot to do to influence your relationships with each other.

Not everybody found this an easy experience. Manufacturing managers were 'very uneasy and uncharacteristically quiet'. But the experience of working across functional divides in 'break-out groups' did introduce a new sense of the possible benefits of participation.

> These mixed groups [mixed across functions] were forced to report back to plenary sessions where they had to say what other functions could do to help them with a particular problem. The tone was completely different [from the usual tone of inter-functional meetings]. It wasn't a functional witch-hunt!

The hidden agenda was no longer 'passing the buck' or 'the search for the guilty'. Montreux introduced the top 100 Ford of Europe managers to a new decision-making mode with unprecedented 'freedom of question and answer during meetings' and to a new management development agenda: 'In management development terms the key objective which is emerging is to develop a capacity for dilemma management among the next generation of executives.' However, despite initial enthusiasm, the organization was not equipped to consolidate the process – 'They [the champions of PM] just weren't supported, they didn't have back-up facilitation or anything to push the thing into reality'. And the initial excitement faded too.

> Of course within two days of coming back [from Montreux] we had all slotted back into the old routine. We had no method for transferring the excitement of Montreux back into the mainstream of company life. So three months later we had a huge anti-climax. Disappointment and frustration inevitably bred cynicism about the possibilities for change.

This mood was consolidated in the 1984 results. 'There was just enough residual enthusiasm to repeat the experience of Montreux' and a further senior executive programme took place in the UK. This proved 'a dreadful experience'. At this low point Product Development decided to take the lead in experimenting with a new approach, something it was to do for the rest of the 1980s in a series of initiatives, with several important study reports and with structural change.

In the wake of 'After Japan', the problematic Sierra launch and the attempted introduction of EI and PM, Product Development initiated its own examination of its management practices – the 'Insight' project. This comprised interviews with over 200 people within Ford to find out what they considered Ford did well, what they could do better and where change was needed. The Insight project team also talked to people from product development in other companies, most importantly in Toyo Kogyo (now Mazda). The message from 'Insight' was a strong indictment of existing best practice. It was summarized as follows:

> increased efficiency can only be achieved by better utilization of available talent through improved teamwork. In our strongly functional organization these improvements require the elimination of artificial barriers to communication and in their place must come a stronger focus on, and identification with, the product and the 'customer'. To facilitate these changes some organization restructuring is needed in order to build cross-functional, multi-discipline teams dedicated to product programs. The organizational change is a means to an end, not an end in itself. Improved efficiencies will result from more delegation, development of broader skills and the substitution of a 'not invented here' attitude by supportive team-goal oriented behaviour.

The comparison with Mazda was crucial to Insight's findings. In Ford of Europe, the project team concluded, there was much evidence of poor communications and inefficiency, due mainly to the 'system' according to which things 'must be done'. The system's formal control was actually dysfunctional in creating blockages in information flow and blockages between different groups who should have been working together: 'Procedure sometimes takes precedence over problem solving'. Mazda, by comparison, had organizational arrangements that functioned smoothly to foster swift flexible responses, employees who were involved in making decisions through consensus, and top management which was committed to delegating decision-making to the relevant working groups. Mazda was characterized as having an 'environment of harmony', based on participative management and employee involvement, in comparison to Ford's 'environment of competition'.

One manager's comments illustrate this difference: 'there is insufficient communication and cooperation between engineering areas and between Manufacturing and PD [Product Development]. Sometimes we get the feeling that different areas work for different companies'. Competition meant that workforce talents were under-utilized at Ford, and time was wasted in feeding information up to the higher levels where decisions were taken and from which they then percolated down. The Insight project found Mazda three times as efficient in terms of hours needed to engineer and style a Sierra-equivalent vehicle. While one third of Mazda managers were in substantive roles, the majority were in flexible project-based teams. For Ford managers accustomed to the ubiquity of immutable hierarchies – to 'thinking structurally' – this was one of the most disconcerting aspects of Mazda organization: that Japanese managers expected to be in transient teams rather than fixed positions, and 'there was no embarrassment about being a minister without portfolio'.

The Insight team examined the various stages of the product development cycle and found major areas for improvement throughout. Key problem areas identified included: lack of early involvement of manufacturing and sales which resulted in late, costly changes in product development; inefficient pre-programme to programme 'handover'; inefficient management of outsourcing; too labour-intensive and slow a cost control system (all parts were being costed approximately four times); under-utilization of scarce resources (such as a failure to integrate development and testing engineers into design development). Recommended changes included: formal involvement of Manufacturing and Sales in a product development programme management team from the initial concept stage; the appointment of project managers to ensure continuity through all programme phases, including the pre-program phase, with a major responsibility for generating greater awareness of pre-program design; a radical analysis of Ford's complex multiple supplier network; a reduction in costing with more immediate feedback, so that product design and manufacturing were optimized; the development of a new process for linking test and development, thus bringing together vehicle development and testing with the aim of fostering the greater involvement of test engineers in the development of products and the elimination of the 'us and them' mentality.

The proposed solution to Ford's endemic problems in product development involved a searching analysis of Ford organization structures and a move to a form of matrix management encompassing vehicle design, planning and finance product functions. But the new approach was not just one of structure. It involved the emphasizing of the crucial importance of the participative management/ employee involvement process. Product development programme teams, it was argued, needed to be strengthened by project managers from the various functions and to include team members from manufacturing and sales/service. The existing organization was conditioned by Ford's strongly functional organization (see figure 5.1). Mazda had a similar functional framework but the key management unit for product development was the programme team (see figure 5.2).

Post-Insight saw major moves in Ford to overcome its highly compartmentalized approach to design. On the basis of the Insight study Product Development senior management established a set of principles for 'forward organization vision'. Organization change was to be geared to generating better teamwork and cooperation. Spans of

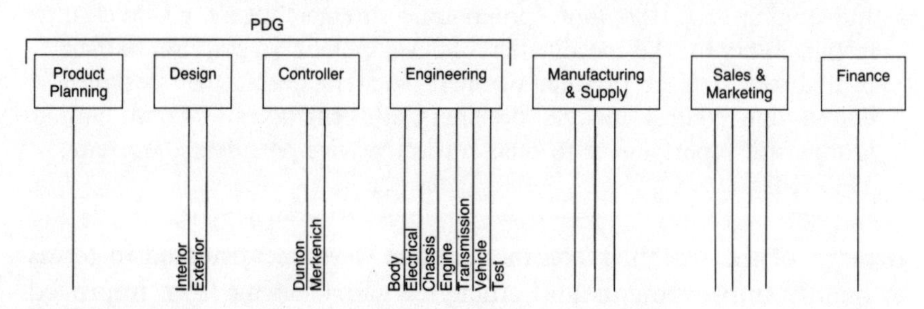


**Figure 5.1** Framework of Ford organization in Europe

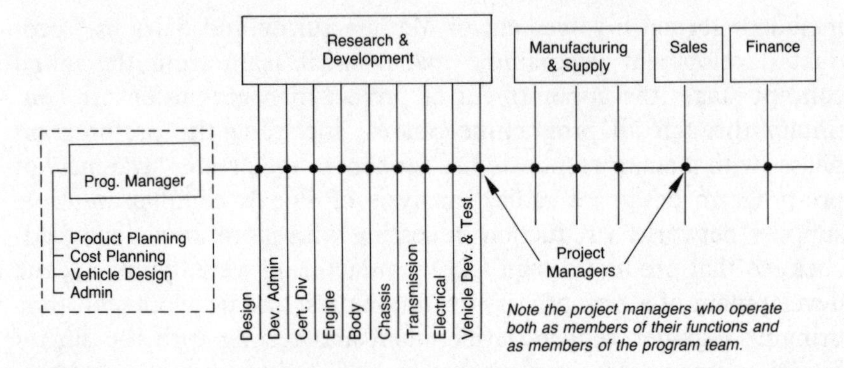


**Figure 5.2** Mazda organization – concentration on program teams within a functional framework similar to Ford

control were to be widened and organization complexity and levels reduced to achieve delegation, job enrichment and process efficiencies; and to avoid duplication and remove structure and its concomitant cost and dysfunctional aspects. A key working principle was that organization change should not be imposed from the top without consultation. Project managers were appointed for each carline. Programme and project manager teams were to provide overall management of the business by carline, with rotation of people between project teams and functional teams to avoid the handover problems of 'not invented here', and the movement of managers between project and functional offices for development and career succession purposes.

> The product planning function was absorbed into four new 'programme offices', one for each of small, medium and large cars, and another for power trains (engine and transmission). Reporting direct to the vice-president of product development, like the heads of design and engineering, the four 'programme directors' were given clear responsibility for the coordination of development. In addition to their own direct staff of product planners and engineers, they assumed dotted line control for the designers and engineers, though both groups still report direct to their respective vice-presidents. (Lorenz, 1986: 102)

Benefits of the Insight recommendations were encapsulated in terms of quality improvements and efficiency gains arising from improved cross-functional coordination, aimed at removing internal product development handover issues and improving 'consensus', thus giving a better product. Teamwork, it was argued, would lead to an earlier identification of issues, therefore more timely decisions and fewer changes, and would provide the basis for more effective support to manufacturing and sales/service. Survival was seen as depending upon a better quality product and 'more product engineering for less engineering cost'.

Restructuring is a typical Ford response:

> In Ford traditionally there's a structural change to meet any and every crisis. We use organization change as a device to bring about a change in the way we work. It was, in effect, a case of structural change as a substitute for process change.

However, Product Development linked change in organizational structure to the need to develop a new style of management. A key conclusion of the Insight study was that it was necessary to change both the structure of the organization *and* the style of management. In the structure, complete car programmes became the basis for management rather than the previous separate functional approach. The desired change in management style was conceptualized as facilitating a change from an internal 'environment of competition' in product development to 'an environment of harmony' based on participative management and employee involvement (figure 5.3). In particular in its communication of its changed thinking on the best structure and management style for effective product development, Product Development emphasized that it was 'evolving to a more participative style of managing change'.

Process intervention followed, with a workshop for senior management spearheaded by a group of external management consultants geared to enabling teams to function in the matrix structure, with its twin organizational bases of function and project teams (Mumford and Honey, 1986). The workshop focused on the desirability of, and the necessary management processes for, a more participative management style. The consultants conducted diagnostic interviews with the top management group, and examined such fundamental issues as:

> What do you understand by 'autocratic' and 'participative' in the Ford context?
>
> What problems and progress have you experienced in attempting to make the new PM principles work?

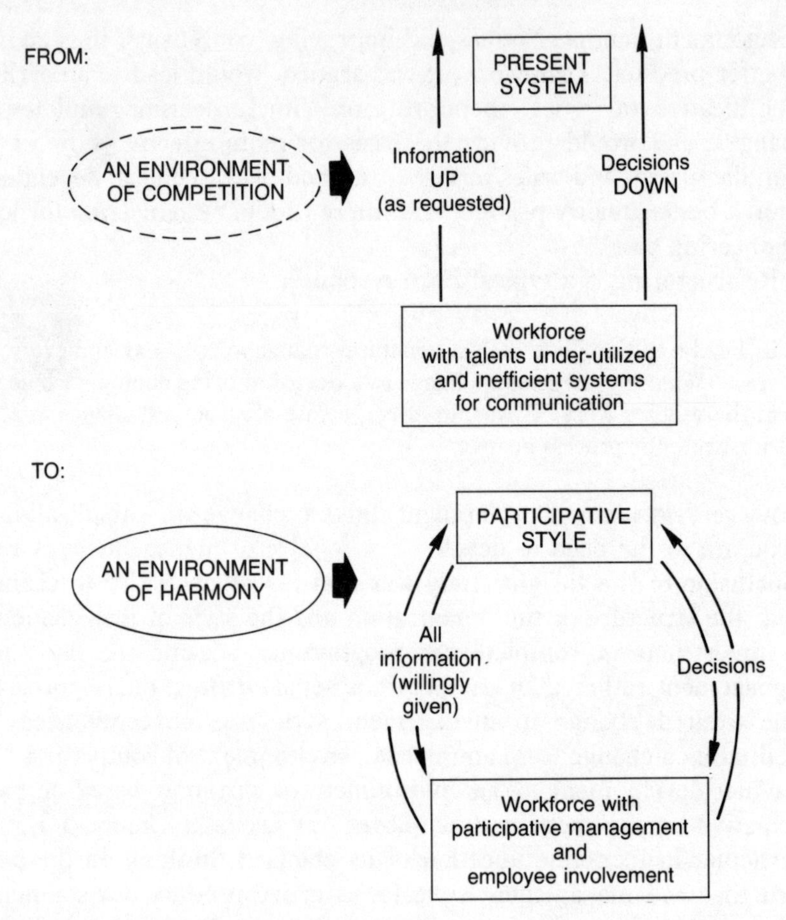


**Figure 5.3** Conclusions of Ford's 'Insight' study

Consider the managerial behaviour of your bosses; what do they do that helps or hinders you in the effective performance of your job?
What kind of managerial behaviour does the organization reward, not reward or punish?

There were major problems, even among the small group of less than 20 senior managers, of a lack of 'the common vocabulary needed to get rid of misconceptions'. Previously, time pressures had worked against the development of 'common yardsticks, understanding and vocabulary' among this group. For example, when they examined their existing vocabulary with the help of the consultants, they found that they had different definitions of basic terms such as 'collaboration' and 'consensus'. With the help of the consultants they examined the meaning of terms like 'participation' and 'consensus', the nature of desirable management behaviour, and whether the top management group actually behaved in a participative manner.

Product Development thus set out to develop 'a new process for operating meetings'. In management meetings, during this transition period, the focus was 'as much on process as content – operating meetings became training sessions'. Participative management based on openness, explicit feedback and the expression of differences, were crucial here. The overall goal was the creation of a 'we agree' rather than an 'I tell' decision-making process and culture. The objectives in the top management group in Product Development at this time can be summed up as follows:

setting aims, objectives, and performance measurements for EI and PM
preparing for the dissemination of EI/PM principles to the rest of the organization
practising the use of PM to reach decisions in the workshop
experiencing the value of open, participative feedback
and, perhaps, most important, agreeing on a common language for EI and PM

For top management participants the workshop experience validated the PM approach and the behavioural skills the approach demanded.

The Insight project significantly advanced the cause of PM in Ford of Europe. Based, initially, on analysis of Japanese management practices, its outcome was not mere imitation of these practices but a new approach to the Ford management process in which learning, not just from Japan but from Ford's own experience, was crucial. In particular the organization learned that

> the matrix is not an organization, it's not an amended version of the Ford system: its an enabling mechanism to help the social processes of management. We wanted to change the way we worked together, not the way we directed each other. We're trying to get away from the formal system, the man in the box mentality.

The next step was for the rest of Ford of Europe, in particular the Manufacturing function, to become convinced that this was the path to follow.

# 6

# Preparing the Future: Program Management and Simultaneous Engineering

## The Transition to Program Management

Historically the focus of product development at Ford has been the integration of highly-developed discrete systems and sub-systems into vehicles. This approach had the advantage of efficient specialist knowledge of those systems but lacked a sufficiently clear whole-product focus. The Insight project prepared the ground for program management, a US initiative, but one that meshed well with the matrix approach pioneered by Product Development, according to which complete car programs rather than their sub-elements were seen as the necessary new focus for integrating product development effort throughout the company.

Program management is an important evolving concept, defined as

> the process which frames all of the events of the product development process which are dedicated to a specific product program. This process deals with setting and achieving the overall product and timing objectives.

Program management using matrix structures is seen as the necessary antidote to and replacement for the traditional sequential functional approach, and as a major step forward in product development, 'because it allows us breadth, to carry a portfolio of projects simultaneously, not just one at a time, sequentially'. Program management assumes a more participative style of managing. Participation based on problem-solving within teams is seen as more conducive to innovation than the traditional bureaucratic approach, and as something Ford needs to continue to develop.

Two managerial roles were seen as crucial to making program management work – those of functional managers and program managers. Program managers are concerned with meeting 'mission objectives' for a vehicle based on technical, cost and timing targets. Functional managers are concerned with the skills aspect of the program. Their role is to provide people with the appropriate skills to achieve the program's mission. Open communication and information-sharing is seen as essential to achieve mission goals. It is seen as particularly important that variance from plans is surfaced early in the decision-making process. Problem solving is based on consensus seeking within the parameters for decision-making set by the mission. Process management is geared to positive conflict resolution and the eradication of the negative effects of politics, personalities and win-lose games. Fundamental to success with this approach is a high level of mutual trust, confidence and respect. 'Achieving these ends is perhaps the most significant challenge facing a traditional, bureaucratic organization' (Hopeman, 1989 – external consultant report on the implementation of matrix management).

Overall program mission goals relate to the design, development, manufacturing, sales and service of vehicles. The mission is to design vehicles which can be successfully engineered and manufactured efficiently ('not just aesthetic masterpieces'), to develop new technologies that are marketable and not just technically interesting, to engineer vehicles to meet or exceed customer expectations including quality and reasonable cost, and to manufacture vehicles that are 'good' not merely 'good enough', thus leading not just to satisfied customers but to customers who become repeat purchasers of Ford products and recommend them to others. Underpinning program management is the notion of 'unity':

> Where [program management] is successful there will be a unity in the vehicle which is evident to everyone: designer, engineer, manufacturer, sales person, and service personnel. Most importantly, unity in the vehicle will be evident to the customer. Their satisfaction is the fundamental key to the current and future success of Ford Motor Company.

After the top management workshops (described in the previous chapter), further workshops were conducted in Product Development to build on the progress made in the top management workshops and to 'cascade' the skills necessary to support the new matrix management principles throughout the organization. In these workshops the focus was not process and management skills *per se*, but a demonstration of how different management approaches (directive, consultative, collaborative and delegative) contributed to effective program management, discussion of the appropriate situations for the use of these different approaches, and obtaining a general understanding of the nature of effective working groups. These workshops were given the task of identifying, clarifying and negotiating effective decision-making processes. Workshops were also run with trade union groups and joint management-union working groups. These workshops were *not* part of any formal Employee Involvement programme but an outcome of the Insight initiative.

What was agreed upon among senior Product Development management and then diffused to the rest of the organization were the key enabling principles and the ideal of a management process geared to the development of successful program management. In practice things were more difficult. Various barriers to program management had to be confronted. There were the inevitable turf battles, functional barriers and resistance to change. There were also issues of organization structure and leadership. Top management leadership was felt to be lacking in trying to get everyone aligned and working toward the same goal. Program management was resisted by Manufacturing:

> Initially when PD [Product Development] went down that road [of matrix/program management] PD wanted Manufacturing and Marketing to join the matrix concept and also have program management groups and people. The Vice-President of Manufacturing said 'No, it's not our business. We are not a program management organization.' . . . That was his view. So apart from a few coordinating people who had an Escort hat on or a Granada hat on just to face off to the PD people we [didn't really get program management then] . . . That's another example of two divisions diverging rather than converging on an objective.

As one manager in Manufacturing described it:

> Because it wasn't invented here, it didn't get any support at all, in fact, quite the reverse. It became a dirty word. It was part of the chimney getting stronger. This was an early attempt to break down the wall of a chimney and it had the opposite effect. It became reinforced. Purely for reasons that it wasn't invented here. And so it worked in PD but it didn't blossom to its full flower.

In a functionally-focused organization, operating in a culture where total company objectives are sometimes obscured by the objectives of individual organizations, Ford was grappling with two linked approaches:

- To create cross-functional teams where joint objectives are to address product design and manufacturing issues
- To define precisely the various development steps and responsibilities

The problem was that the means of achieving these objectives had yet to become clear. Further learning was necessary.

Major problems post-Insight arose from the lack of clarity of team responsibilities, and conflicts between team and existing organizational objectives. The resource demands to support what was seen as incremental work seemed exorbitant in some quarters. And there was the added difficulty of actually defining the myriad interfaces between the various functional organizations, particularly Product Development and Manufacturing. There were inevitably conflicting objectives between organizations whose mission definition was functionally based. This, an outcome of the old organizational chimneys, was accepted by Product Development as a real difficulty in its dealings with Manufacturing.

> This, by virtue of management performance and reward/punishment systems that focus sharply on individual, measurable goals, causes the behaviour of leaders of the existing functional organization to be mutually antagonistic. Over time, this behaviour can become a subculture of the two organizations. Attempts to address this problem, including team-building, management behaviour modification and more shared objectives can go some way towards reducing the organizational conflicts, but the fundamental cultural shifts required to overcome it are long lead and uncertain. (Hopeman, 1989)

As an aid to understanding the change process it was negotiating, Product Development, with the help of an external consultant, developed a map of the journey it needed to make. The evolution to full program management was seen as a series of seven phases. In phase 1, the traditional approach to organization is perceived as problematic. The key issues emerge as the dysfunctional effects of hierarchy, bureaucracy, autocracy, functional myopia and a preoccupation with territorial boundaries. In phase 2 the organization attempts to develop informal ways of coping with these problems, primarily informal team approaches to working to promote flexibility and adaptiveness. As a result major issues of authority and responsibility begin to surface. Phase 3 sees the development of more formal arrangements to address these issues; new forms of organization and management are developed, such as program management. A major problem at this stage remains the issue of responsibility/authority. In particular the new program managers 'become concerned about having a lot of responsibility without commensurate authority'. In phase 4, the desired authority shifts finally begin to occur:

> The organization becomes more accustomed to teams, and engages more consistently in participative decision making. The authority to acquire needed resources shifts to the program managers. There are several consequences of this shift which must be resolved regarding authority, responsibility, reward systems, and mechanisms for conflict resolution.

In phase 5 functional units, the previous repositories of power, become 'resource pools' as projects become the key organizational entity. Functional units now become 'the repository of knowledge, skill, experience, and judgment which may be drawn upon to meet program requirements.' In phase 6 program managers become responsible for the management of resources over the life cycles of multiple programs. The key issue now is the balancing of these multiple programs and the efficient allocation of limited resources to their mutual advantage. In phase 7 'the programs flow through the organization, their life cycles balanced. The organization emerges as flexible, adaptive, and mission driven. The organization climate exhibits high degrees of cooperation and integration.'

Ford of Europe is currently negotiating the transition from phase 4 to phase 5. New attitudes are slowly developing.

> In terms of participative management that I think at the higher level it has been a difficult one for people to understand, to be involved in because of the way in which we organized it. We had a Vice-President of Product Development who sees his responsibility as being that for the product, designing the product, releasing the product and saying to Manufacturing, 'Here it is, you go and make it. Don't question why we've designed it that way'. On the other hand you had a Manufacturing Vice-President who says 'You give me a good design and then if it doesn't work it's your responsibility'. What we have

> done in terms of participative management is gradually to bring the people together but we're not there yet. The organization structure does not allow it. You've still got the autonomous groups.

Certain aspects of program management are working well. The organization is seen as having become more flexible and adaptive, and, therefore, more able to respond rapidly to changing market conditions. Integrative and cooperative efforts are working to broaden people's perspectives and to reduce functional myopia. New technologies are being incorporated more quickly into design to shorten product development cycle times. Program management has promoted earlier 'buy-in on decisions' concerning the mission of the program and integration of viewpoints from various contributing organizations both within and without Ford, thus creating a more unified and efficient effort as the program develops. Teamwork has been enhanced, thus making working together more effective: 'Getting to know people in other departments and sharing planning and decision-making tasks makes getting results and resolving conflicts easier. The traditional bureaucratic and autocratic approach seems to induce competitiveness and risk-avoidance which does not enhance program effectiveness.' New team structures are emerging to replace bureaucracy and cross-functional teams provide a clearer perspective on how expertise – be it from design, development, manufacturing, sales or service – 'fits' into the vehicle design. Problems on technical, timing and cost matters are coming to the surface earlier: they are 'brought out into the open to be dealt with instead of being hidden until it is too late to do much to correct them'. Decisions are being made lower down the organization, closer to the activities involved, rather than having to be referred constantly up for adjudication to the higher levels. As a result decision-making is improving and top-level managers are having their time freed to think more strategically about the long-term health of the business and develop a new non-functional mind-set – 'If your manager starts thinking about totality then we can change the culture.'

But there is still considerable confusion over roles and responsibilities during the attempts to implement program management. There are problems of allegiance. Program directors complain that the members of their team, drawn from functional organizations, 'cannot deliver their organization' and that they 'only serve as representatives of the functional area'. There is a lack of a pool of experienced program managers and a turnover of staff that affects program continuity. There is also the problem of an evolving reward structure which is ambivalent in whether it favours functional allegiance or program commitment which creates tensions in performance appraisal – should it reflect functional or program achievements or some form of combination of the two? Senior management also finds it a problem stepping back from the day-to-day decision-making arena. The shift of authority from functional manager to program manager remains incomplete. Program managers, crucial players in the new approach, feel that they have considerable responsibility for their programs but insufficient authority to get resources to support their programs. This reflects the problem of shifting authority from functional managers toward the program directors.

The goal is for program directors to determine what needs to be done and when it should be done, while the functional managers determine how the tasks should be done and who should do them. The role of functional management will be to provide people with experience, knowledge, and skills to support the program director in achieving the mission of the program. Program managers will have an 'integrative', 'mission driven' role. Budgeting previously done by functional unit needs to be transferred to a program team which can contract in functional services. Senior management has to learn how to really devolve responsibility: 'once decisions are made by senior management at a particular point, then the authority and responsibility is delegated to others until the next review point.' But this does not mean senior management abrogates its responsibility to the overall mission of the total organization: 'It may be necessary to subordinate functional and/or program goals at times to achieve total organizational goals. This is necessary to create an organization which is adaptive and flexible.' Despite inevitable problems and frustrations Product Development managers feel that the changes implemented in the wake of Insight and with the introduction of program management have created a positive momentum for change and that the major issues of the company's competitive disadvantage are, as a result, being confronted. Ford of Europe's ability to manage three major projects simultaneously at the end of the 1980s – the Fiesta, Escort and Sierra replacements, the Sierra design being for the two major markets of Europe and the United States – would have been impossible, senior managers argue, without these changes. Problems with these products – namely the 'qualified success' of the new Escort – are attributed to 'perhaps having bitten off more than we could chew', but the real proof of the value and the success of the new working practices is the replacement, Sierra the Mondeo, 'the jewel in the crown' in 1993.

## From Concept to Customer

The changes in product development in Ford of Europe reflect the progressive reanalysis and reconstruction of the heritage of Fordism that we have highlighted in previous chapters. Product development in the 1990s is still in a state of evolution in the wake of 'After Japan' and Insight, the primary impetuses to change from which the other change initiatives of the 1980s flowed. Product development under the old Fordist mode of management and organization came to be seen as inevitably and irrecoverably flawed in the light of the new strategic imperatives of the 1980s. The key product development issue is to design a set of mechanisms for continuous horizontal information flow among manufacturing, supply systems, product development, technology acquisition, and distribution. The emerging consensus is that the best way to put these mechanisms in place is to develop strongly-led teams for product development, which bring these skills together with a clear objective (Womack et al., 1990: 220).

What we see in Ford of Europe during the 1980s is the development of a capacity for continuous learning and ongoing change to replace the old certainties of the Fordist approach to product development. Changes in product development are now being influenced by the recent company-wide Concept to Customer (CTC) initiative, piloted on the 1994 Fiesta facelift and the 1994 Transit, and led initially by Product Development, but this time with the participation of Manufacturing. CTC is the name given to a new, 'more orderly logic' for the design, development and manufacturing-launch of new products and has as its main aim the ongoing reduction of the time required to conceive a new product, design it and place it in dealer showrooms – the time from 'Concept to Customer'.

CTC has as its major focus the elaboration and improvement of the discipline necessary to define precisely and achieve the various steps and responsibilities of bringing products successfully to market. It is predicated upon the definition of a new 'backbone' of key checkpoints and 'gateway reviews' to guide the product development process. The key objectives of CTC, therefore, are to reduce both program execution costs and program execution time while further improving vehicle quality, in line with company commitment to continuous quality improvement, in order to satisfy customer needs. The goal is to increase the rate of change within the company: 'we must make a "quantum leap" forward and to do this we must look fundamentally at new ways of working'.

CTC targets two major areas for improvement:

> Our current system [despite the major improvement already achieved] [still] tends to generate many late design and process changes as well as too many practices which are completed in series rather than in parallel.

The approach is still too sequential with lack of overall program teamwork. More 'up-front' work needed to be done before program approval so as to avoid later design/process changes. Conflicting objectives need to be eradicated from the system at the earliest possible stage. The timing plan was seen as still encouraging too slow a build up of activity.

Important here is the redefinition of quality in terms of conformance to customer requirements. This emphasis ensures that the quality assurance process takes in both design and manufacture and includes marketing as 'a central driving force of corporate strategy' (Lorenz, 1986). Participative management is seen as a crucial part of this approach. Indeed the argument is that PM and customer focus have a symbiotic relationship.

> [PM] is essential, there is no doubt about that, if you are going to have the concept within your organization or division that you care about the customer. If you care about the customer at all levels you then have to have participation. You then have to have working groups where all of the people are involved from the guy who finally produces the product to the guy who has the responsibility of thinking of the product and designing and they have to work together because manufacturing, manufacturing design, manufacturing sales, service, parts, all of the people involved in either bringing the product to market and servicing it in the after-market, you have to get all of these people together so it has to be truly participative. You have to have faith in the working groups, you have to give them the resources and responsibility, and you have to make them think that it is their product. And it is their product, their responsibility. . . . It is above all maximum joint ownership. It's joint ownership and applying the commitment of joint ownership.

This requires a major change in management attitudes. The following view comes from Manufacturing.

> What the managers have to do, they have to see their people being involved with somebody else making the decision rather than them. If you've got a manager sitting here [Manufacturing] and you've got another manager sitting the other side and he's done all the advanced planning, he's taken the thing through the costing and presented a paper to management that says 'In 1995 we want to make this car . . . it's a billion dollars'. . . . That gets approved. Then you hand over to this guy who is the manufacturing engineering manager for the production process. Now traditionally he will have said 'I'm the guy who's going to put it into production. I don't like what you've done. Change it. I recognize we're going to have this car and it's going to be these dimensions but I'm going to change what you've done. I'm going to change the process . . . it's my responsibility'. He's responsible to the vice-president of that part of the organization for that product. *Now* what he's got to do, what he's got to say is 'These guys here, although they work for me, they're going to be influenced by this lot and once they have made up their mind I'm *not* going to be able to change the process. If I do attempt to change it I'm going to be in trouble. Someone is going to say 'You were part of the commitment'. To that extent there is a big mental organizational change in the way we do our business.

The alternative is the old intolerable situation where 'product development is the meat in the sandwich', a vicious circle of reactive problem-solving, with 'constant changes of direction from management, pressure from manufacturing to release . . . increased cost, timing delays, no time to do the real job, too busy chasing problems . . . reactive rather than interactive process'.

CTC requires a new, disciplined approach.

> The process is a framework of logic, the key planning discipline in which individuals are better able to contribute to the success of the programme with clearer and common understanding of product objectives. [CTC] promotes better understanding of the overall plan and of individual roles and responsibilities within it and strengthened in-house teamwork. That's what it's about and that's the barrier we have to break down.

The vision for the CTC process is to deliver high quality products that customers want to buy, on time – 'products with greater excite-

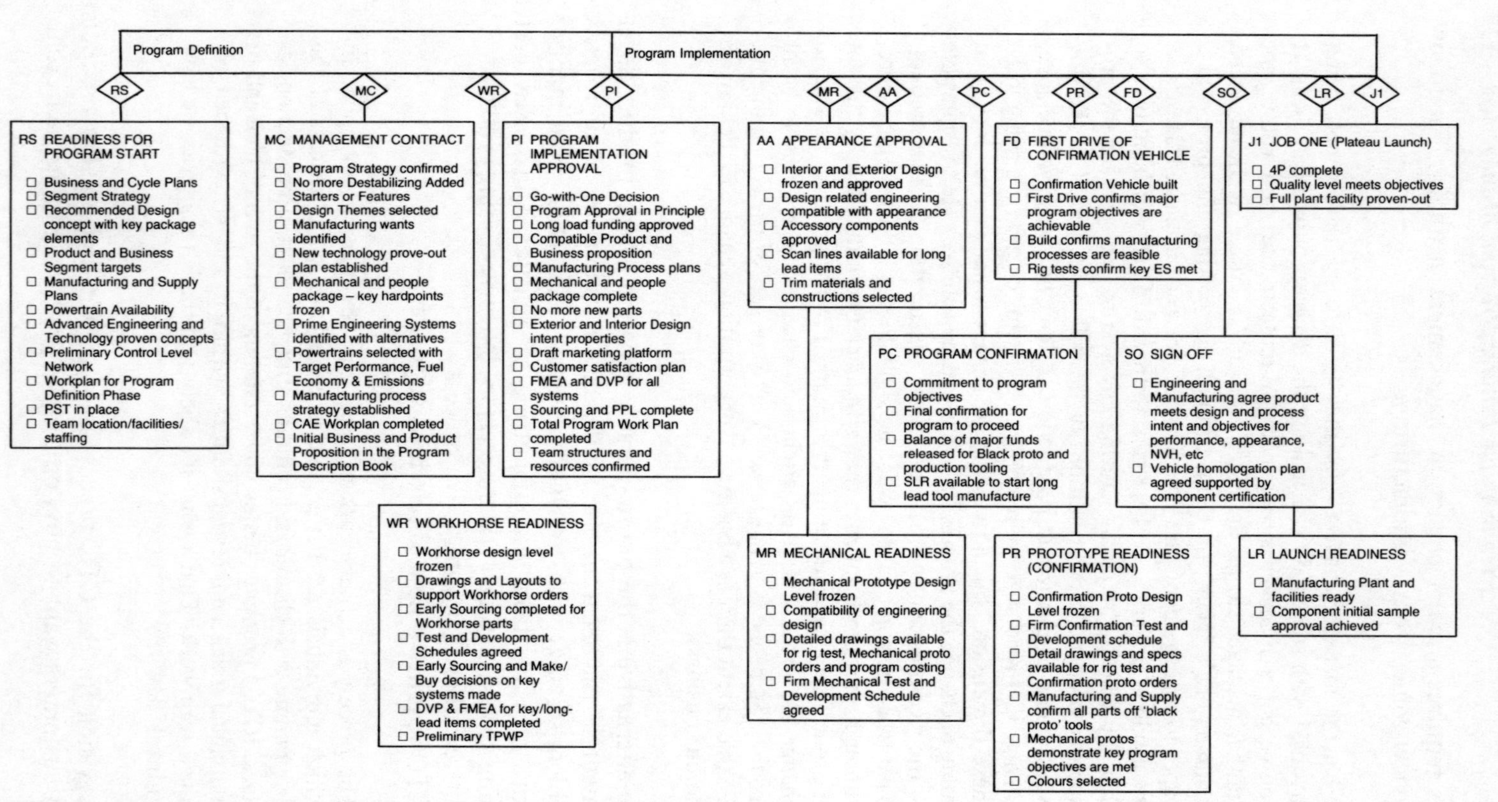


**Figure 6.1** Total program work plan – 'Concept-to-Customer'

ment, charisma and technology content; and a broadening of our product range'. The objective is to have a well documented process that can be managed with greater precision and discipline *and* executed with fewer resources in a shorter time. CTC documentation describes the steps required to deliver a new product to market. The process contains a number of checkpoints or gateways which are positioned at points in the process where a number of interdependent actions come together or where decisions are required. To pass through a gateway/checkpoint the program team must confirm that they have met a number of criteria, the 'deliverables' against which progress from concept to customer is measured (see figure 6.1).

The 'go-with-one' principle of decision-making – achieving consensus and commitment before proceeding to the next stage of the process – is reminiscent of the Japanese *nemawashi* decision-making approach, in which, once alternatives have been considered and a decision arrived at, the team involved is responsible for implementing that decision in the way in which they have agreed it. 'Shortest possible program execution timing' is based on team agreement that once gateways have been negotiated there will be 'no further inventions'. A major aspect of CTC is the development of supporting sub-processes. These are:

*Ongoing processes*: These take place prior to the formal start of a program and depend upon consistent strategic planning to support technology (product and process) and business plans. They determine the product cycle plan needs based on benchmarking of best competitors.

*Total program workplanning (TPWP)*: This requires all areas to plan their work recognizing their interdependence upon other areas. The program workplan allows progress to be monitored and potential problems to be identified early before the program is destabilized.

*Enhanced teams*: Enhanced teamwork with cross-functional 'buy-in' ensures that all relevant inputs are received at the appropriate time in the process.

*Early sourcing* to involve suppliers at the earliest stage of the process to ensure design and engineering incorporates supplier inputs.

*Compatible targets*: This is the process which balances the requirements of the customer against the business needs of the company. The objective is to define the product which delivers maximum customer satisfaction within the business resources available to the program team. It is intended to force trade-offs to be made using customer satisfaction as the prime criteria and to determine program stability through the implementation phase.

*Program parts list (PPL)*: This is a common database which provides information by part to all members of the program team. Its use enhances control over key program parameters such as weight, cost and release timing, thus helping to avoid late changes which destabilize programs.

*Product process*: This is the process by which product targets and knowledge are translated into hardware of required quality.

Ten factors differentiate CTC from previous approaches:

1 Customer satisfaction (internal and external) is the key driving force.
2 Customer requirements need to be understood upfront and incorporated into product targets.
3 Compatible product and business targets drive and stabilize the design process.
4 Only proven technology is carried into programs.
5 Enhanced cross functional teams are empowered to make decisions.
6 Mandatory gateway reviews provide program management discipline.
7 Clear measurement criteria are provided at gateways to assess quality of deliverables.
8 Product design decisions are made early in the development cycle and kept stable.
9 Upfront engineering is required to accelerate the development of program knowledge.
10 A 'right first time' discipline drives the whole.

## Japan Revisited – the Simultaneous Engineering Study

The dysfunctions of Ford's product development system again came under the spotlight in a searching report of the late 1980s – The Simultaneous Engineering Study. This was conducted in 1989 (the study group reported on 31 October 1989) with extensive interviewing of managers and executives primarily in Product Development and Manufacturing. Its charter was to 'Recommend changes necessary to facilitate the aims of best product/best process/first time by simultaneous planning and thinking'. The focus was on the upstream side of the product development process and the key areas of interface between Product Development and Manufacturing with significant potential for improvement. It is this study that has defined the product development agenda for Ford as a whole and encapsulated the major managerial and organizational issues of the 1990s.

The Simultaneous Engineering Study took its leader, the champion of 'After Japan', Bill Hayden, back to Japan. After a decade of change he reached a different conclusion, succinctly summarized by the then Chairman of Ford of Europe, who situates the Simultaneous Engineering Study on a learning curve starting with After Japan and encompassing Insight: '[The new message was] that you guys got to re-organize. That wasn't implicit in AJ. AJ didn't take us far enough . . . Insight told us some of that but even then we didn't have the whole response together.' One of the most important challenges for managers in the 1990s is to get manufacturing expertise contributing directly to product development early on (Gomory, 1989). Design for manufacture has become a key strategic issue and the strategic management of the human resource to facilitate product development is a major factor in the ongoing search for competitive advantage. This involves a major rethink of relationships between various functional groups, for example, various kinds of engineers. For Ford the acceleration of the product development cycle has become a major strategic concern in contributing to its ability to respond rapidly and flexibly to the increasing differentiation of consumer choice. It remains a concern that it is to the forefront of the Ford management agenda:

> We're talking about survival. Its not about taking two months out of the cycle time, its much more than that. Its about achieving a quantum leap: we need to take eighteen months out of the cycle time to be competitive. And we can't do that by putting more committees in place. We have to say, 'Stand back, its fundamental change'. You get small efficiencies by evolutionary change but to get the quantum leap you've got to do something completely different. The Simultaneous Engineering study team is a concrete manifestation of the company saying, 'Let's stand back and look what's going to get us the quantum leap in organizational process time'.

In Ford, program management and Concept to Customer were predicated upon the integration of product development and manufacturing processes. The exact nature of this integration has proved extremely problematic. It was the nature of the integration that the Simultaneous Engineering study addressed.

Simultaneous engineering describes a process of identifying and developing the sources, processes, facilities and tools that will be used to manufacture and assemble vehicles and their components using the most efficient and effective methods possible. In Ford simultaneous engineering is the logical outcome of the process of change that started with Insight; it is the antithesis of sequential processing. Its goal is to bring together the design and engineering functions that used to work separately, sequentially and often at cross purposes. The movement is towards 'a more cooperative, simultaneous, computer-aided process' (Butman, 1991: 11) with the aim of moving beyond the old mentality that viewed product development as akin to assembly-line manufacture, proceeding through a predetermined and preplanned set of stages. The approach involves 'compressing' responsibility for the various steps involved and assigning it to the relevant cross-functional team (Hammer, 1990). The aim is to link parallel activities rather than integrating their results.

Simultaneous engineering reflects a growing manufacturing trend, the shift from purely functional forms of organization to more integrated structures (Clark and Fujimoto, 1991: 103). As such it represents a move beyond matrix forms of coordination to actual structural integration of previously separate functional groups, namely Product Development and Manufacturing. The new approach emphasizes communication.

> The distinction between Engineering as we understand it today (sequential Product and Manufacturing Engineering), and Simultaneous Engineering, is that communication has to be simultaneous, not sequential nor sporadic. Communication is the key to improved relationships and performance at all levels throughout the organizations. (Clark and Fujimoto, 1991)

The process of product development involves continuous communication from the initial customer requirements fed into the company, through to the complete vehicle, delivered to the customer as the company's realization of his or her requirements. The effectiveness of simultaneity of product and process engineering – working on product and process design in parallel – is dependent upon communication, cooperation and skill (technical and social).

> The parallel approach . . . heightens the importance of coordination and communication between product and process engineering. Product engineering must comprehend implications of their designs for manufacturability, and process engineering must clarify constraints and opportunities in the process and develop a good measure of flexibility to cope with the changes inherent in the product design process. Though it can be a source of improved product quality and lower costs, emphasis on manufacturability without flexibility in the attitudes and skills of process engineers can negatively affect a product's competitiveness. Process engineers dream of product engineers who take manufacturability fully into account in the early stages of development and then freeze the design. But paraphrasing what one process engineer said of this dream: 'If the voice of manufacturing dominates product design, the car may be great in the factory but a dog in the market'. (Clark and Fujimoto, 1991)

Attitudes of customer orientation, joint responsibility and mutual trust on both product and process side are the basis for effective communication. In the West analysts have argued that culture change is required to promote communication to diffuse throughout the organization a shared sense of competitive reality and customer orientation (Clark and Fujimoto, 1991: 123–6). The way to achieve this, Ford decided, was a blend of new structures and a new participative working culture.

The Simultaneous Engineering study group analysed what Ford had already achieved and how it compared with its competitors. The company's traditional strength had always been economies of scale and specialist expertise. To reorganize into wholly self-sufficient and autonomous car-line engineering divisions would be inefficient and would weaken specialist expertise. The goal of the program management matrix had been to reconcile expertise and product focus. Program management had allowed engineering activities to find a better fit of their component efforts into the total vehicle. The extensive use of product-line-focused functional working groups in the matrix structure, to communicate and integrate the efforts of various component areas, had been effective, but it had also increased the number of dedicated coordination resources and the non-dedicated time commitment. Program management, the study group concluded, was still some way from realizing its potential due to insufficient isolation of dedicated resources to major programs, especially early in the process, and because of 'a multitude of demanding near-term problems and minor programs'.

This organizational approach had tried to grow along a third axis, involving Manufacturing much more closely in the program process than the historical approach of loose linkages and handovers. This was linked to increased manufacturing participation in working groups, and more recently, where a special problem or opportunity has been identified, participation in the formation of Simultaneous Engineering Teams. The study group considered this directionally sound, but it had led to overstretching of engineers, and the underlying risk was still present that functional organization objectives could weaken the effectiveness of the teams' and management's buy-in to their recommendations.

But program management was soundly endorsed in the study, which concluded that it was a firmly entrenched organizational characteristic among Ford's key competitors. Although there was no direct relationship between organizational structure and product development success, successful volume manufacturers were characterized by the use of program management and by solving problems in an overlapping, rather than sequential, manner. Companies successfully using simultaneous engineering possessed these features:

- Educational focus on cross-disciplines
- Geographic co-location for easy communications
- Reward/incentive systems that rely on team performance *vs* individual performance
- Strong, culturally-based sense of interdependence
- Highly disciplined engineering processes
- Considerable reliance on ad-hoc meetings and teams as well as more formal cross-functional teams

There is no reason why Ford of Europe could not, in theory, achieve all of the above conditions, except perhaps those associated with Japanese culture. However, in practice, the study argued, Ford at present had very few of the above characteristics. It was also questionable, given the serious competitive deficiency of its total program process in relation to that of the Japanese, if it was making the necessary pace of improvement. To implement simultaneous engineering a cultural change was required involving management leadership, good communication, skilful management of organizational change, and 'training on how to make it happen'.

The study group concluded that the major barriers to full cooperation between Product Development and Manufacturing were insufficient Manufacturing involvement, product development process deficiencies and competing organizational objectives. Process definition, different management goals, resource constraints, organization structure as well as geographic separation and communication difficulties were identified as the cause of the barriers. Most frequently suggested solutions to resolve these problems were the adoption of a more disciplined, 'front-loaded' product and development process (CTC was often mentioned as a conceptually correct approach), and a reorganization bringing Manufacturing and Product Development closer together. Manufacturing, it was argued, needed to become more involved earlier in the product development process. The major reasons given for missing Job No. 1 dates were late engineering changes, due to inadequate up-front engineering work, and lack of discipline in holding process gateway reviews during program execution.

In the Simultaneous Engineering Study Japan again provided the main point of critical comparison. Mazda, Toyota and Honda were identified as leaders in program management. They all had different approaches but also important points in common.

> All three companies adopt a structured process for their product programs. The program director works with the functional area to reach a clear understanding on who will contribute what at each point in the program and in this way they construct a structured work plan. This identified the level of achievement which must be reached by the functional area at each stage of the program and becomes the basis for the functional areas to plan their work and control the outcome. In this process the program director acts as a catalyst, one who communicates and coordinates to ensure that the efforts of the functional areas are synchronized.

In Ford program management had been implemented in Product Development only. (The study found that Product Development managers were more convinced that PM had become 'embedded in its structure and culture' and that 'participative decision-making at executive level is proven and firmly established'. These views were not shared by Manufacturing.) In Japanese companies program management was company-wide. (Of Ford's European competitors, Opel too had company-wide program management, with cross-functional project teams but no formal matrix structure.) Mazda introduced program management into Product Development in 1975 and extended it to embrace Manufacturing in 1979. Mazda also had Product and Manufacturing Engineering on one site with a manufacturing plant. Some Japanese companies had functional organizations but they also had structured cross-functional training and a relatively unitary, integrated company culture.

> The Japanese companies have distinctly separate Product Development and Manufacturing Engineering organizational divisions. They rely, very successfully, to judge from results, on their company culture of teamwork, dedication and personal relationships and on Program Management teams to avoid 'chimney' issues with this approach.

Mazda stressed the importance of four factors to successful simultaneous engineering:

| | |
|---|---|
| *Communication* | – Co-location, classmates, joint social evenings, to link Product Development/Manufacturing. |
| *Formal cooperation* | – Team meetings. Joint Product/Manufacturing management meetings, cross-functional career move planning. |
| *Team culture* | – Family loyalty, human values, shared responsibility. |
| *Customer driven* | – Establish process customer relations and agree what is needed. |

Simultaneous engineering needs a background of 'suitable conditions'. Mazda enhances communication through a 'classmate system' of recruitment, hiring people from the same school or university into interfacing organizations to improve cooperation across functional boundaries. Informal meetings (drinking parties) are encouraged to foster team building. In Mazda 'No one is a Big Boss', a stark contrast to Mazda's view of the Western firms being over-dependent on the 'Big Boss, with great authority'. In Mazda a leader is not expected to be perfect. All involved in the team share responsibility in an atmosphere of mutual respect. Many joint meetings serve to foster a 'buy-in' philosophy. Every member of the team has full responsibility for the team's success with freedom to criticize and a responsibility to improve.

The power/authority of the program director is an important issue in the Simultaneous Engineering Study. Mazda's view was that the program director is 'powerless'. His main job is to keep channels of communication open through the clear definition of program tasks, including timing and responsibility. The Japanese deal with this as a priority at program inception, through participation among functional areas. This provides the plan against which functional areas themselves compare their work and report any 'off-standard' event likely to cause delay and consequently needing management attention. Ford signalled this as a characteristic they should seek to emulate:

> The product development process is like Kanban the production process, a self regulating process giving visible control at all times and greatest opportunity for improvement because problems are found and fixed, not concealed and ignored. In such a well regulated environment, power for the program director is irrelevant. There is need to achieve this culture change in Ford. Extend Program Management to Manufacturing and Sales/Marketing.

In Mazda, cross-functional training supports this environment. The company's basic training philosophy is summed up as follows:

> The Company conducts education and training which it considers necessary for character-building, knowledge acquisition and skill learning of the employees. The upper echelon of employees shall participate actively in the education and training programs and give guidance to the subordinates and junior workers in their respective workplaces.

The study team concluded that fundamental organizational and geographic changes were required to accelerate the process changes that Ford was trying to make. It recommended (1) the extension of program management to include Marketing, Manufacturing and Supply and (2) the need for greater involvement of functional chiefs to resolve areas of conflict with the Program Office. There was also a need for stronger leadership of programs to generate early consensus on product and technology strategies. This required Manufacturing involvement from the concept stage.

The optimal structure of the matrix linking Product Development and other functions was a crucial concern of the study. At the top level it was clear that full time people were required both as functional chiefs and product program managers. However, lower in the organization the situation was less clear-cut. The goal was to increase the product-focus of the organization in line with the principles of program management at the expense of its functional focus. To this end the replacement of separate Product Development and Manufacturing Units was recommended with a separate Vehicle Division whose mission is to produce the best value, highest quality vehicles in the world, and a Powertrain Division whose mission is to produce the powertrains needed by the Vehicle Division to fulfil its mission. As one Manufacturing manager put it, 'If we truly want to be participative, if we truly want to work simultaneously with all of the activities it is no good having those activities under two separate heads of departments . . . that doesn't work. One guy has got to have the responsibility to be totally participative. He has to have the authority and the know-how and the wherewithal to get all of the people involved together.'

In addition, separate Vehicle Programs were seen as the means to provide strong, company-wide product-focused leadership to the Vehicle and Powertrain Divisions through matrix management. The Vehicle Program activity should be separate because:

- Vehicle Division would become too large and dominant if it incorporated Vehicle Programs, and this in turn might lead to a dilution of management focus between manufacturing efficiency and future programs.
- There is a risk that Vehicle Division could over-value internal constraints (e.g. existing facilities versus customer's needs), and less risk that a separate Vehicle Program area would do this.

A vehicle program focus gives a balance so that no single activity can be dominant: Vehicle Engineering, Design and Finance are equally charged with providing services to the Program Directors for their functions. The matrix structure provides the mechanism to integrate Vehicle Division and Powertrain Division by Vehicle Program with the integration of product and manufacturing engineering activities to the greatest practicable degree (in order to eliminate or reduce conflicts caused by differing objectives, encourage efficient early and informal communications and reduce the complexity of technical interfaces). The extended program management matrix gives responsibility for resolving conflict to the Program Director, who can go to the level of Vice-President as a last resort.

The study group recommendation constituted major surgery. In the words of Lindsey Halstead

> We recut the organization which had traditionally been Manufacturing and PD, we sliced it and we took the two heads and said 'You take the vehicle engineering side of the business and you take the produc-

> tion side' and we took the other guy and said 'You take the powertrain and transmission and engines and the manufacturing', we also gave him program management responsibility. Bill [Hayden]'s study said 'Make three legs, Program Management in the centre, Vehicle and Powertrain' . . . The key thing is we resliced the organization with two guys who had a reasonable capacity to work together to make it work and some matrix function in this program office in between. That was reorganizing workgroups on a massive scale. We're in the process of diffusing this through the organisation gradually.

In the summer of 1992 the structure was altered again in line with the study's recommendations to create 'three legs' – Engineering and Vehicle Manufacturing Group, Powertrain Group and Product Programs (including Vehicle Engineering and Design). The logic of the changes is clear. They are process-driven. In Halstead's words

> In the final analysis the manufacturing engineer way down the organization has to be sitting beside and communicating with the product engineer responsible for that piece or system of the vehicle. Jack Welch at GE calls it the borderless, the seamless organization that doesn't have traditional functional structure. Now many Japanese companies have functional structures . . . Mazda, for example, but they seem to overcome that through program management and the way the Japanese culture works. For us that's a very tough change process because for us, for us in key positions, for as long as we can remember, we've been organized in the other way. We've virtually had to relearn how we operate. . . . We've had to, complementary to the EI/PM process, recut the organization . . . Organization by itself doesn't get you very far. The organization ought to reflect the system, ought to reflect the process first and then decide on the organizational structure.

Bill Hayden, the architect of the study, describes it in these terms.

> Hopefully it's a better way of working but the most important thing is getting people to think afresh. They've got to be challenged and that is what Simultaneous Engineering [the study] was about. It was a chimney-busting exercise. Chimneys are a monstrous problem in this organization.

Another important proposal was the 'co-location' of product development and manufacturing activities. Ford of Europe suffers significantly greater geographic dispersion of core engineering activities than key competitors, who regard geographic co-location as important to simultaneous engineering. It is unusual in having 'split site' product development in the UK and West Germany. This is the historical legacy of uniting the UK and German companies to form Ford of Europe. General Motors took a different approach, rationalizing its product development into one country (Germany) and its Opel subsidiary, rather than Vauxhall (its UK arm) during a period of financial trouble.

> It didn't have the volume of sales or profits to support the increasing cost of developing new models, and although GM invested in Vauxhall, they paid more attention to Opel. Beginning in the mid-seventies, GM began shifting design and engineering operations from the UK and consolidating them at Opel. From being a complete auto manufacturer – capable of designing, engineering and manufacturing a car from scratch – Vauxhall became a marketing and assembly operation only. (Butman, 1991: 40)

It was to General Motors and the Vauxhall Cavalier that the Sierra lost market share in the 1980s. Ford justifies its position while seeking improvements.

> We believe that our presence in Britain and Germany is an advantage which most of our competitors do not share and politically we cannot significantly change it anyway. There remains an opportunity, however, to improve efficiency by bringing our engineers closer together. We propose to consolidate all Product and Manufacturing engineers in Britain on the Dunton site and physically realign the Product and Manufacturing engineers in Germany.

## Conclusion

The Simultaneous Engineering study concluded that communication and teamwork have improved in Ford, that the organization is more flexible and adaptive and more customer-focused. However, it also recognized that planning of how a product program should be implemented is currently incomplete and that there is still a problem of people 'buying into it'. This reflects a lack of clarity about where individuals and previous functional groupings fit into the process of development and the mission of the vehicle. Discipline was essential, based on performance meeting concept-to-customer 'diamond points' to ensure steady progress was maintained throughout the program.

The problem of 'buy-in' also reflects a continuing problem of trust. Trust between individuals and groups is essential if people are to help each other resolve problems rather than blame each other for their existence.

Trust emerges as a key issue. There is a residual cynicism that 'front-loading' is possible as the necessary resources to manage the process have never looked likely to be implemented. Program management is still seen as excessively Planning and Finance oriented. The full implication of the transition to program managements still needs to be addressed. Significant numbers of engineers feel the company does not recognize the value of engineers. Also, there is a tendency for the Program Office, which has significantly richer grading, to 'steal' the best engineers and demotivate those left in the component areas. This suggests the need to create more grading equality between all areas within product development to allow easy cross rotation of people. There is also the problem of overall fatigue in product development personnel as a result of increasing program demands.

The process is far from complete but product development in Ford of Europe has moved beyond the old Fordist emphasis on cost reduction as an end in itself (Frey, 1991). A new perspective has emerged.

> In PD [product development] the balance between innovation and efficiency has changed dramatically. It's not just about cutting cost as an end in itself. It's about cutting cost in relation to the defined output. Now it's 'Let's keep the product exactly the same in terms of quality and specification but cut the cost of development. So it's no longer a zero-sum trade-off between efficiency and innovation. It used to be, but no longer. If we take 25 per cent out of costs through PD or better engineering planning during pre-production then we now plough back 23 per cent to enhance the product. The terms we use, 'efficiency' and 'quality', may sound the same as they did 15 years ago but their meaning has changed.

The strategic need now is to make this newly emerging perspective a permanent and pervasive part of the collective Ford consciousness.

The company is currently coming to terms with the radical rethinking initiated by the Insight project and legitimized on a company-wide basis by the Simultaneous Engineering study. In some ways the conclusion of this study, with its emphasis on a balance of structural and process change, is an expression of pessimism about Ford's capacity for fundamental cultural change. What the company identifies as very difficult if not impossible to create, certainly in the short-term, is the strong culturally-based sense of interdependence that they see in Japanese competitors. But Ford is now clear about the dysfunctional consequences of its old bureaucracy. It is too slow and inflexible for today's dynamic competitive environment. It also perpetuates division.

> A pyramid-type organization with vertical authority/accountability chimneys is the antithesis of Japanese operating practice. Pressures to achieve consensus and harmony dictate that complete consideration of other functions' views and needs must be incorporated in a plan or idea *before* it goes very far as a proposal.

The Japanese launch 'many trial balloons' that 'are punctured at very low levels before going higher in the organization to a management committee'. By the time the senior executive needs to sanction projects this approach means that consensus about a best solution is close to emergence. Senior management's function is to 'confirm that the consensus process works and that the proposal is in line with overall policy direction established by the top management and the Executive Committee': 'The traditional Ford approach was to manage *through* levels and tasks, now the intention is to manage *across* levels and projects.' Program management and simultaneous engineering attack head-on the problem of organizational 'chimneys'. The new approach to organization emphasizes proactivity and innovation rather than reactivity and blame.

> The boxes on the organization chart had a double purpose: for the individual they provided the certainty of task and responsibility; for the manager it meant he knew who to kick hardest.

Program management is based on a new notion of teamwork and responsibility. It gives them the space to contribute beyond a narrow role definition: 'That's the problem with chimneys. When a problem falls from the top it lands heaviest at the bottom. The matrix diffuses this by dispersing the downward force laterally.' 'Dilemma management' requires the surfacing of problems rather than narrow conformity to role. It demands a new approach to problem-solving and conflict resolution that avoids 'smoothing, withdrawing, avoidance, or exercise of dominance'. 'Negotiation' should replace 'paperwork';

'Problem solving should utilize consensus seeking where the focus is always on the mission, not on politics, personalities, or win-lose games within the organization structure.' An environment of open communication and sharing of information is seen as essential to achieve mission goals. This requires high levels of trust, respect, and confidence. Ford accept that achieving these ends is perhaps one of the most significant challenges it has to face and that it requires a fundamental shift in organizational values to generate the willingness to pursue cooperation and integration rather than internal competition and separation. A new way of thinking about product development demands a new way of thinking about products – the car as a 'totality' rather than a 'collection of individual components'. Concept to Customer dictates that creative conflicts now have to be resolved in terms of what is best for the customer.

What one clearly sees emerging in product development in Ford of Europe in the 1980s is a new willingness to learn, an acceptance of the need for critical self-analysis and a desire, fragile at first but growing stronger, to innovate. This new will was evident in the constitution of the product development study teams of the period. 'For the first time [they used] our stars, our best individuals. For thirty years study teams were used as dumping grounds for underperformers and people about to retire.' 'Study' and 'learning' were no longer marginal activities.

The ultimate success of the transition we have examined in chapters 5 and 6 has still to be demonstrated. Critics of the company in Europe have long maintained that its past success has been chiefly due to the lack of competent competitors, a situation that, in the wake of the recent performance of General Motors and the incursion of new Japanese competition, no longer applies. Has Ford changed enough? Has it created the capability for ongoing change? In the 1990s we will see whether Ford's performance is product-led, reflecting new product development skills, as it needs to be. Ford in the past has achieved successful products when it has managed to balance technical, managerial and financial demands. Its future depends upon its skill in reconciling these demands on a consistent basis.

# 7
# Top Management at Ford

Explanations of Ford's transformation in the United States during the 1980s have emphasized the role of top management (Pascale, 1990), particularly that of Don Petersen, President of the company from 1980 to 1985 and Chairman between 1985 and 1990. In this chapter we analyse the literature on the top management role in general, paying particular attention to leadership characteristics and organization mission before turning to the role of top management at Ford in the United States and in Europe. Our major focus is upon the participative nature of the top management process. Our research traces differences in the constitution of the top management groups in Ford of Europe and in the US which had a significant effect upon the unfolding of the new corporate strategy/human resource management agenda.

## Strategic Leadership

In a landmark *Harvard Business Review* article, 'Managing our way to economic decline', Hayes and Abernathy (1980) blame America's productivity crisis on management failure. It is the failure of both managerial vision and leadership, they argue, that erodes the inclination and the capacity to innovate, thus leading to decline. Peters and Waterman (1982) began their seminal study on excellence with the conviction that it was a unique set of cultural attributes rather than leadership that distinguished excellent organizations from the rest in their ability to evolve and change. What they concluded was that in almost every excellent company there was a strong leader who was decisive in making the company excellent. The recent strategy literature has also emphasized strategic leadership (Schendel, 1989).

Peters and Waterman also emphasize the important role of the founders of companies in establishing organizational culture and a sense of mission. In excellent companies the values and practices introduced by the 'founding fathers' persist. But in some cases this is counter-productive over the longer term. In Ford's case the legacy of Henry Ford, refined by Henry Ford II – the Fordist system – was, as we have suggested previously, an ambiguous gift, extremely successful at first but, later, an obstacle to change.

Top management's beliefs concerning the company's sources of competitive advantage – its distinctive competence, its significant resources, financial and human, its strengths and weaknesses, its market standing, its technological base, its mode of management and its interpersonal processes – are crucial. Beliefs and the vision they sustain can create a form of strategic myopia, limiting the managerial gaze, focusing managerial attention too narrowly. One can illustrate the strategic significance of this aspect of management in the experience of Imperial Chemical Industries under the Chairmanship of John Harvey-Jones (Pettigrew, 1985). ICI had to overcome the inertia created by a particular heritage of beliefs that highlighted its undoubted technological prowess as *the* source of ICI's strategic strength. The company had to learn, under Harvey-Jones, that new, broader business skills rather than narrow technical skills were necessary to awake it from its slumber. The company had to develop a sharper market focus, fundamentally question its existing product range and geographical spread, develop more entrepreneurial qualities and reduce stifling bureaucratic and central controls to allow it to become truly competitive in a much harsher global environment than that in which its traditional culture had been shaped.

The recent experience of Glaxo reinforces the point (Myers, 1991). The company, like ICI, set itself a similar challenge of cultural change. First, there was the existing hierarchy to eliminate. This had made Glaxo a successful company in the 1980s but in the 1990s time and energy were being wasted in internal competition between different interest groups without a sense of shared objectives. There were major cultural differences, for example, between the two trading subsidiaries. The company's main pharmaceutical markets were in the process of major shake-up with Europe moving towards 1992, while Glaxo's major customer, the British National Health Service, was itself going through radical change. The company redefined its core values as role clarity, a more sharply focused results orientation, team working, acceptance of change and innovation, and set about a major change initiative based on 'destructuring' hierarchies and generating the shared sense of ownership of issues as a driver to cultural change.

Top management serve as role models for the rest of the organization. Bennis and Nanus (1985), in their study of leaders, cite a Taoist story from ancient China to illustrate the importance of top management analysing its own attitudes and behaviour as a prelude to change in others:

> When Yen Ho was about to take up his duties as tutor to the heir of Ling, Duke of Wei, he went to Ch'u Po Yu for advice. 'I have to deal,' he said, 'with a man of depraved and murderous disposition. . . . How is one to deal with a man of this sort?' 'I am glad,' said Ch'u Po Yu, 'that you asked this question. . . . The first thing you must do is not to improve him, but to improve yourself.'

Top decision-makers bring their cognitions and values to their decision-making and these create a 'filter', between the situation and the decision-makers' perceptions of it, through which information is interpreted. As managers rise to the senior levels of an organization a general management perspective is increasingly required. Ironically, functional loyalty, so important in the earlier career stages, now becomes an obstacle to this general perspective because it generates a tendency towards a particular decision-making bias, be it marketing, finance, product or manufacturing oriented. The composition of the top management team will also have an impact upon decision-making. Homogeneous teams, composed of individuals from similar backgrounds, will tend to make decisions more quickly, but these teams will make their best decisions only in stable environments. In dynamic, complex environments team heterogeneity is a positive factor, although heterogeneous teams will have to learn to live with their differences and use them as an aid rather than a barrier to more complex decision-making.

## Vision

The old managerial motivational 'tool kit' based on hierarchy, career promotion, power and fear is no longer adequate. New and more effective incentives are needed to build commitment and encourage high performance. Sir John Harvey-Jones, in *Making It Happen*, emphasizes that he considers himself a leader rather than a manager and that his key role in change at ICI was in leading by example – persuasion and hard work took the place of power, authority or rules. His most important skill, he argues, was his ability to help others release their energies and focus their efforts on corporate objectives by creating conditions in which people wanted to give of their best. This view emphasizes a fundamental shift in thinking about the basis of managerial power, to personal power and the importance of vision.

> Leaders need to be able to persuade both their immediate colleagues and the workforce as a whole. They must be able to drive change through the systems and structures via the strategy of the organization. Individuals who possess both a vision of the future and personal and formal power are likely to have a significant impact on the culture of the organization. (Williams et al., 1989: 52–3)

Of the new managerial 'tools' that Kanter (1989) and others identify, most attention has been given to the importance of mission. Management guru Peter Drucker argues that the most common cause of organizational failure is the inability of top management to instil in organizational members a sense of direction. The stress is on the visionary aspects of leadership and the symbolic aspects of the executive's work, in marked contrast to the previously prevailing view in the strategy literature of the manager as rational final decision maker (Westley and Mintzberg, 1989). The alternative to the machine bureaucracy is the 'missionary' organization where the driving strategic force is a top management with a rich system of values and beliefs shared by its members. The key feature of such an organization, most common in Japan, is the shared sense of mission that binds individual and organizational goals into a common purpose others in the organization accept as their own (Mintzberg, 1983).

Chester Barnard (1938), himself a CEO, pioneered the view that the top manager's role is to harness the social forces of organization through shared vision and values. The most effective managers, he argued, are value-shapers; they give organizational members a sense of collective purpose and shared norms, thus binding them into collective forms of behaviour. With this kind of executive, work is not anomic or alienating, individuals find a sense of purpose in working with others in a cooperative endeavour. This is an important theme in the literature on the new managerial work. 'The leader's task, as Chester Barnard recognized long ago, is to develop a network of cooperative relationships among all the people, groups, and organizations that have something to contribute to an economic enterprise' (Kanter, 1989: 90). Pascale's (1990) analysis of Ford's American turnaround makes the same point – what emerged in Don Petersen's era was collaboration and teamwork at all levels of the company.

The new image of top manager is that of the coach or facilitator. Peter Senge (1986: 134) approvingly quotes Bill O'Brien, president of Hanover Insurance Companies:

> As we move from the traditional authoritarian organization to the vision-oriented, value-driven organization, the skills required of effective leaders will change dramatically. . . . The effective leader in a traditional work environment is above all else a strategist and decision-maker. In the type of work environment we are creating at Hanover critical decisions are made throughout the organization. My job is more and more becoming that of a teacher and a coach rather than a decision-maker.

It is top management's task to define a mission, express a vision, inspire their employees and provoke change. There are two essential preconditions for change. Significant people need to feel there is a need for change. They then have to convince others of this need before meaningful, lasting change can occur. The need must be felt throughout the organization. A key leadership task is motivating. Peters and Waterman argue that managers in excellent companies are adept at motivating by compelling, simple values. These managers demonstrate transformational leadership – leadership that builds on humanity's need for meaning and creates a sense of purpose in belonging to an organization and pursuing its goals. They induce clarity, consensus and commitment regarding the organization's basic purposes. The major faults of leadership are failure to set goals and setting goals that enjoy only superficial acceptance (Wrapp, 1967; Selznick, 1957). People need to be challenged and motivated by strategy, excited by its goals or methods (Rumelt, 1988). The best form of competitive advantage is to improve existing skills and develop new ones in search of a meaningful, even inspiring, goal. The major management challenge of the 1990s is to empower employees to invent the means to accomplish ambitious ends (Hamel and Prahalad, 1989).

'Visioning' can be broken down into three distinct stages: first, envisioning – generating an image of the desired organization and strategy; then articulating and communicating this vision to the rest of the organization; and, finally, empowering the organization to enact the vision (Westley and Mintzberg, 1989). Visionary leaders therefore need to be skilled communicators, able to motivate people to high achievement through appeals to both rationality and emotion, capturing their hearts and souls as well as their minds. Steve Jobs, co-founder of Apple computers, motivated his workers with a vision of democratizing the computer industry by making computer power accessible to the masses. Apple employees, he convinced them, were going to change the world with a great product and democratize an industry dominated by giant corporations such as IBM. Apple's purpose was 'to make a contribution to the world by making tools for the mind that advance humankind' (Collins and Porras, 1991: 39).

Organizations are, in the final analysis, systems of meaning and belief. A critical administrative activity involves the construction and maintenance of shared belief systems (Pfeffer, 1981). Management is increasingly the negotiation of meaning in complexity through the exercise of symbolic skills.

> If management involves the taking of symbolic action, then the skills required are political, dramaturgical, and language skills more than analytical or strictly quantitative skills. . . . Language, symbols, settings, stories, ceremonies, and informational social influence to produce socially constructed realities are as much the tools of managers as are economic analysis, finite mathematics, and theories of leadership and organization design that stress the rational, objective results of managerial action'. (Pfeffer, 1981: 44–6)

Top managers in their figurehead role symbolize the meaning of the organization and the sources of its sense of order (or disorder) for their employees and the outside world. To the extent that they provide a sense of order in this symbolic role, top management helps organizational participants to 'successfully contend with the highly charged, affect-ridden, intensely human aspects of their lives' (Astley, 1984: 269–70).

## Charismatic Leadership

Vision has usually been seen as the preserve of top management. In particular vision has been associated with 'charisma'. Indeed, charisma and vision have tended to be seen as interdependent. The term refers to a special quality that enables the leader to mobilize and sustain activity within an organization through specific personal actions combined with perceived personal characteristics (Nadler and Tushman, 1990: 82). The charismatic leader articulates a compelling vision that challenges, is meaningful and is worthy of pursuing. He or she energizes and motivates people to act through example. Finally he or she serves an enabling function, supporting others and giving them confidence through his or her support.

But charisma has drawbacks. Potential problems include creating unrealistic expectations which set yourself and your organization up for failure, creating too much dependency on one individual or, conversely, creating a strong countervailing culture based on counter-dependency among those who are uncomfortable with strong leaders. A strong charismatic leader runs the risk of disenfranchising others who lose their own innate ability to lead because they lose the belief that a sense of direction or a vision can come from anybody but the leader. The charismatic leader thus may end up under-leveraging his or her management and/or creating passive and dependent followers; or perhaps they may be too strong-willed and dominate all aspects of their organizations, running their companies autocratically with little delegation of authority or participation in strategic decision-making. Peters and Waterman's 'excellent' companies, where strong leadership was a key factor, have been criticized for demanding too much of their employees and for expecting them to submerge their individuality in a common mission. This has been condemned as unethical, even a form of dictatorship, however benign.

Also, individuals (even supermen or superwomen) have limitations. Individual contribution is necessarily limited by time, energy, expertise, and the attention span of that individual. Different types of strategic changes make different demands and call for different personal characteristics. The single-minded pursuit of a vision can create major problems when that vision needs reexamination or revision. One of the problems Peters and Waterman's excellent companies experienced in trying to sustain excellence is attributable to a fault of leadership. There was too much emphasis on charisma, an over-reliance on one form of vision. There are limits to the number of strategic changes that one individual can lead over the life of an organization (Nadler and Tushman, 1990: 85). Charismatic leaders run the risk of burning out or, in the long run, revealing their feet of clay. Charismatic visionaries can get organizations into trouble – as happened, for example, at Apple, eventually leading to the departure of its charismatic founder, Steve Jobs, from the company. Michael Edwards at British Leyland assumed the mantle of charisma in his much publicized battle with the unions, yet he failed to turn the company around because he over-emphasized labour problems at the expense of long-term strategy (Williams et al., 1988).

Another type of leadership behaviour is also necessary to complement vision, one which focuses not on exciting a sense of purpose in individuals and changing their goals, needs or aspirations, but on making sure that individuals in the senior team and throughout the organization behave in ways needed for change actually to occur. This kind of leadership has been described as 'instrumental' (Nadler and Tushman, 1990). It builds competent teams; structures the operating rules of the organization, defining roles and responsibilities; controls, measures and monitors; rewards and punishes. Charismatic leadership excites, creates aspirations, mobilizes energy. Instrumental leadership shapes behaviour to support aspirations. Instrumental leadership is needed to balance charismatic leadership as a means of ensuring that visions are actually operationalized.

David Kearns at Xerox set a new agenda for the company, inspiring new behaviours with his strategy of 'Leadership through quality' (Giles and Starkey, 1988). He himself served as a role model for appropriate interpersonal behaviour, so that the new management process could cascade through the organization. Kearns also used instrumental leadership to support Leadership Through Quality.

> Kearns and his Quality Office developed a comprehensive set of roles, processes, teams, and feedback and audit mechanisms for getting customer input and continuous improvement into everyday problem solving throughout Xerox. Individuals and teams across the corporation were evaluated on their ability to continuously meet customer requirements. These data were used in making pay, promotion, and career decisions. (Nadler and Tushman, 1990: 86)

## The Dynamics of Top Decision-making

Given the limitations of any one individual charismatic leader and the need to balance charisma and vision with substance, the organizational challenge is to 'broaden the range of individuals who can perform the critical leadership functions' (Nadler and Tushman, 1990: 88).

> The ability to co-create a collectively chosen vision is perhaps the weakest link in even our very best organizations. Our organizations are populated at senior levels by leaders who can be very masterful personally; that is, when the realization of their vision is dependent solely on themselves, they easily create what they want. However, when the vision involves mobilizing the committed union of numerous other people, this mastery declines dramatically. (Kiefer, 1986: 186)

A shared sense of vision is important but it does not necessarily require charisma for its generation. What *is* necessary is a kind of leadership whose goal is 'not to establish the vision, but to catalyze visioning among members of the organization. Recognizing that clarity and power of vision can come from the creative output of any individual, it becomes the leader's responsibility to ensure that everybody in the organization is envisioning their personal future as well as that of the organization' (Kiefer, 1986: 188). In this kind of organization the emphasis is on managing in a way that fosters difference and creative disputes rather than suppressing both. The leader empowers and coaches others to create what they want and helps create structures and processes that make this possible. The image of top decision-making that emerges from this perspective is one of teamwork.

Particularly important are those managers one or two levels below the top team, the senior operational managers who are seen as senior management by the rest of the organization. This group can be particularly problematic, especially in times of change. 'They may be less prepared to change, they frequently have moulded themselves to fit the current organizational style, and they may feel disenfranchised by the very act of developing a strong executive team, particularly if that team has been assembled by bringing in people from outside the organization' (Nadler and Tushman, 1990: 92). They have to be convinced and motivated to work as an extension of the top management team. Middle management can prove a particularly problematic area. At General Motors in the US, Ford's major competitor, it was the white-collar bureaucracy that proved resistant to the reforms of the 1980s. CEO Roger Smith described this as 'the frozen middle'. It is difficult for those in formerly secure positions in traditional hierarchies to give up their attachment to the status quo.

It is unrealistic to expect such altruism on any large scale. So times of change are likely to be times of overt or covert conflict and pain as many managers are forced to critically re-examine their cherished assumptions about the organization and their careers.

Here the 'cascade' principle of the senior team acting as change agents in their own teams is particularly significant. Communication is critical, as well as involvement in the process of preparing for change, diagnosing the need and planning actual strategies, so that team members feel like owners and not victims of the process. Through this careful process of management development the team building and the management systems and processes needed to support the leadership – 'to leverage and add substance to his vision and energy' (Nadler and Tushman, 1990: 94) – can be established.

The broadening of the leadership cadre can help organizations combat strategic myopia (Lorsch, 1986). It is very difficult for one individual to see beyond his or her own core beliefs or to reflect critically on the core beliefs of an organizational context. The tendency to awareness is impeded by individual denial. The surfacing of key existing beliefs is therefore a major step on the road to change. Top managers need to share their beliefs with each other in a context of experimentation with new ideas. The challenge is to balance the retention of the best elements of the old culture – which, after all, has got you where you are – with the development of new elements and sloughing off of old elements that are now a liability. The quality of top level participation is particularly important in times of shared uncertainty. There is a large proportion of managerial work where teamwork is unnecessary, a small proportion where it is vital. This is strategic work or any form of work characterized by high levels of choice and by conditions of great uncertainty. In this context the top team of an organization needs to pool the entirety of each individual's wisdom and experience, if it is to achieve quality and commitment in its decisions about future directions.

The key here is *not* reacting to a problem in terms of functional knowledge and experience. The circumstances are not reducible to these categories. What is necessary is the admission of uncertainty and the struggle to build shared perceptions and, out of them, a new sense of possibility.

> This is where that much abused word 'sharing' really comes into its own. In this context it is not merely a value-laden exhortation, it is vital to the future of the organization. Ideas and opinions are all we

> have to inform our view of the future, but if we are to take a risk with a fragile idea or opinion, unsubstantiated by facts, we will only take it if the climate is right. Conversely, if we take the risk and the sheer airiness and vulnerability of the idea attracts forth a volley of ridicule and abuse, then it will die on the instant, lost forever, snuffed out like Tinkerbell.
>
> Most functional executives, brought up on the hurly-burly of politics and inter-functional warfare, find the transition from the functional to strategic mode very difficult to make. They do not see the difference, and if they do, they are reluctant to leave their mountain-top, the summit of knowledge, experience and hence power, for the equality and shared uncertainty of strategic decision making. And yet this is one area where real teamwork is not only necessary but vital. (Critchley and Casey, 1984)

The distinction between two possible modes of working in management groups is crucial here. These modes are cooperation and shared uncertainty. The key drivers determining appropriate mode of working and kind of suitable teamwork are levels of uncertainty and the need to share. The key distinction in terms of levels of uncertainty is between 'complex puzzles' and 'problems'. Complex puzzles can be solved by each group member working from the certainty of a professional knowledge base and making the necessary inputs based on this knowledge into a collective decision-making process. The manager is sharing the unambiguous fruits of knowledge and experience. The conditions necessitating decision-making in the 'problem-solving' mode of shared uncertainty are different. This mode is appropriate only where nobody knows what to do, uncertainty is rife and full sharing between members is the only way out. 'The attitude of members has to be "the good of the whole outweighs any one member's interests – including mine. I carry an equal responsibility with my colleagues for the whole, and for this particular work. I am not able to rely on my specialism, because my functional expertise is, for this problem we all face, irrelevant"' (Critchley and Casey, 1984: 169).

Shared uncertainty is the most difficult mode of working, and the managerial and interpersonal processes needed to accomplish it are also more difficult. The nature of the social process required is different. It is necessary to distinguish among polite social skills and processes (all that is required in conditions of shared certainty); task processes such as cooperation, negotiation and coordination (to facilitate the exercise of current expertise in conditions of understood complexity); and feeling processes (required to cope with the anxieties and other emotions that arise in conditions of shared uncertainty). People's feelings become a crucial part of the work.

Here trust and mutuality are essential to the development of the managerial process. Joiner (1986) emphasizes 'open integrity' as a key aspect of the organizational learning that is the prerequisite for an effective strategic decision-making process. Open integrity is based on the premise that the integration of difference depends on openness. What is needed are 'non-manipulative ways to bring differences into contact with each other. Each party needs to remain clear about its own purpose and perspective while also understanding opposing viewpoints. This requires centred questioning and exploration, attending to conflicts and tensions without closing them off or being absorbed by them' (Joiner, 1986: 50). The result is a 'collaborative culture', an essential condition for ongoing organizational learning and adaptation to the demands of new environments. Bennis and Nanus (1985) highlight the importance to a healthy management process of creating a shared sense of vision, as well as the importance of open communications, the frank sharing of information, the development of trust through constancy, and the importance of a sense of positive regard for self and others.

Unlearning the lessons of the past is crucial. Hurst *et al.* (1989) analyse creativity in top decision-making. They propose that the traditional approach to management in general and strategic management in particular only allows managers to maintain existing activities or to improve them incrementally. The conventional strategic management framework which has evolved over the past 40 years and has come to dominate Western thinking about the principal functions of senior managers is based on a logic developed from past experiences. This is an appropriate methodology, in Miles and Snow's (1978) terms, for 'defending' an established business but is not suitable when a firm needs to 'prospect' because it cannot cope with novelty and ambiguity. Strategic thinking within this framework is limited by the existing structure of the managers' understanding. Prospecting requires a new logic of understanding, a new mind-set. Conventional strategic thinking 'incorporates no means to unlearn what has been learned'.

> At the intuitive level a vision or insight into a new way of doing business does not by itself result in action. Because it is outside the established logic of the business, it cannot be evaluated by the

> thinking process. Therefore its worth, whether positive or negative, cannot be logically derived and must be based upon personal or group values. A positive feeling must be created for the idea if it is to overcome the established logic, result in action and thus change the understanding of the business. (Hurst et al., 1989: 87, 91)

This view emphasizes the centrality of both feeling and intuition as well as thinking in the process of top decision-making.

## Participative Management at the Strategic Level in Ford

A reaction against the 1980s charisma trend is beginning to emerge. Collins and Porras (1991) challenge what they describe as one of the great 'myths' of modern management, the myth that building a visionary organization *requires* the presence of a charismatic leader, blessed with almost super-human visionary qualities. For many managers this myth is positively demotivating because they themselves do not fit the stereotypical mould of the 'visionary'.

> Charisma's role in setting vision is vastly overrated. In fact, attempting to substitute charisma for substance is destructive. The function of a leader – the one universal requirement of effective leadership – is to catalyse a clear and shared vision of the organization and to secure commitment to and vigorous pursuit of that vision. This can be accomplished with a variety of styles and does not require charisma. The key is to build an organization with vision, not simply to have a single charismatic individual with vision as the CEO. And without vision, organizations have no chance of creating their future, they can only react to it. (Collins and Porras, 1991: 51)

The experience of Ford in the US illustrates the positive outcomes of a mix of managerial styles and strengths at the top of an organization in the context of a necessary shift in the organization's vision.

Ford was fortunate to have at a time of major change a chief executive, Don Petersen, with a transformational leadership style based on the generation of a new company vision, the goal of which was 'to reap the benefit of all the accumulated knowledge, experience, dedication and creativity of our people'. Petersen's management style was complemented by that of the then president, Red Poling, who emphasized the managerial virtues of control, discipline and commitment to agreed targets (Pascale, 1990: 156–7). Their joint leadership of the company was based on a positive synthesis of these two opposites. Pascale describes it as a match between 'enlightened discipline' and 'compassionate pragmatism'. They combined 'task' and 'social' leadership (Zaleznik, 1989: 61–2).

Petersen was, by most accounts, quiet and unassuming, a leader who kept a low profile and was low-key in his dealings, yet who accomplished one of the most significant turnarounds in corporate history:

> Picture the opposite of Henry Ford II, Lee Iacocca, and a host of other egotistical and dominating managers who have played significant leadership roles at Ford, and you get the man who could be Detroit's first Japanese-style executive. He lives and breathes participative management, taking to heart suggestions from vice presidents and assembly line workers. Most remarkably, he subordinates his ego to the needs of the company. Asked how he turned Ford around, he emphatically attributes he success to others. Says Petersen: 'I want you to remember one thing, the credit here goes to our team, not me.' So low [was] his profile that even after becoming chairman in 1985, the company proxy statement misspelled his name. (Pascale, 1990: 159)

One of Petersen's most significant contributions at Ford was to set in place the participative approach to top decision-making, thus broadening, deepening and enriching the company's strategic decision-making. He was also responsible for the motivation and excitement of individuals and for changing their goals, needs and aspirations through the redefinition of company mission and values. Poling provided another form of leadership – the instrumental leadership responsible for making sure that behaviour throughout the organization was consistent with the new goals necessary to transform the company. Instrumental leadership ensures that the envisioned changes actually occur. It does this through three means: *structuring* – building the teams and structures necessary to operationalize change; *controlling* – creating the systems necessary to monitor necessary achievement; *rewarding* and punishing appropriate and inappropriate behaviour.

We have discussed Petersen's account of change in Ford in the US in chapter 3. An important management task was to distinguish between form and substance. He raised the point when discussing the introduction of statistical process control, giving an important insight into the existing Ford culture.

> [Deming] warned me that a lot of people inside Ford would tell me that they knew all about it, that they were already using statistics. . . . A group of young managers known as the whiz kids had come into Ford after World War II and tried to put statistical process control into place. But it was the same old story: the effort was initiated by the people at the top; the employees in the plants didn't buy it and they didn't use it. They just papered their bulletin boards and office walls with graphs and charts of statistics that they could show to any management people who might stop by. But nobody believed in it. (Petersen, 1991: 7–8)

The cover-up was motivated by fear. The next step identified by Petersen, again with the help of Deming, was the need to eliminate fear from the workplace and give workers the opportunity to do a better job by building relationships of trust between management and employees. Employees had to be convinced that management meant what they said about the need for new behaviours. Driving the changes at Ford was the growing belief that incrementally improving the way things had been done in the past was no longer enough. This view led to the fundamental reappraisal of the company's core beliefs out of which came the new Mission, Values and Guiding Principles.

Petersen himself appreciated the importance of a balanced management team that was comfortable with its own internal differences. Difference was to be seen as a virtue rather than a threat. Ford used the Myers–Briggs personality test in its participative management training seminars to focus on the issue of different management styles and the extent to which individual managers are extroverted or introverted (E or I), sensitive or intuitive (S or N), thinking or feeling (T or F), perceiving or judging (P or J). The Myers–Briggs test taught managers about the differences between themselves and illustrated how different types of individuals operate differently. One manager likes to collect a lot of information to analyse before making decisions, others are more intuitive, ignore a lot of detail and choose on the basis of instinct or past experience. This can create tensions in their relationships with each other but if each knows how the other thinks this can help prevent breakdowns in communication.

Petersen himself came out of the Myers–Briggs test as a rare personality type:

> Most managers are TJs (thinking and judging), extroverts who are prone to making sharp analytical decisions and telling their sub-

> ordinates what to do. The test identified me as an introvert inclined to be intuitive and feeling (NF). I'm told that my personality type – the INFJ – is found in only one percent of the population. The Myers–Briggs people say that INFJs 'listen well and are willing and able to consult and cooperate with others. . . . they value staff harmony and want an organization top run smoothly and pleasantly. . . . If they are subject to a hostile, unfriendly working condition or to constant criticism, they tend to lose confidence, become unhappy and immobilized, finally become physically ill'. (Petersen, 1991: 55)

Insight into his own personality and that of his peers helped Petersen refine the management style of the top management group. Petersen and Poling learned how different they were and concluded that this helped them work better together, despite the expectations of their corporate peers.

> They were aware that Red and I emphasized different things. They thought that I would be after them for not putting this or that and who knows what else into the product. Then Poling would be all over them for spending too much money. . . . We became a team whose ability exceeded the sum of the parts. (Petersen, 1991: 55–6)

Poling concentrated on the quantifiable, on getting the quality and the numbers right. Petersen dealt with the unquantifiable, such as issues of product styling.

An important part of the development of a new management style was the introduction of the participative management approach to the workings of the top decision-making forums of the company, such as the crucial Policy and Strategy Committee. When Petersen joined this committee in 1975 as head of diversified products the approach was non-participative in the sense that committee members spoke only about their own businesses and did not intrude on the views expressed by members from other areas. For example, the rule was that if the manager in charge of cars was discussing product problems, it was inappropriate for Petersen himself to contribute to the discussion, despite his experience in product development.

> The way we changed the dynamics of the Policy and Strategy Committee pretty much followed the pattern of our efforts at the plant and operations levels. We just started making changes to encourage participation. For example, Red and I held back from expressing any personal opinions at the beginning of the discussion. Also, I made

> the point of telling the committee members that they should feel encouraged to speak up regardless of the subject. This was hard for them at first; they certainly hadn't had any practice. I often polled the members individually for comments and suggestions, in effect serving as the facilitator. (Petersen, 1991: 61)

To facilitate the free exchange of ideas committee meetings were sometimes conducted away from traditional committee meeting venues such as the Board of Directors' room. Breakfast meetings were particularly successful in this respect, and occasionally top management meetings were conducted off-site 'dressed in sweaters and slacks to get an even broader base of discussion. As time went on, I think we had some of the most candid conversations in Ford's history' (Petersen, 1991: 61–2). The shedding of conventional modes of behaviour was symbolic of a shift in managerial role expectations.

To appreciate the novelty of the collaborative atmosphere fostered under Petersen, consider Lee Iacocca's account of the management dynamics at Ford under Henry Ford II in the mid-1970s, when fear and conflict were endemic. The following was a representative incident.

> As president of Ford, one of my duties was to chair the committee on product planning. In the meetings, Hal Sperlich sat on my left and Henry sat on my right. Every now and then, Henry would give a nod or a grunt. He never talked much at these meetings, but his gestures and noises spoke volumes. In fact, people generally paid more attention to Henry's facial expressions than to whatever ideas were being presented at the time.
>
> It was clear that Henry didn't like Sperlich or his proposals. Hal was brash and he didn't show much deference to the king. . . . Sperlich, who knew a great deal about cars and had incredible instincts about the future, kept pushing us in the direction of smaller models – which was about the last thing in the world Henry wanted to hear.
>
> One day, after a product committee meeting, Henry called me into his office. 'I hate that goddam Sperlich,' he said, 'and I don't want him sitting beside you. He's always pissing in your ear. I don't want the two of you ganging up on me like that.'
>
> I had little choice but to call Sperlich in and tell him the news. 'Hal,' I said, 'I know this sounds ridiculous, but you can't sit next to me anymore.' (Iacocca, 1986: 128–9)

Iacocca describes Sperlich as the most valuable player on the team. Soon after he had to fire him on Henry Ford's orders.

Hal took it very hard. Although both of us could see it coming, you always live in the hope that if you do your job well, justice will prevail. Hal genuinely believed that his talent was enough to keep him at Ford, even if the boss didn't like him. But he forgot that we worked in a dictatorship.

'This is a chickenshit outfit,' I told Sperlich. 'And I should probably be getting out with you. I'm higher up than you are, but I have to put up with the same garbage. Maybe Henry's doing you a favor,' I said. 'In a more democratic environment, your talent will be recognized and rewarded . . .'. (Iacocca, 1986: 129–30)

In 1978 Iacocca took his own bitter farewell from the company, ousted by the 'dictator'.

Despite his undoubted influence Ford senior management now qualify Petersen's role and point out the important roles of Philip Caldwell, who was chairman when the crisis first hit, and Harold 'Red' Poling.

At executive meetings in Detroit for the top fifty or so managers worldwide . . . we used to look at each other and wonder how long the company could survive with our cash flow. Phil Caldwell was great at the time in terms of keeping people's feet on the ground, and saying stick to the basics, get the quality right, keep costs down, you've got to get your product right and so on. . . . That was his parting shot at the end of meetings, 'Would you please look after the basics!' A lot of people don't find that much of a turn-on but it's very valid because every day you've got to watch your quality, every day you've got to watch your costs, every day you've got to watch your product programmes, every day you've got to watch your headcount controls. You have to do these things. . . . And so all the process of change really took place quite a long way before MVGP [the new Mission, Values and Guiding Principles]. . . . I remember in one meeting Phil Caldwell talking us through why we should be optimistic about the future – we had a good truck programme coming, we do have Europe, NAO [North American Operations] was committed to a billion dollar cost reduction that year.

This particular executive was sceptical about the bottom-line effects of EI/PM and MVGP. He added, 'None of that was EI or PM.' Caldwell's key role was in convincing the company 'to accept that we really had to do something fundamentally different'.

Indeed, some executives see Poling's role as more important than Petersen's:

> Red deserves a great deal of credit . . . because he provided all the drive in getting the headcount, the cost structure, the performance and everything moving. . . . Red to me was the strong man of the 1980s. Phil [Caldwell] was the guy who kept our feet on the ground and kept the organization steady while the finances were rocky. . . . And Red was the guy who did the hard work. Pete [Petersen] was a product man and he concentrated on product and he became an advocate of Deming. Pete focused on the company's management process and its people process. And in that situation you do need a slogan, a rallying point. The impetus dies if you don't have a focal point. . . . Petersen was the new Messiah and EI/PM was the new religion.

But, despite the differing views on the relative importance of individuals, the complementarity of the top management team is unambiguously regarded as crucial.

> Ford was lucky to have this dynamic of individuals who somehow complemented each other. Phil had his tremendous ability not to panic and to keep stressing the basics. While Red looked after the North American cost structure, Pete became an EI diplomat.
>
> Ed [Poling] was very much cost-focused and Caldwell very much the 'by-the-numbers disciplined manager, hands-on, tell me in detail', Petersen trying to promote cultural change and a product vision, so it was a sort of blessing.
>
> I don't think you can do one without the other, I really don't. If Petersen had absolute 'I'm going to run this the way I want to without any pressure either this way or this way' I'm not sure that it could have been so successful. By the same token, I don't think Poling without that other pressure [of Petersen and participative management] could have done it on his own.

Pascale (1990) emphasizes the creative tension that existed in the top management team at Ford in the US. His view is that the problems that beset a large proportion of Peters and Waterman's excellent companies were due to the inability of those companies to deal creatively with conflict and contradiction. Creative tension was submerged under the impact of the charismatic leader. He suggests that contention can be a positive force for change in organizations as new definitions of appropriate strategies develop in opposition to the *status quo*. This suggests an either/or opposition between the old and the new. We have tried to suggest during the course of our study that this is too simple. What one sees at Ford in the US in the 1980s is the complicated working out of a dialectic between old and new, forming a new synthesis composed in part of new elements but with important points of continuity with the old. If Petersen was the new guard, Poling represented the best of the old with his emphasis on efficiency and discipline. Caldwell was the bridge between the old and the new, a steadying influence in the crisis and a key player in getting the issue of change onto the agenda. In Europe it was a very different story.

## Ford of Europe: Executive Tourists?

Zimmerman (1991) in his analysis of the turnaround experience focuses on three elements – low cost operation, product differentiation and leadership – or what he terms 'appropriate turnaround organization'. Poling's role of stripping costs out of Ford's operations reminds us that the cost and efficiency aspects of turnaround should not be ignored. Low cost operation depends upon operational and inventory efficiency, modest overhead and lower cost through design. Ford's ruthless benchmarking against its key competitors led it to major rationalization, restructuring and reduction in headcount. HRM principles such as flexibility had a major contribution to make here. Product differentiation – Petersen was the product champion in the US – is based upon distinguishing features, superior reliability and performance, product quality and a sharp product market focus. In Ford US Petersen championed the product, Poling dealt with the operations.

In Europe there was no comparable balance of champions. What we do have is a marked difference in top management tenure of position in Ford of Europe and in experience of the European environment. We have already mentioned the role of Bob Lutz in Ford of Europe's radical design initiative, the Sierra. Lutz transferred back to the US before the Sierra went into production and was then sent back to Europe to try to sort out its launch problems. He left the company soon after. The European champion of operational efficiency was Bill Hayden, Vice-President of Manufacturing from the creation of Ford of Europe until 1991, when he became the first 'Ford' Chairman of Jaguar after its acquisition. Hayden provided an important source of continuity in the Ford of Europe management cadre, indeed in some ways the only constant source during the steady turnover of American presidents and chairmen in the 1980s.

One of Zimmerman's key sources of turnaround leadership is managerial stability:

> Because of the long-drawn-out nature of the turnaround process, managerial stability is often present among successful turnaround cases while instability and internal turmoil often characterize failure. Most successful turnarounds involve a top-management team that is essentially constant for at least 7 or 8 years following the period of crisis. Unsuccessful firms have frequent managerial changes, sometimes even when progress is being made. (Zimmerman, 1991: 16)

Of course Ford of Europe was not in the same state of overt crisis that tested the managerial skills of its parent. But what motivated the change process in Europe in the 1980s was a sense of imminent and inevitable crisis, inaugurated and championed by Hayden in the 'After Japan' campaign. It says much for Hayden's vision that he actually championed this perspective and challenged the Ford of Europe *status quo* at a time of record profits and 'fat complacency'. But in some senses Hayden was operating in a top management vacuum. He himself says of his experience in the Ford of Europe boardroom,

> Ford of Europe is not a very stable organization. By that I mean if you look at the number of chairmen and presidents of the organization over the last twenty odd years then there's been a change of personnel every two or three years. And it's not like an ordinary organization where the guy tends to come up [through the ranks]. They've come over and gone back. If you come up through the ranks then you're part of the culture and you're less of a shock to the system. . . . [they] arrive and you've never met, never worked for or with them. . . . It slows down the decision-making process. Because when people arrive they have to buy into the current agenda. Unsettling is a strong word but if you're setting long-term objectives and changing three of the top five players in Europe every other year then it makes it very difficult.

He found the effort of keeping up with the changes in top management personnel an increasing chore.

> I had met most of them in Dearborn, but it wasn't a working relationship. We didn't *know* each other, hadn't worked together. When they arrived I'd usually go and introduce myself. But with time – it would

register that a new guy had arrived – but I didn't bother going down the corridor to knock on his door. The business went on as before, new chairman or not.

The lack of a top management team with a long term stable membership creates particular problems of institutionalizing change. If the tenure of change agents is transitory then the ownership of the change process becomes difficult if not impossible. In Ford of Europe Europeans refer to American managers as 'executive tourists': 'This is seen as a place that people need to come for experience to move them up the ladder in the US.' Consequently, Hayden, despite the fact that he was never president or chairman, has exerted a disproportionate influence in Ford of Europe as a whole, not only by sheer force of personality, but also because European postings are used as career staging-posts by fast-track American executives. Hayden has been a constant feature in an otherwise rapidly changing executive team in Ford of Europe, a constancy which gave him enormous power not only in Europe but also through personal contact with Dearborn.

Viewed from Detroit, Hayden's role is 'an interesting story':

> If you look at it from a rational perspective, there is no one in the Ford Motor company that can be that indispensable. Nobody! Yet he's managed to maintain his power position. I have my own assumptions about him . . . one of the assumptions is that if you look at the people who go over to Europe, they're all Americans and they're all going for a short time. Why would they want to shake anything up? Obviously he produces.

There is a perception in the US that Europe resisted EI/PM and MVGP. Again, Hayden is mentioned.

> People resisted. Bill Hayden is one of the worst. He had his own way of operating. He's an interesting person. On the one hand he's described as being a genius and the only one who can run manufacturing, and on the other hand he's described as being a son-of-a-bitch and everybody's fearful of him. He's not, as far as I'm concerned, the idea of participative management – it's alien to the way he operates. But he's also very effective in the way he operates. . . . Bill Hayden was a pivotal figure. If he agrees with it, you're in good shape. I think now he's decided to buy into process improvement, well . . . it'll happen!

Hayden himself asserts that Ford has always been participative. Of the 1980s he argues forcefully:

> Let's get back to fundamentals. How did the company achieve its success? If people believe it achieved success simply by writing up MVGP that's rubbish. If people think they did it by inventing employee involvement or participative management they forget that there always was employee involvement and participative management. In an organization this size there *has* to be! One man can't run this company. Fifty men can't run this company. 500 men can't run it. There has to be participative management. If you go back 20 or 30 years, Ford could have been a scared company but I've never been in an environment in which I didn't feel I could speak my mind.

Hayden 'stories' are legion. He is the major source of recent mythology in the company either as hero or anti-hero.

> There are lots of horror stories about Bill Hayden. But I think he's so stuck in the Ford mould that no matter how hard he tries to be different, the men below him would not allow him to be. . . . He's ruled with an iron hand . . . On the other hand, he's the man that got manufacturing into shape – so give the devil his due. Its easy to blame Bill for the ills of the world, he's a very powerful figure. He obviously has some Godfathers in the US.

It is a significant measure of the influence of PM that some Ford managers now assert that 'even Hayden has tried to change his spots!'

Hayden, furthermore, is associated with the urge to centralized control:

> He has been running manufacturing in a way which is almost unbelievable that one man could run an organization that large in such a centralized way. . . . you would find it difficult to believe how all the decisions have been funnelled into him. . . . Extremely centralized. And of course a man of tremendous ability, not many like him.

Centralization was, at times, important; for example, in the early 1980s when Hayden brought powertrain and body and assembly together:

> Powertrain and Body and Assembly were two very large teams wearing different coloured shirts and they weren't as cooperative with

> each other as they should have been. They didn't, I think, recognize that they were in a sense reliant upon each other because without the one you didn't have the complete vehicle – that applied in both directions. And Hayden found it increasingly frustrating through the late 1970s to have to go to these two separate groups to get a coherent total manufacturing picture. So in the early 1980s he decided he'd had enough of this and he took his opportunity when the heads of those two groups [retired] . . . He said 'Right, this is my chance. I will now centralize the manufacturing group into one unit. . . . I think without question it has produced a much leaner, tighter, more efficient manufacturing operation.

Hayden's role in Europe was comparable to that of Poling, the champion of operational efficiency in the US, but with no strong countervailing force for change.

> Europe didn't have a Petersen, it didn't have a big name champion of change throughout the 1980s in anything like the same way [as the US] so it missed out on that healthy tension, it remained cost-driven. There were change initiatives, there wasn't the same advocacy of change.

Hayden symbolizes the old discipline, the emphasis on cost as the focus of strategy. He was quite willing to innovate in search of efficiency but was more wary of other kinds of innovation. One senior manufacturing executive offered the following anecdote as encapsulating the deep-seated tensions of the period in Europe:

> There is conflict between quality and cost. We were having a discussion about our objective of being the lowest cost vehicle producer in Europe and was that right or should we really be designing the best quality vehicles and sales would come from that rather than cost? Lou Lataif [then president] made a statement that our objective was to be the lowest cost producer but also the best quality producer. Bill Hayden stood up and said, 'Yes, I agree with you Lou, but Manufacturing is totally committed to being the lowest cost vehicle producer in Europe'. And Lou Lataif said, 'Thank you Bill, would anyone in Manufacturing who disagrees with Bill please stand up . . .' It was a nice blend of Bill saying, 'This is Manufacturing, and this is what we do' and Lou saying, 'Well, perhaps there should be some debate about that'. Everyone laughed because everyone knew damn well that nobody would stand up and contradict Bill. To me it was indicative of some of the conflicts between what we say we're trying to do and what we actually do, especially at the highest level!

One can construe this dialogue in a variety of ways. There are none of the subtleties of 'problem-solving' and 'dilemma management' in the participative management mode. It represents the old politics – the manufacturing function protecting its power base within the corporation. The event also has important symbolic significance. Such dramatic moments pushed the real nature of strategic decision-making 'into the public domain, not . . . the privacy of the board-room'. When Product Development wanted Manufacturing and Marketing to join the matrix concept and also have programme management groups, 'Hayden said "No"!'

This is not to suggest that Hayden was the 'villain' of the piece. It is far more complex than that. In psychodynamic terms Ford needed and, indeed, had created Hayden as a crucial point of stability and as a symbol of the old system in which his subordinates at least knew their place in the scheme of things. Another manager recalled Hayden summing up a presentation on EI/PM:

> So Hayden said, 'Now, you've all heard this EI stuff. But at the end of the day I'm paid to run this bloody place and I'll listen to all you've got to say if there's time, if there isn't time I won't listen. I make the decisions that I think are right and you'll just have to learn to live with that: that's your contribution to EI'.

For this manager, perplexed by the emerging managerial agenda of a new mission, new values, new guiding principles, employee involvement, participative management and all the other change initiatives, this response was a source of grim satisfaction and some relief – 'And I thought, well thank Christ for that – at least I know where I am!' Some senior managers clearly were reassured by Hayden's insistence on established verities.

Others suggest that Hayden was true to himself and the vision of the best way to manage Ford which he had always espoused:

> Ford published what it wanted to be rather than what it was . . . It still hasn't achieved anything close to full MVGP definition. . . . That's been something . . . that Bill always genuinely had a problem with . . . He has always said since MVGP was issued, 'How could you expect me to go to one of my plants and look the people in the eye and quote from the Mission Statement, "People are our most important asset", that we believe in integrity and we believe in the whole approach to EI and to be customer-driven and everything, when I am having to share the painful decision with them that we can no longer keep the Thames

> Foundry going and it has to close and the forge has to close and the Woolwich plant has to close, the Cork plant in Ireland and the Amsterdam plant in Holland, they all have to close. Now all for totally valid business reasons and I am very "happy" to sit and debate the business scenario with these people and assure them that we will take care of them as best we can within the limitations of reality but don't ask me to spout Americano at them.' . . . The States got rid of their people before they started doing EI/PM. They laid off 80,000 people in 1979. . . . So I can understand Bill's reluctance in the early 1980s when the whole MVGP was coming at us, huge US enthusiasm, to say I can't look my people in the eye and give them two conflicting messages on the same day.

Hayden's major contribution of the early 1980s was 'After Japan'. One can now see AJ as very much in the traditional Ford cost-focused mind-set.

> It *was* cost-driven. It was benchmarking. I don't think we quite fully realized – it was a tremendous step. Don't get me wrong, I don't mean to demean it – but in the context of PM/EI I don't think 'AJ' took that step. Because it didn't diagnose that we had a fundamental cultural change problem . . . it didn't focus on cultural change . . . 'AJ' didn't take us far enough. It was a revelation for the US by the way in terms of cost focus. Until 'AJ' we didn't understand how far off the cost objectives we were so it served an enormously useful purpose but I don't think it focused on cultural change. . . . it was a hell of a good start. But I don't know that before we did MVGP we knew what a fundamental change it really was, how thorough throughout the organization it had to become.

The timing of the diffusion of PM to Europe did not help the smooth unfolding of the process of change. At the strategic level the American experience was transmitted through senior executive conferences in late 1983 and 1984, precisely the moment at which Ford of Europe's relatively poor financial performance was generating massive tension at board level. The diffusion of PM was hindered by 'highly dramatic stuff going on on the sixth floor' with major bitter and public disagreements at board level during the troubled launch of the Sierra. Rather than serving as examples of PM in action, dissemination conferences became vehicles for very public displays of internecine strife in the executive team. As one manager bluntly expressed it: 'they were kicking the shit out of each other'.

> These conferences gave us a real window into what our management culture was *really* like. We had fooled ourselves into thinking that at Ford we had a task culture, a can-do culture. It was that, but there was more to it than that. There were all these hidden – and not so hidden – resentments and power struggles just beneath the surface. And as soon as we gave them the opportunity to surface all these tensions became painfully obvious. This pulled us all up short.

Manufacturing management was thrown onto the defensive, under intense pressure to achieve still further efficiencies and manpower reductions while at the same time being implicitly pilloried for its rigid adherence to Ford's traditional authoritarian managerial style. Debates about PM became intertwined with debates about the poor 1984 business results. In this debate Hayden emerged not just as the champion of further rationalization but was also perceived as the standard-bearer of an authoritarian managerial style that was at odds with the philosophy of the new approach. This, not surprisingly, created scepticism lower down the organization.

> Our executive team are having real difficulties appreciating the depth of cynicism among Ford managers. There is a huge gap between the Ford of Europe Executive Committee and most of the rest of the company. The executive process is much more open and effective than before and that touches managers who report to Directors but then there's a vacuum. They travel as a cloistered group around Europe and the world and they try to make contact with the rest of management but I don't think it's very successful. They'll never meet plant managers, for example. They're like high-level tourists. Even if we wanted to give them bad news – and we don't – we don't have the opportunity. They receive their information about the *process* in sound-bites, half-hour briefings. But the budget process, the *hard* figures are pored over for weeks on end. We're still driven by the numbers at the executive level no matter how hard we try.

But despite relatively poor results Ford was doing well in Europe and continued to do so until the late 1980s. The crisis, although identified as imminent by Hayden himself, had yet to hit.

> Knowing what I know now, I've asked myself, why didn't we get on with this sooner? Because it's such a massive change that you have to go through. Why have we been slow? The honest truth . . . we didn't feel the pressure for change, we weren't in trouble, we weren't in

> crisis. . . . we didn't feel the need, we were doing alright, leave us alone. And they did. By and large that was the case. Would we have benefited from that? Sure we would. Would we have torn down the functional barriers and chimneys quicker? YES, we would have. . . . The whole logic of the process would have forced us to examine that aspect of how we managed. . . . In the final analysis Pete [Petersen] would say this, you have to live PM.

In Europe there were no top level champions of the new change agenda with the power to make this the centre of the management agenda. In the US, European champions of EI/PM were seen as politically naive.

> There's something else that I discovered. The concept of PM wasn't new in Europe either. A group within the UK had written an excellent paper on the need to change the way they managed. It was written about 1976. But what happened is they didn't understand the politics of how to bring about change. They thought they could just write the paper and hand it to somebody. It doesn't work that way! They didn't bother to identify who would be the sponsor of their change process and bring operating management into the discussion and get some support. The problem was they didn't know how to gain acceptance. But I was impressed by the quality of the thinking.

The emphasis on cost and efficiency that Hayden represents, the strength of this mind-set and the weakness in political terms of the new change perspective also have to be seen in terms of the relationship between Europe and the parent company. There were pressures from the US that slowed down the European change process.

> I think probably that the pressures even from Dearborn caused it to be that way. . . . Remember Europe was producing profit, it was sort of salvaging North America, the rest of the company was in significantly difficult shape. Part of that you can explain away by the economic conditions and the fact that the Japanese hadn't attacked here. There's a whole bunch of reasons. Therefore I don't think that there was that pressure for change even from Dearborn. The pressure was to keep producing profit and keep doing the job that you're doing. You're doing it well so keep at it guys. Well what kind of pressure was that? That was a cost-profit pressure, primarily.

In the final analysis, the lack of champions tells us something important about the composition and tenure of the Ford of Europe top management group of the time. Two major factors contributed to the weakness of the impetus to develop the new initiatives and the strength of local resistance: the composition and tenure of this group and the way in which US management used Ford of Europe as a convenient 'staging-post' in American top management development. In the US, of course, there were the top-level champions, 'competing' perspectives had the time to gel, and operating management was brought into the process as were top union representatives. In short, the process was managed. This just did not happen in Europe in the same coherent manner. It was not made to happen.

We mentioned early on (in chapter 1) the problems facing the multi-national, problems of resolving the tension between central control and local autonomy. In their analysis of the transnational solution, Bartlett and Ghoshal (1989) emphasize the *joint development and worldwide sharing* of learning. The key management tasks in the transnational include the legitimization and balancing of diverse perspectives and the building of individual commitment in pursuit of a shared vision. If the learning concerns technology this is relatively uncontroversial. If what is at stake is a challenge to a strong, long-established culture and mode of managerial behaviour then this is a far more difficult process. Creating the right organizational context for transnational learning involves establishing clear corporate objectives, developing managers with broadly-based perspectives and relationships, and fostering supportive organizational norms and values. In Ford of Europe the management of the top management process was at odds with this learning agenda insofar as it involved creating innovative ways of linking corporate strategy and human resource management.

# 8

# Conclusion: Beyond Japan and America

## Achilles Heels

In 1990 Don Petersen resigned as chairman and CEO of Ford Motor Company. In 1989 Bill Hayden left Ford of Europe to become chairman of Jaguar in the wake of Ford's acquisition of the UK luxury car manufacturer, a position he retired from in 1992. These events heralded the end of an era in both branches of the company. In the US the era spanned the 1980s, Petersen's decade at Ford in many people's eyes. (Fellow American CEOs voted him the most effective business leader in a 1988 *Fortune* poll.) In Ford of Europe the Hayden era – it is fair to describe it in these terms although he never became chairman of the company – has been longer, spanning the period 1975 to 1989 and beyond. Even though he has retired from the company Ford of Europe is still coming to terms with his final legacy – the Simultaneous Engineering study. In the US Petersen was the champion of change embodied in employee involvement, participative management and the new 'Mission, Values and Guiding Principles'. In Europe, Hayden, until his late conversion on the road to Damascus to program management with the Simultaneous Engineering study, had been the champion of continuity in the old Ford tradition, with the emphasis on cost, efficiency and discipline. The departure of these influential figures raises the question: what next?

In the US Petersen has been replaced by Harold 'Red' Poling, whose role in the top management team we have discussed in the previous chapter. The reasons for Petersen's departure are unclear. *Fortune* (11 February 1991) described it as 'the odd eclipse of a star CEO'. Although Petersen claims he retired of his own volition some insiders suggest he was forced to leave in a boardroom coup and that there was a major worry, at the highest level of the company, that Petersen was not the man to lead it through a gathering recession. Whatever the reasons Petersen's departure raises questions about the balance of Ford's top team. If Petersen was the champion of innovation, Poling seems to be the champion of efficiency and strong financial control, an American Hayden. Hayden, incidentally, declares himself Poling's 'biggest fan'. There is a worry inside the company that under Poling the efficiency imperative might again become too powerful and damage the company's capacity for innovation as it has in the past.

In Europe the situation is different. Europe never had a Petersen. No chairman has been there long enough to stamp his authority and vision on the company. It was Hayden who, until his departure, represented the dominant forces of tradition and stability. Ford in the US entered the 1990s much stronger than it started the 1980s. Under Caldwell and the leadership of Petersen and Poling the company achieved a famous turnaround based on the principles of EI, PM and MVGP. It developed an innovatory fusion of corporate strategy and human resource management and, as a result, now enjoys a new image for high quality and innovation. Ford in Europe is not in this happy position.

Ford of Europe was very successful on one level – the financial – for much of the 1980s, with the UK as its most profitable arm. In 1988 Ford of Europe pasted record profits, but since 1989 it has under-performed a market struggling with the effects of a deepening recession. In 1991 the company achieved record sales in Europe but went into loss. Although Ford claims major improvement in its other main European markets – Germany, France, Spain and Italy – the UK, for so long the mainstay of its European financial strength, performed particularly badly. Overcapacity and excess stocks, the comparative strength of rival products, and falling market share plunged Ford UK into its first losses in twenty years. Its performance was not helped by the acquisition of Jaguar – seen by the company as a long-term necessity in its effort to move its image up-market and to compete with German and Japanese luxury cars – although Jaguar ownership has now been transferred to the parent company.

The company still faces the twin strategic imperatives of efficiency and innovation. Costs continue to be stripped out of operations and the workforce reduced. In 1979 Ford of Europe had 150,000 employees who produced 1.4 million vehicles. In 1991, 100,000 produced 1.8 million units. The company is still striving to reduce its middle management headcount, the 'frozen middle', in what *The Financial Times* (17 February 1992) described as 'management blood-letting'. The intention is to reduce the number of indirect salaried staff, foreign service employees and some management layers by 30 per cent according to the '30/30/30' plan, in pursuit of the 'leaner, more effective and less bureaucratic organization' (Cochrane, 1991). Ford has greatly improved the productivity and the quality of output of its UK factories, despite industrial relations problems, but still cannot match the levels achieved in Germany with exactly the same facilities and higher individual wages.

Its product development record in the 1980s has been patchy. It continues to make massive investment in this area and has ambitious plans to replace most of its engine range by the mid-1990s. In part this is to be achieved through a joint venture with Yamaha. Much rests on the fate of the Sierra replacement (the Mondeo) to be launched in 1993. It faces increasing Japanese competition as firms such as Toyota develop a manufacturing base in Europe, although it can perhaps take some comfort that the major Japanese manufacturers are themselves suffering at the moment. The most successful, Toyota, reported its worst performance in ten years for the year to June 1992 (*Financial Times*, 27 August 1992). Honda has introduced emergency management measures, including a degree of autocracy new to the company, to cope with its increasing problems, and, like Ford, is going through a process of major restructuring with particular emphasis on flattening the corporate hierarchy (Butler, 1991). Nissan too faces 'a hard slog to lift profitability' (*Financial Times*, 6 July 1992).

It has been suggested that organization adaptation is the Achilles heel of Japanese multinationals, and that having used their highly centralized organizations as the means to penetrate world markets, they are now hampered by an over-centralisation which works against the local adaptability necessary to respond to fast-changing and very different markets. As a result, Japanese multinationals are faced with the need to decentralize both decision-making and resources. They have to overcome the strong cultural forces that gave rise to centralization in the first place but without destroying the strength and cohesion that culture provided. This offers an opportunity for Western organizations. As Bartlett and Yoshihara (1988: 40) note: 'This period of organizational adjustment represents a breathing space in which European and American managers can regroup and prepare for the next stage of the global battle.' A regional approach to product development, for example, has the potential to provide a competitive advantage in local responsiveness over the Japanese approach of centralized worldwide responsibility for product development and manufacturing.

Ford of Europe served the crucial role of 'corporate cash cow' in the early 1980s, but this left it without a clear vision of its *own* future. Its problems of the late 1980s were certainly exacerbated by the failure to clarify its role and also by its own senior management's slow awakening to the magnitude of the change agenda it had to address. In the early 1980s there was little generally-felt need for fundamental change. The belief persisted that the company only needed to do better what it had always done well. This was understandable but, with the benefit of hindsight, myopic. In the words of one manager, 'When you're making two billion dollars a year it's tough to say our system is inadequate. And suddenly when you're not making two billion dollars profit it's too late.' There is much uncertainty in Ford of Europe, as it comes to terms with the heritage of the turbulent 1980s, the restructuring necessitated by simultaneous engineering report, program management, rationalization and the legacy of the turmoil of changing ideas that marked the last decade. In conjunction with its US parent, Ford of Europe still has to negotiate an appropriate governance process at the highest level that will allow it to optimize its development and become master of its own destiny. The parent company has still to fully assimilate the lesson that it has 'ceased to be primarily an American manufacturer and must now consolidate its position as a multinational organization with a world-wide role to play' (Seidler, 1976: 61).

## Past Imperfect

We have dealt at length with the legacy of Fordism. Ford, by its own admission, is 'a very cautious, conservative company. We look many times before we leap.' Its administrative heritage, embodied in its planning system, represents a formidable barrier to change. Ford has always been criticized for having too many administrative layers. We now realize that they were not, as they seemed to the outsider, layers of effective control. They were layer upon layer of reporting and review (institutionalized by managers forced to justify regularly their existence) which actually pushed up costs. The system, ironically, was both self-perpetuating *and* self-defeating. The company 'got into the habit of *reporting* the costs rather than *controlling* them'. The real problem was that planning and perfectly rational processes had been developed too far, beyond their rational limits. The formal process squeezed out dissenting voices, challenges to the established wisdom. Innovators 'just got worn down'. In the words of one Finance veteran, 'We'd bludgeon every investment proposal until it stopped moving.' Ingenuity, accountability and personal responsibility were stifled by fear. Individual initiative suffered 'because they [knew] the bureaucracy [would] review the hell out of it'.

Ford brought to the 1980s a very peculiar mixture of authoritarianism and bureaucracy, of politics and planning, of rationality and irrationality. Politics was important as 'territory protection', what and who you 'controlled' determined your grading and grading determined salary and perks. Structures were predicated upon the misplaced notion that specialization is synonymous with expertise. Functional behaviour and thought ruled, creating divergent cultures based on the goals of the organizational sub-unit and not the superordinate goals of the firm.

## Present Learning

In USA the human resource management initiatives of employee involvement and participative management were 'born of catastrophe'. The US parent exerted pressure on Ford of Europe to adopt EI/PM which, as a result, was experienced not as an 'organic' initiative but as a 'dictate'. The formalism of attempts by EI/PM advocates to sell the process also worked against it. The format confirmed the distance Ford's European management lagged behind their American counterparts in process management. In the US, EI/PM principles were championed by industrial psychologists adept at the process of gaining 'buy-in' from senior management and acting as consultants and facilitators to them in the EI/PM process. These facilitators were skilled at convincing sceptics and cynics of the strategic imperative of change. As one of them explained, 'The two old issues for industrial psychology are productivity and satisfaction. And you've gotta deal with the ones who say, "I can give orders and get it done faster".' In Europe these skills of organization development are relatively rudimentary. Even Ford's established presentational style for disseminating new ideas embodied the company's top-down hierarchy.

> But that was how we did things; that's how we had *always* done things. We had already hit the limits of our own practical knowledge of how to involve people, how to integrate a management team. We understood *why* we had to do it but had no conception of *how* to achieve those objectives. We were stuck before we had even got started. Perhaps that was a good thing in the long run as it taught us a real humility and reinforced just how big our problem actually was, both conceptually and organizationally.

In the US the groundwork had been done and the initiatives were given more direct resources.

> Certainly they got started a lot earlier over there and have a lot more resources than in Europe, no question about that. These factors *are* contributory factors to the relative pace of change in Europe and the USA. Plus the motivation was quite different over there. In the early 1980s . . . people will say that Ford was in deep trouble and that's why they did it. The fact of the matter is that the policy of Employee Involvement was written in 1978, which was a good year, and it was ready to sign in early 1979, again before things were going sour. It was decided to hold on it until the negotiations were completed that year by which time the clouds were on the horizon. And the business hit bottom over there in 1980 and there's no question that was important: people were in deep trouble and they were looking for anything to save the company. From a historical standpoint, the work – the desire to do it – preceded the collapse in the US.

The HRM initiatives found their roots in a pre-existing cultural need and 'desire'.

In Europe there was the problem of 'not invented here', the lack of a sense of ownership because they had not created the initiative. This was exacerbated by European cynicism and antipathy to some of the values the HRM initiatives seemed to represent, symbolized in the 'plastic card mentality':

> We often say in a rather superior fashion, 'Well first we have to translate it into English.' Part of it is just being toffee-nosed but part of it has a genuine substance . . . There are certain things, words and phrases which a British audience will instinctively react against. The

> best illustration I can give is what I would term 'the plastic card mentality'. You go to a conference or any kind of group seminar in the States and I guarantee at the end of it you will be given either a plastic card with the basic Greek homilies on it or a baseball hat or a folder of some kind which is a memento . . . You try and run a conference in Britain and dish out plastic cards and just see what they do to you. . . . X [an American on assignment in Europe] has a cupboard full of plastic cards. He'll give you a thousand if you want them. He'd be delighted to get rid of them. He imported them literally by the thousand and nobody would take them. The last thing we wanted was to stick it on a plastic card and exhibit it proudly in our offices. . . . And that is the US way, which is fine for them and they genuinely believe in it. It does good things for them and they benefit from it.

There was also resistance in Europe to using an EI/PM process to address real business issues.

> I think we were far too restrictive. In the States EI was a good thing – a signal went out. In the UK a set of ground rules went out which proved to be very restrictive. There are supervisors and managers who have EI going on around them but it's directed towards the potted plants, the coffee machines and that sort of thing. And they don't feel they can use EI to address business issues. Very frustrating. So I'm a busy manager with a heavy workload and if I let my people go to attend to the potted plants that's a lot of productive time. So there's some resistance. You can't blame these guys. I don't think we prepared the organization as well as we should have.

The 'bad times' in the US forced people to look more deeply at themselves, to go beyond recriminations pent-up under the old regime. In Europe involvement and participation were more superficial. From the American point of view, 'They [Europeans] don't like to accept anything that was "Made in America".' One American consultant in Europe described the distance she felt Europe had to travel:

> When I first started here it was like the theory of Maslow was like something from outer space. How long has that been around? They want everything fast, easy and not complicated. They see it as more of a threat than an opportunity. It takes more time to be human with people.

Yet, for all the hesitation, mistakes and resistance, the agenda was inexorably, if slowly, changing. Post-1984 managers discerned new elements in Ford of Europe's strategic planning process. Qualitative aspects of manpower planning, such as the organization's skills base and less tangible factors such as morale were now included. The yardstick for strategy is no longer simply 'the numbers'; 'There is a human resource element in all the business plans. Ten years ago you just didn't see that.' There is hope for the future because a rising generation of managers has been exposed to the new principles. The previous generation ruefully acknowledge the problem they experience with change.

> It's very difficult for the people at the top of the organization to change. I think that those people who have been involved in the participative style on their way up will find it very easy. They will just look for that style. But people who have traditionally had the responsibility for running a large organization, a large group of people, can't easily change.

> It's very difficult to change. You find . . . I still find it . . . I mean I say to this guy 'Where did you get that from, you must be dreaming, what the hell's this?' The guy will say 'I've talked to so and so, so and so, and our view is . . .' and you sit back and you think 'What am I doing?' But there's still a tendency . . . very much so.

Understanding and behaviour need to be aligned.

> There are two different issues here. One is understanding and the other is behaviour. And I think unquestionably that the knowledge base of people in the organization has increased dramatically about such things as how to involve employees and the concept of participative management but the behaviour is more difficult to evaluate. Everyone would say, I imagine, 'I am a participative type of manager but it's those bastards above me . . .' So it's two things. . . . And of course there's a fair amount of cynicism in the organization so the behaviour doesn't match the words. But Ford is changing, Ford has changed!

> The bedrock of the company was specialized technical expertise, be it finance or manufacturing. And now Ford are saying that softer skills, interpersonal skills are . . . very important to the survival of the company. You've got to have a motivated organization in which all the brainpower in the company is used to its maximum. And it's very difficult to do that when you have an autocratic organization. So the

style of management has to change and it is. If you ask around then I'm sure people will say that this company is a hell of a lot better that it was ten years ago, no question about that.

Some things have changed for ever.

> Certain things have become almost second nature. Now at any time in this building you could cut the front off like a doll's house and you would see all over the place groups of people with flip-charts indulging in some sort of meeting process that prior to 83 would have been unthinkable. There wasn't a flip board in this building in 83. There must be fifty of them now, even more, I don't know. So that kind of change in our behaviour has emanated from those early days and, of course, since then various groups in an EI sense or in any other sort of sense recognize the need to acquire skills of listening and group process. . . . Certain aspects of those early participative management meetings have become a way of life. . . . So it would be unfair and untrue to say the arrow fell on the ground at the same altitude that it was fired from. And I think it's come at a higher level but it hasn't maintained the heights that it had at the apex.

Skills and values are now central managerial concerns. Learning new skills that reconcile functional and program responsibilities is recognized as a strategic necessity. New 'instinctive values' are very much a part now of the organizational agenda that started with the After Japan study. This broke the ice for Ford of Europe. It was 'the first of the big focuses on the fact that we weren't as good as we thought we were in virtually any sense of the word, [that] we were driven by cost rather than product satisfaction'. After Japan was a crucial starting point – 'We used to rule by fear, and fear breeds cynicism. It was that vicious circle which After Japan and all that followed tried to break' – but only a starting point. It did not diagnose that there was a fundamental cultural change problem. But for the first time Ford looked outside itself, broke the bounds of its old insularity. The nature of the dialogue in the company changed.

> Some of the questions we asked were very basic. Is our prime objective cost control or increased quality? And hours of debate went on around that single issue. The point is that as a manager you can't expect a clear answer: the terms of the question are ambiguous and can conflict. The business answer is you balance cost and quality – its a trade-off. You can't enforce the full Ford cost control disciplines while

> you pursue enhanced quality. The point is that these issues are the subject of free debate whereas [before After Japan and the ensuing initiatives] they were not. Not only would they not have been debated, the issue would not have arisen: cost reduction took overriding priority.

To be competitive the company realizes it cannot afford its previous 'enormous' bureaucracy based on the fetish that it has to 'police everything'. Managers lamented 'the amount of paperwork that circulates with no one actually being accountable for it because I know if someone else has to sign it I'm not going to review it'. 'Hot paper' is no longer compatible with the view that employees 'are important and we trust you':

> what's changing now and hopefully it's going to change even more is that the manager begins to understand that his success is more interdependent with some of his colleagues, his peers, rather than his own. . . . that whole psychology drove the cost system we had, the fact that individual performance and the need to excel were very complementary to this cost system, the cost focus we had. That was a . . . deadly combination . . . one of the biggest contrasts would be a core understanding that teamwork and team involvement is going to get you better solutions.

In the words of another manager, 'we've got to stop doing business with ourselves and do more business with our customers.'

An American HRM consultant described the slow learning she had witnessed in Europe:

> The issue here is that they have never taken and are only beginning to take human resources seriously as a business issue. They're beginning to grasp that the mechanistic model where they moved people in and out of the places and it didn't really matter . . . that maybe that wasn't right.

The change of mind-set is reflected in the 'myths' of the organization. There are fewer stories about the 'really tough characters, usually from Manufacturing'. One manager said that there was 'more pleasure, more laughter – I've never been so relaxed or productive'. Another spoke of a new freedom.

> Now there is a freedom which allows us to try and find out what other people are doing and to compare our processes . . . before you needed

> an act of Parliament to get out of the plant. You are now encouraged to go and see what other people are doing, encouraged to participate in what other people are doing, get out and visit other plants, let people see you . . . let people know you are there to provide a service.

There is a real seriousness about breaking down the 'not invented here' syndrome, a growing willingness, born of business need, to accept 'that somebody else can do a job just as good as you can and you shouldn't change it for the sake of change . . . we can share each other's knowledge. The key is to feel you are part of the decision, [to] believe in releasing the talents that are out there.'

> You've got to spend time. You've got to bring people together freely to discuss what you want to talk about . . . it's easier just to say 'Go and do it' whether the position is right or wrong, which is the old style of management – 'I accept responsibility, I made the decision'. It takes a lot longer to think about and discuss issues . . . but hopefully we save on the implementation. . . . It is frustrating from time to time, especially when you're confident you know the way to go. But it's not frustrating when someone convinces you it's not the way. I like to be persuaded their position is better than mine and I feel it's worthwhile. When I've gone in with a preconceived idea and it's not changed, I think why did I waste my time going through it, and I look back and think maybe my input was too strong to convince people that I really did want an open view.

There is, too, realization that 'We've still got a fair way to go. We've got to work it through the organization better', that it is 'not well rooted yet because we had a very strong culture':

> It's the old, old story that if you've got a big boat and you want to get it across the bay and that's all I want to do, get it across the bay as quickly as possible, then it's not a bad idea to fill it full of oarsmen with a great big guy with a bull-whip at the back. It works pretty effectively. But if you need these guys to use a bit of technology to get that boat across and to use a bit of navigation skills and all the rest of it, then that big bull whip will just confuse them and get them scared and they won't be able to think straight. The more sophisticated the thinking processes and decision-making . . . the less the autocratic and the more the participative techniques are suitable. I think that's where we are now.

## Future Conditional

> In management development terms the key objective which is emerging is to develop a capacity for dilemma management among the next generation of executives.

> My only concern is whether we have long enough to make the change because the threats are very severe.

> When the chips are down there's still a propensity to maintain very top-down management, very quick and reactive and pretty short-term. How sensitively and in what sort of modern framework will Ford manage the next downturn? . . . Will we have learned our lesson at all or will our sharp-pencilled friends in Finance do all the usual things we've always done and let all the training expense and the staff fall away because we can't afford any more . . . To me that's the kind of scenario that presents the test because have we changed as a company because some of us suspect that we may not have changed very much at all.

> You are removing crutches that people have been used to using all these years so not everybody is happy.

These views capture some of the ground Ford has still to cover.

Product delivery and world-class cost-competitiveness remain the major imperatives. There is still the industrial relations problems of the United Kingdom side of the business to be improved.

> We are reaping the whirlwind of the old-fashioned complacency and over-manning of British plants to allow all the restrictive work practices and the job schemes and all the militant, defensive union behaviour by organizations who have yet to come out of the 1920s confronted by management who haven't come out of the 1920s either.

In Germany co-determination, a key issue in the consideration of governance issues, has made employee involvement easier. In the words of a UK plant manager: 'a sharing of purpose, continuity, consistency. That's the thing the Continental plants have always had that we've never had. Forget the traditional roles, we're either going to go on together or we're not.' The future of UK plants remains a major problem for the company, given their relatively poor productivity record, despite the improvements of the 1980s. But a new employee relations agenda is emerging.

> The IR fraternity is starting to ask itself questions like 'Are we policemen or are we supposed to be innovators in terms of creating a work climate in which people can fulfil their own ambitions and gain self-awareness?' In a twenty year career in [industrial relations] in Ford Motor Company I haven't heard that sort of question [until recently]. 'Are we policemen or innovators?'

The Employee Development and Assistance Programme announced in late 1988 represents a significant new strategy in the company's attempt to win over the hearts and minds of its employees. It introduces non-pay benefits in the form of funding for personal development through participation in education courses, to be run in addition to the job-related training programs, and the provision of paramedical services designed to promote healthier lifestyles. Employees are free to pursue non-vocational courses to improve the quality of their education as they see fit – 'Not just to improve their career prospects – though it can certainly help – but to make the most of them as individuals'.

Elements of the HRM approach based on employee involvement and participative management have become part of the company agenda while the formal attempts to introduce them have passed. The company understands the issues better – 'We're quite clear about what EI is as a philosophical statement. But the jury is still out as to whether we can translate that philosophy into changed behaviour'. Further progress depends upon a clear-eyed assessment of where the company is and a refusal to give in to pessimism, scepticism or cynicism.

> Ford published what it wanted to be rather than what it was, some people would say, what it still is. It still hasn't achieved anything close to full MVGP definition. And that's a fairly brave, potentially dangerous thing to do. . . . Some people, the cynics, have said 'But Petersen thought that's what we were!'

At the same time one has to acknowledge the ground that Ford of Europe has covered. If elements of the old Ford survive – and only an incurable romantic would expect them not to, given the company's history – the underlying principles of involvement and participation feed the changes we have examined in chapters five and six concerning product development and the ongoing restructuring of relationships within the company. The chairman wrestles with the task of participative management at the highest level. Here Lindsey Halstead describes changes he made in the Ford of Europe boardroom:

> [How was it possible] to be able to answer any questions in that damn boardroom? . . . There was a horseshoe table and a hierarchy of seating. It's a very cold room. We used to assign seats literally, by tradition, because the damn thing is arranged this way. There would be a name card and the chairman would sit there, and so it went down in pecking order. We stopped this. We created another conference room. It's got a round table. We don't have any assigned seats, deliberately, we sit wherever there's an empty chair. That's what I would call PM in action, it's living it . . . it makes a statement.

## Lessons?

How representative is the Ford experience? A former vice-president of product development is in no doubt.

> Watching the company under Mr Ford during the 1970s, I alternated between sorrow and outrage over what was happening. The company grew only more Byzantine, with a chief executive fighting with his president and principal lieutenants who were, at best, inwardly focused; people who fostered functional isolation among the company's best employees, usually to divide and diffuse power – all antithetical to innovation. . . .
>
> This was a personal sadness, but it also made me sorry for our country. In the story of Ford during the 1970s, there was a bigger story of failure, which led to our taking for granted such unacceptable concepts as 'rust belt'. Is it not a shame that we need to ask whether manufacturing matters at all to our commerce and our culture? (Frey, 1991: 56)

A heritage of Byzantine politics, functional isolation and the lack of an outward focus is by no means unique to Ford. What does make Ford unique is the courage with which it has attacked these problems.

In terms of the overarching issue of fundamental changes in traditional approaches to management and organization – the putative demise of Fordism, the experience of Ford in the 1980s, given its pivotal role in the evolution of this system, is particularly symbolic. In the prophetic words of Carl Rogers nearly 25 years ago,

> It is becoming increasingly clear to the leaders of any complex modern industry that the old system is obsolete . . . What takes its place? The only road to true efficiency seems to be that of persons communicating freely with persons – from below to above, from peer to peer, from above to below, from a member of one division to a member of another division. It is only through this elaborate, individually initiated network of open human communication that the essential information and know-how can pervade the organization . . .
>
> I see many industries, by the year 2000, giving as much attention to the quality of interpersonal relationships and the quality of communication as they currently do to the technological aspects of their business. They will come to value persons as persons, and to recognize that only out of the communicated knowledge of all members of the organization can innovation and progress come . . . What I have said will apply, I believe, not only to management but to labor. The distinction grows less with every technological advance. (Rogers, 1968)

Don Petersen said that he wanted Ford's performance to be measured by its human as well as its economic enterprise. He wanted Ford to be recognized as a 'people company'.

## Coda

Like Ford, we have to constantly remind ourselves that there is no one easy answer, that if one thing is certain it is that the future will be uncertain. But it does seem clear that emerging out of our current uncertainties is a new strategic imperative concerning human resources and a new managerial lexicon containing such terms as strategic integration, involvement, participation, commitment, stakeholders, learning, humility, quality, pride in work, knowledge, shared vision, responsibility and values. Governance issues are also of increasing concern. The chief executive has to take the lead in securing commitment and communicating and sharing the organization's vision. This is particularly problematic in the complexity of multinational management, with potential clashes of interest between parent and subsidiary, a situation made more difficult when the top management team is constantly changing.

The new competition demands a new order of commitment, employee and manager. Organizations that possess the capacity for continuous learning are most likely to survive and prosper in the dynamic, complex environment of the 1990s (Hampden-Turner, 1991). Visionary leaders stuck in one mode of thinking are not. Fundamental to the creation of enthusiasm toward a vision is top management's ability to inquire into and harmonize diversity, to encourage people through the difficult tensions of negotiating the gap between the vision and reality, to make sure current reality is not ignored and to create a quality of relationships that sustains enthusiasm and ongoing inquiry (Senge, 1990). Japan, despite its current problems, 'points towards the next frontier of management: one in which the social system is finely tuned to become a precise instrument for adaptation and continuous learning' (Pascale, 1990: 261–2). The success of Japanese firms is based upon the ability of their managers to match cultural, organizational and strategic imperatives in an integrated management system (Pucik and Hatvany, 1983).

A new image of leadership is emerging, that of someone who is not omniscient, despite what followers expect, who does not have the answers but who does have the questions, a consensus-builder, a healer in an age of 'trust gaps and morale crises' (Kiechel, 1992), adept at what the Americans call 'grief work', building trust in the survivors, lancing the boil of rage, resentment and fear as a first step to giving a new sense of commitment and purpose, giving hope for the future. Concern with responsibility and business ethics is growing. It was Chester Barnard (1938: 283, 259) who warned us that it is 'the creation of organizational morality [that] is the spirit that overcomes the centrifugal force of individual motives' and that 'cooperation, not leadership, is the creative process; but leadership is the creative indispensable fulminator of its forces'. The CEO needs to create a sense of culture, morality and purpose, a balance between organizational goals and good of society, rather than exemplifying the triumph of a sort of nihilistic will to power (MacIntyre, 1981).

The integrated European market is destined to become the world's most important trading arena. Ford started preparing for this market a quarter of a century ago with the establishment of Ford of Europe. Ford of Europe also has to be seen in its broader international aspect. The issue of global strategy is one of the most important on the strategic management agenda. Its multinational talent (Lataif, 1989) is one of Ford's great potential strengths but it still has to learn how best to capitalize on it. The development of a worldwide learning capability that drives continuous innovation is crucial (Bartlett and Ghoshal, 1989). A central managerial issue that the multinational corporation must resolve is the tension between central control and local autonomy so that assets, resources, responsibilities and decisions are both dispersed *and* interdependent and there is *joint development and worldwide sharing* of learning in search of innovation. Perhaps the main management task here is the legitimization and balancing of necessarily diverse perspectives without central over-dominance and in the context of a shared vision. This demands more than mere structural change. What is most pressing for today's managers is 'the constantly haunting issue of finding a connection between organization designers (structure) and organization developers (process)' (Greiner, 1977).

In the words of Lindsey Halstead:

> I don't think any one answer in the complicated environment we have is going to solve our problems. It's a whole series of answers. EI/PM is an important ingredient, stating MVGP is an important ingredient, organizational destructuring and restructuring are. A key part of PM is to provide decision-making capability down at the level where decisions are best made, provide them with direction, strategy and objectives but get the decision-making off a hierarchical onto a horizontal plane and down lower . . . that doesn't mean you don't control the process, it doesn't mean you don't have key objectives . . . [You need] meaningful participation . . . make them a meaningful part of the process.

Ford of Europe is a wholly owned subsidiary of the US parent company incorporated in Delaware. The sense of being owned is strong, perhaps too strong.

> You can walk out of the door after 40 years service and be no more a part of the company than the day you walked in. We've still got the philosophy that you pay for service and when the service is finished the pay stops and that's the end of the contract. A large number of management, supervision, salaried staff would like to feel part of the company. . . . I think we will have to look at that radical change because if we want employee involvement what better way of involving them than having them take a piece of the company in terms of shares. That's real involvement.

What is necessary is a stronger sense of *ownership*. It is difficult to see how this sense of ownership can be fostered by a top management who, for the most part, experience Europe mainly as a rite of passage on the way to higher things.

But Ford, for all the problems it has experienced in its search for competitive advantage, is in the throes of a 'quantum leap' in management thinking stimulated by, in the words of Bill Hayden, 'the sudden stark realization in 1980 that if we didn't change we wouldn't survive.' Alas, there are no comforting nostrums to prescribe for the brave reader who has come with us this far. We started the book warning against the easy but unfulfilling seduction of quick fixes. The starting point of change, if it is to reach to the heart of an organization, is that its leadership adopt new ways of thinking (Pascale, 1990: 262). Change demands that existing paradigms of thought are challenged. Managers do not save their companies just by championing cost reductions. They save their companies by championing new ways of thinking about and confronting the world. Bill Hayden himself, probably much to the surprise of his critics, now advocates continuous revolution. This, he explained, is the goal of simultaneous engineering – 'The point . . . is to keep on forcing people to re-evaluate their "natural" ways of thinking'. 'Natural' in this context means the way of thinking the traditional Ford approach to management engenders.

A change of mind and heart takes time. As one Ford manager, closely involved with the initiatives we have examined, told us, 'It will take a generation for the organization to change completely'. But things, he felt, had changed irrevocably.

> If you go around the organization today the whole lexicon of terms that people use are significantly different now. They talk about participative management and employee involvement and value systems, mission, values and guiding principles, management styles and employee attitudes. All these terms which were foreign to the organization fifteen years ago.

In the words of one HRM activist,

> We're still trying to break down the division, between departments and divisions and operations. We're also talking about breaking down the barriers between countries and cross-cultural issues. This doesn't happen overnight but we're moving that way. The important issue is if we're moving in the same direction, not if our approaches are all the same.

It is appropriate to leave the last word to Bill Hayden, a man whose long shadow still marks the company.

The most important change is that the company no longer believes today – as it did ten years ago – that its quality was sufficient to match the competition, that customers were loyal to Ford and that our efficiency was more than a match for the rest of the world. It's as basic and fundamental as that. The Japanese have caused us to completely rethink our policies and behaviour patterns and that's what we're desperately trying to do.

# Appendix: Notes on Research Methodology

The authors came to this research project from both shared and divergent backgrounds – a shared training as social scientists and researchers and experience as university teachers of business strategy and organizational behaviour; individually, experience spanning psychology, psychotherapy and labour and business history. As social scientists we had learned the importance of rigorous and systematic data collection. Our inclination was towards qualitative research (Starkey, 1990) with the emphasis on the lived experience of managerial work and the factors conditioning the quality of organizational life.

Our core research method was the semi-structured interview. As a result of previous research (Starkey and McKinlay, 1988), we felt we knew enough about the issues we were researching to identify those of most importance but we knew we did not know enough to be prescriptive in designing a closed questionnaire that would tap the rich variety of experience. We focused our interviews on several areas:

individual career experience of the company
individual assessment of crucial factors in the company's history as he or she had experienced them
individual experience and assessment of company initiatives in the core areas of strategy and human resource management
individual reflection upon the current and likely future strategic and HRM issues facing the company

In all we conducted several hundred hours of interviews. Where the nature of the dialogue with the interview subject demanded we conducted follow-up interviews. There were also numerous follow-ups by telephone or letter for clarification, elaboration upon interview discussions or supporting material.

The interview process focused upon senior management with experience up to and including board level. Our data thus provides a source of reflection on managerial experience at the highest levels. Interviews were conducted over a year period between 1987 and 1992, primarily in the United Kingdom and also in Continental Europe and North America, in corporate head offices and manufacturing and research and development sites. A large majority of the interviews were tape-recorded and subsequently transcribed for purposes of analysis. Interviews were supplemented by an extensive review of both academic and business literatures. We were also allowed generous access to in-house company materials – business plans, reports, both internal and those by external consultants, and other forms of written communication. Individual recollection was corroborated wherever possible by reference to Ford archives, but, inevitably, the line between fact and myth becomes blurred. For us this is not a problem. A company's myths are often as indicative of corporate reality as the 'facts'.

We wholeheartedly agree with the observations of another researcher when she writes of her research experience that 'only a spirit of mutual collaboration in search of deeper understanding would merit the kind of generosity I sought' (Zuboff, 1988). Our over-riding impression of our interviews was that they represented a generous and brave attempt by our 'subjects' to make sense of their experience and to share it with us as would-be analysts of that experience.

In analyzing the data our approach was very much inductive. We sifted through the material we had collected over a period that now, for some of it, stretches into years, seeking to discern from what can now only be described as voluminous data – over two hundred hours of taped discussion, transcripts and other material, company-specific or more general – patterns on which to structure the book. Material was analysed and cross-referenced thematically as these patterns began to emerge. The quotations included in the text are, we feel, representative of these patterns and of range of responses that we received.

The book attempts to bridge the gap between the abstract and the concrete in the spirit suggested by Nichols and Beynon (1977, viii):

> so much of what passes for 'theory' . . . fails to connect with the lives that people lead, whereas most descriptive social surveys too often fail to grasp the structure of social relations and the sense which people

> make of them. It is almost as if another way of writing has to be developed; something which 'tells it like it is' even though in any simple sense this is not possible; something which is theoretically informed yet free from theoretical pretentiousness, and which destroys the gap between the abstract and the concrete.

The final outcome is a mixture of fact and myth, of narrative and themes, of history and theory. As we said at the beginning, if the answers are not yet clear the issues are now better understood. The important questions have been raised!

# Bibliography

Abell, D. F. and Hammond, J. S. (1979) *Strategic Market Planning: Problems and Analytical Approaches*. Englewood Cliffs, NJ: Prentice–Hall.

Abernathy, W. J. (1984) abstract to 'The anatomy of the product development cycle: an historical perspective'. Colloquium on Productivity and Technology, Harvard Business School, March.

Abernathy, W. J., Clark, K. B. and Kantrow, A. M. (1981) 'The new industrial competition'. *Harvard Business Review*, September–October, 69–77.

Abernathy, W. J., Clark, K. B. and Kantrow, A. M. (1983) *Industrial Renaissance*. New York: Basic Books.

Argyris, C. (1991) 'Teaching smart people how to learn'. *Harvard Business Review*, May–June, 99–109.

Astley, W. G. (1984) 'Subjectivity, sophistry and symbolism in management science', *Journal of Management Studies*, 21, 259–272.

Auerbach, P. (1989) 'Multinationals and the British economy'. In F. Green (ed.) *The Restructuring of the British Economy*, Brighton: Harvester Wheatsheaf.

Bamber, G. and Lansbury, R. (1989) 'Co-determination and technological change in the German automobile industry'. In G. Bamber and R. Lansbury (eds) *New Technology: International Perspectives on Human Resources and Industrial Relations*, London: Unwin Hyman.

Banas, P. (1984) 'The relationship between participative management and employee involvement'. Dearborn: Ford Motor Company.

Banas, P. (1988) 'Employee Involvement: A sustained labor/management initiative at the Ford Motor Company'. In J. P. Campbell, R. J. Campbell and Associates, *Productivity in Organizations: New Perspectives from Industrial and Organizational Psychology*, San Francisco: Jossey–Bass.

Banas, P. and Sauers, R. (1988) 'Participative Management and Employee Involvement: Model and application'. Dearborn: Ford Motor Company.

Banas, P. and Sauers, R. (1989) 'The relationship between Participative Management and Employee Involvement'. Dearborn: Ford Motor Company.

Barnard, C. I. (1938) *The Functions of the Executive*. Cambridge, Mass: Harvard University Press.

Bartlett, C. A. and Ghoshal, S. (1989) *Managing Across Borders. The Transnational Solution*. London: Hutchinson Business Books.

Bartlett, C. A. and Yoshihara, H. (1988) 'New challenges for Japanese multinationals: Is organization adaptation their Achilles' heel'. *Human Resource Management* 27, 1, 19–43.

Bayley, S. (1983) 'The car programme: 52 months to Job One or How they designed the Sierra'. London: Victoria and Albert Museum.

Beckett, T. (1975) 'The European motor industry in the seventies'. *Business Economist*.

Beer, M., Spector, B., Lawrence, P. R., Mills, D. O. and Walton, R. E. (1984) *Managing Human Assets*. New York: Free Press.

Bennis, W. and Nanus, B. (1985) *Leaders: Strategies for Taking Charge*. New York: Harper and Row.

Best, M. H. (1990) *The New Competition. Institutions of Industrial Restructuring*. Cambridge: Polity Press.

Beynon, H. (1984) *Working For Ford*. Harmondsworth: Penguin (2nd edn).

Beynon, H. (1987) 'Dealing with icebergs: organisation, motivation and efficiency in the 1990s'. *Work, Employment and Society* 1, 2, 247–59.

Bhaskar, K. (1979) *The Future of the UK Motor Industry*. London: Croom Helm.

Bradley, K. and Hill, S. (1983) '"After Japan": the quality circle transplant and production efficiency'. *British Journal of Industrial Relations* 21, 291–311.

Buckley, P. and Enderwick, P. (1985) *The Industrial Relations Practices of Foreign-Owned Firms in Britain*. London: Grafton Books.

Butler, S. (1991) 'A multinational changing gears'. *Financial Times*, 12 August.

Butman, J. (1991) *Car Wars. How General Motors Europe Built 'The Car of the Future'*. London: Grafton Books.

Carroll, R. (1987) 'Organizational approaches to strategy: an introduction and overview'. *California Management Review* 30, 1 (Fall), 8–10.

Casson, M. (1987) *The Firm and the Market: Studies on Multinational Enterprise and the Scope of the Firm*. Oxford: Basil Blackwell.

Chandler, A. D. (1962) *Strategy and Structure*. Cambridge, Mass.: MIT Press.

Clark, K. and Fujimoto, T. (1991) *Product Development Performance. Strategy, Organization, and Management in the World Auto Industry*. Cambridge, Mass.: Harvard Business School.

Clark, P. and Starkey, K. (1988) *Organizational Transitions and Innovation-Design*. London: Pinter Publishers.

Cochrane, A. (1991) 'Desperate times for managers at Ford'. *Management Week*, 18 September, 26–7.

Collins, J. C. and Porras, J. I. (1991) 'Organizational vision and visionary organizations'. *California Management Review*, Fall, 30–52.

Cowans, N. (1986) 'The future role of the personnel manager'. University of Warwick: Warwick Papers in Industrial Relations, no. 4.

Critchley, B. and Casey, D. (1984) 'Second thoughts on team building'. *Management Education and Development* 15, 2, 163–75.

Crozier, M. (1964) *The Bureaucratic Phenomenon*. London: Tavistock and University of Chicago Press.

Cusumano, M. (1985) *The Japanese Automobile Industry. Technology and Management at Nissan and Toyota*. Cambridge, Mass.: Harvard University Press.

Cusumano, M. (1988) 'Manufacturing innovation and competitive advantage: reflections on the Japanese automobile industry'. Working Paper no. 1996–88, Alfred P. Sloan School of Management, Cambridge, Mass.: MIT.

David, F. R. (1989) 'How companies define their mission'. *Long Range Planning* 22, 1, 90–7.

Davis, S. M. and Lawrence, P. R. (1977) *Matrix*. Reading, Mass.: Addison–Wesley.

De Vos, T. (1981) *U.S. Multinationals and Worker Participation in Management: The American Experience in the European Community*. London: Aldwych Press.

Deming, W. E. (1982) *Quality, Productivity and Competitive Position*. Cambridge, Mass.: MIT Center for Advanced Engineering.

Dohse, K., Jurgens, U. and Malsch, T. (1985) 'From Fordism to Toyotism? The social organization of production of the labour process in the Japanese automobile industry'. *Politics and Society* 14, 2, 115–46.

Done, K. (1992) 'From design studio to new car showroom'. *Financial Times*, 11 May, 15.

Doyle, J. L. (1985) 'Managing new product development: how companies learn and unlearn'. In K. B. Clark, R. H. Hayes and C. Lorenz (eds) *The Uneasy Alliance. Managing the Productivity–Technology Dilemma*. Boston, Mass.: Harvard Business School Press.

Drucker, P. (1973) *Management. Tasks, Responsibilities, Practices*. New York: Harper and Row.

Drucker, P. (1990) 'The emerging theory of manufacturing'. *Harvard Business Review*, May–June, 94–102.

Eli, M. (1990) *Japan Inc. Global Strategies of Japanese Trading Corporations*. London: McGraw–Hill.

Enderwick, P. (1985) *Multinational Business and Labour*. London: Macmillan.

Fombrun, C. J., Tichy, N. M. and Devanna, M. A. (eds) (1983) *Strategic Human Resource Management*. New York: Wiley.

Fox, A. (1973) *Beyond Contract. Work, Power and Trust Relations*. London: Faber.

Freeman, C. (ed.) (1984) *Technological Trends and Employment, volume 4: Engineering and Vehicles*. Aldershot: Gower.

Frey, D. (1991) 'Learning the ropes: my life as a product champion'. *Harvard Business Review*, September–October, 46–8, 52–6.

Friedmann, H. and Meredeen, S. (1980) *The Dynamics of Industrial Conflict*. London: Croom Helm.

Fulop, I. (1991) 'Middle managers: victims or vanguards of the entrepreneurial movement'. *Journal of Management Studies* 28, 1, 25–44.

Giles, E. and Starkey, K. (1988) 'The Japanisation of Xerox'. *New Technology, Work and Employment* 3, 2, 125–33.

Gill, C. (1985) *Work, Unemployment and the New Technology*. Cambridge: Polity.

GLC [Greater London Council] (1985) 'The Ford Report'. London: greater London Coucil.

Gomory, R. E. (1989) 'From "ladder of science" to the product development cycle'. *Harvard Business Review*, November–December, 99–105.

Grant, R. M. (1991) *Contemporary Strategy Analysis*. Oxford: Basil Blackwell.

Greiner, L. (1977) 'Reflections on OD American style'. In C. L. Cooper (ed.) *Organizational Development in the UK and USA*. London: Macmillan.

Guest, D. (1987) 'Human resource management and industrial relations'. *Journal of Management Studies* 24, 5, 503–21.

Guest, D. (1988) 'Human resource management – is it worth taking seriously?'. London School of Economics, First Annual Seear Fellowship Lecture.

Guest, D. (1989) 'Human resource management: its implications for industrial relations and trade unions'. In J. Storey (ed.) *New Perspectives on Human Resource Management*. London: Routledge.

Guest, D. (1990) 'Human resource management and the American Dream'. *Journal of Management Studies* 27, 4, 377–97.

Guthrie, G. (1987) 'After Japan and beyond'. *Production Engineer*, May, 29–31.

Hackett, D. (1976) 'The big idea – The story of Ford in Europe'. Brentwood: Ford of Europe.

Halberstam, D. (1987) *The Reckoning*. London: Bloomsbury.

Hall, W. K. (1980) 'Survival in a hostile business environment'. *Harvard Business Review*, September–October.

Hamel, G. and Prahalad, C. K. (1989) 'Strategic intent'. *Harvard Business Review*, 75–85.

Hammer, M. (1990) 'Reengineering work: don't automate, obliterate'. *Harvard Business Review*, July–August, 104–12.

Hampden-Turner, C. (1991) *Charting the Corporate Mind. From Dilemma to Strategy*. Oxford: Basil Blackwell.

Harvey-Jones, J. (1988) *Making It Happen. Reflections on Leadership*. London: Collins.

Hayes, R. H. and Abernathy, W. J. (1980) 'Managing our way to economic decline'. *Harvard Business Review*, July–August, 67–77.

Hendry, C. and Pettigrew, A. (1990) 'Human resource management: an agenda for the 1990s'. *International Journal of Human Resource Management* 1, 1, 17–44.

Hofer, C. W. (1986) 'Designing turnaround strategies'. In J. B. Quinn *et al.*, *The Strategy Process*. Englewood Cliffs, NJ: Prentice–Hall.

Hopeman, R. (1989) 'The evolution of program management' EAO Presentation, Dagenham, 31 August.

Hurst, D. K., Rush, J. C. and White, R. E. (1989) 'Top management teams and organizational renewal'. *Strategic Management Journal* vol. 10, Summer, special issue, 87–106.

Iacocca, L. (1986) *Iacocca. An Autobiography*. Toronto: Bantam Books.

Income Data Services (1986) *Report*. No. 468, March.

Imai, K., Nonaka, I. and Takeuchi, H. (1985) 'Managing the new product development process: how Japanese companies learn and unlearn'. In K. B. Clark, R. H. Hayes and C. Lorenz, (eds) *The Uneasy Alliance. Managing the Productivity-Technology Dilemma*. Boston, Mass.: Harvard Business School Press.

Jaikumar, R. (1986) 'Postindustrial manufacturing'. *Harvard Business Review*, November–December, 69–76.

Jary, S. (1985) 'New technology: the union response at the local level'. Unpublished M. Sc. thesis, Imperial College, London University.

Johnson, G. and Scholes, K. (1989) *Exploring Corporate Strategy*. New York and London: Prentice–Hall (2nd edn).

Johnson, R. H. (1988) 'How Ford's HR staff supports strategic planning'. In Y. K. Shetty and V. M. Buehler (eds) *Competing through Productivity and Quality*. Cambridge, Mass.: Productivity Press.

Joiner, W. B. (1986) 'Leadership for organizational learning'. In J. D. Adams (ed.) *Transforming Leadership*. Alexandria, VA: Miles River Press.

Jones, D. (1983) 'Technology and the UK automobile industry'. *Lloyds Bank Review*, no. 148, April.

Kanter, R. M. (1989) 'The new managerial work'. *Harvard Business Review*, November–December, 85–92.

Kaplinsky, R. (1988) 'Restructuring the capitalist labour process: some lessons from the car industry'. *Cambridge Journal of Economics* 12, 451–70.

Katz, H. (1985) *Changing Gears: Changing Labor Relations in the US Auto Industry*. Cambridge, Mass.: MIT Press.

Kester, W. C. (1991) *Japanese Takeovers. The Global Contest for Corporate Control*. Cambridge, Mass.: Harvard Business School Press.

Kiechel, W., III (1992) 'The leader as servant'. *Fortune*, no. 9, 4 May, 81–2.

Kiefer, C. (1986) 'Leadership in metanoic organizations'. In J. D. Adams (ed.) *Transforming Leadership*. Alexandria, VA: Miles River Press.

Kochan, T., Katz, H. and McKersie, R. B. (1986) *The Transformation of American Industrial Relations*. New York: Basic Books.

Kochan, T. A. and Chalykoff, J. B. (1987) 'Human resource management and business life cycles: some preliminary propositions'. In A. Kleingartner and C. S. Anderson (eds) *Human Resource Management in High Technology Firms*. Lexington, Mass.: Lexington Books.

Kotler, P. (1984) 'Design: a powerful but neglected strategic tool'. *Journal of Business Strategy*, Fall, 16–21.

Lataif, L. (1989), 'Ford and the Development of the International Manager'. *European Review* 5, 1/2, 48–51.

Lawrence, P. R. and Lorsch, J. W. (1967) *Organization and Environment*. Cambridge Mass.: Harvard Business School.

Lawrence, P. R. and Lorsch, J. W. (1969) *Developing Organizations: Diagnosis and Action*. Reading, Mass.: Addison–Wesley.

Legge, K. (1989) 'Human resource management: a critical analysis'. In J. Storey (ed.) *New Perspectives on Human Resource Management*. London: Routledge.

Lengnick-Hall, C. A. and Lengnick-Hall, M. L. (1988) 'Strategic human resource management: a review of the literature and a proposed typology'. *Academy of Management Review* 13, 3, 454–70.

Lever-Tracy, C. (1990) 'Fordism transformed: Employee Involvement and workplace industrial relations at Ford'. *Journal of Industrial Relations*, June, 179–96.

Lorenz, C. (1986) *The Design Dimension*. Oxford: Basil Blackwell.

Lorsch, C. (1986) 'Managing culture: the invisible barrier to strategic change'. *California Management Review* 28, 2, 95–109.

MacIntyre, A. (1981) *After Virtue. A Study in Moral Theory*. London: Duckworth.

Marsden, D., Morris, T., Willman, P. and Wood, S. (1985) *The Car Industry: Labour Relations and Industrial Adjustment*. London: Tavistock.

McLoughlin, I. and Clark, J. (1988) *Technological Change at Work*. London: Open University Press.

Miles, R. E. and Snow, C. C. (1978) *Organizational Strategy, Structure, and Process*. New York: McGraw–Hill.

Miller, P. (1989) 'Strategic industrial relations and human resource management – distinction, definition and recognition'. *Journal of Management Studies* 24, 4, 347–61.

Mintzberg, H. and Quinn, J. B. (1991) *The Strategy Process*. Englewood Cliffs, N.J.: Prentice–Hall.

Mintzberg, H. (1983) *Structure in Fives: Designing Effective Organizations*. Englewood Cliffs, N.J.: Prentice–Hall.

Morgan, G. (1986) *Images of Organization*. Beverley Hills: Sage.

Mumford, A. and Honey, P. (1986) 'Developing Skills For Matrix Management'. *Industrial and Commercial Training* (UK) 18, 5, Sept/Oct, 2–7.

Murray, R. (1988) 'Life after Henry (Ford)'. *Marxism Today*, October, 8–13.

Myers, V. (1991) 'How a cultural revolution can lift the spirits'. *The Independent on Sunday*, 13 January, 20.

Nadler, D. A. and Tushman, M. L. (1990) 'Beyond the charismatic leader: leadership and organizational change'. *California Management Review* 32, 2, Winter, 77–97.

Nichols, T. and Beynon, H. (1977) *Living With Capitalism. Class Relations and the Modern Factory*. London: Routledge and Kegan Paul.

Nonaka, I. (1988) 'Toward middle-up-down management: accelerating information creation'. *Sloan Management Review*, Spring, 9–18.

Nonaka, I. (1991) 'The knowledge-creating company'. *Harvard Business Review*, November–December, 96–104.

Ohmae, K. (1983) *The Mind of the Strategist*. New York: Penguin.

Ouchi, W. G. (1981) *Theory Z*. Reading, Mass.: Addison–Wesley.

Pascale, R. T. (1984) 'Perspectives on strategy: the real story behind Honda's success'. *California Management Review*, Spring, 47–72.

Pascale, R. T. (1988) 'The Honda effect'. In J. B. Quinn, H. Mintzberg and R. M. James, *The Strategy Process*. Englewood Cliffs, NJ: Prentice–Hall.

Pascale, R. (1990) *Managing on the Edge*. London: Viking.

Peters, T. and Waterman, R. H. (1982) *In Search of Excellence*. New York: Harper and Row.

Petersen, D. E. (1991) *A Better Idea. Redefining the Way Americans Work*. Boston: Houghton–Mifflin.

Pettigrew, T. J. (1985) 'Process quality control: the new approach to the management of quality in Ford'. *Quality Assurance* 11, 3, 81–8.

Pettigrew, A. (1985) *The Awakening Giant. Continuity and Change in Imperial Chemical Industries*. Oxford: Basil Blackwell.

Pfeffer, J. (1981) 'Management as symbolic action: the creation and maintenance of organizational paradigms'. *Research in Organizational Behavior* 3, Greenwich, Conn.: JAI Press, 1–52.

Piore, M. (1986) 'Perspectives on labor market flexibility'. *Industrial Relations* 25, 2, 146–66.

Piore, M. and Sabel, C. (1984) *The Second Industrial Divide*. New York: Basic Books.

Poole, M. (1990) 'Editorial: human resource management in an international perspective'. *International Journal of Human Resource Management* 1, 1, 1–15.

Porter, M. (1980) *Competitive Strategy*. New York: Free Press.

Porter, M. (1985) *Competitive Advantage*. New York: Free Press.

Porter, M. (1987) 'From competitive advantage to corporate strategy'. *Harvard Business Review*, May–June.

Prahalad, C. K. and Hamel, G. (1990) 'The core competence of the corporation'. *Harvard Business Review*, May–June, 79–91.

Pucik, V. and Hatvany, N. (1983) 'Management practices in Japan and their impact on business strategy'. In H. Mintzberg and J. B. Quinn (1991) *The Strategy Process*. Englewood Cliffs, NJ: Prentice–Hall.

Pugh, D. S., Hickson, D. J. and Hinings, C. R. (1983) *Writers on Organizations*. Harmondsworth: Penguin.

Purcell, J. (1989) 'The impact of corporate strategy on human resource management'. In J. Storey (ed.) *New Perspectives on Human Resource Management*. London: Routledge.

Purcell, J. and Gray, A. (1986) 'Corporate personnel departments and the management of industrial relations: two case studies in ambiguity'. *Journal of Management Studies* 23, 2, 205–23.

Quinn, J. B., Mintzberg, H. and James, R. M. (1988) *The Strategy Process*. Englewood Cliffs: Prentice–Hall.

Rapp, S. and Collins, T. L. (1987) *Maxi Marketing: the new direction in advertising, promotion and marketing strategy*. New York: McGraw–Hill.

Rappaport, A. (1990) 'The staying power of the public corporation'. *Harvard Business Review*, January–February, 96–104.

Ray, C. A. (1986) 'Corporate cultures: the last frontier of control'. *Journal of Management Studies* 23, 3, 287–97.

Rogers, C. R. (1968) 'Interpersonal relationships: USA 2000'. *Journal of Applied Behavioral Science* 4, 3, 265–80.

Roots, P. (1984) 'Do companies get the trade unions they deserve?' Trent Business School Open Lecture, 6 November, Nottingham.

Roots, P. (1986) 'Collective bargaining: opportunities for a new approach'. Warwick Papers in Industrial Relations, no. 5.

Rumelt, R. (1988) 'The evaluation of business strategy'. In J. B. Quinn, H. Mintzberg and R. M. James, *The Strategy Process*. Englewood Cliffs: Prentice–Hall.

Ryder Report (1975) *The Future of the British Car Industry*. Central Policy Review Staff, London: HMSO.

Sabel, C. (1982) *Work and Politics*. Cambridge: Cambridge University Press.

Scarborough, H. (1984) 'Maintenance workers and new technology: the case of Longbridge'. *Industrial Relations Journal* 15, 4, Winter, 9–15.

Schendel, D. (1989) 'Introduction'. In *Strategic Management Journal* Special Issue, 'Leaders and Leadership', 10, Summer.

Seeger (1984) 'Reversing the images of BCG's growth/share matrix'. In H. Mintzberg and J. B. Quinn (1991) *The Strategy Process*. Englewood Cliffs, NJ: Prentice–Hall.

Seidler, P. (1976) *Let's Call It Fiesta. The Auto-biography of Ford's Project Bobcat*. Lausanne: Edita.

Selznick, A. (1957) *Leadership in Administration*. New York: Harper and Row.

Senge, P. M. (1986) 'Systems principles for leadership'. In J. P. Adams (ed.) *Transforming Leadership*, Alexandra, VA: Miles River Press.

Senge, P. M. (1990) *The Fifth Dimension. The Art and Practice of the Learning Organization*. New York: Doubleday.

Shook, R. L. (1990) *Turnaround. The New Ford Motor Company*. New York: Prentice–Hall.

Silva, E. (1988) 'Labour and technology in the car industry: Ford strategies in Britain and Brazil'. Unpublished Ph.D. thesis, Imperial College, London University.

Sloan, A. P. (1986) *My Years With General Motors*. Harmondsworth: Penguin (originally published 1963, Doubleday).

Soeters, J. L. (1986) 'Excellent companies as social movements'. *Journal of Management Studies* 23, 3, 299–312.

Souder, W. E. (1988) 'Managing relations between R&D and marketing in new product development projects'. *Journal of Product Innovation and Management* 5, 6–19.

Starkey, K. (1990) 'Studies on transitions: meanings and methods'. *Journal of Management Studies* 27, 1, 97–110.

Starkey, K. (1992) 'Durkheim and organizational analysis: two legacies'. *Organization Studies* 13/4, 627–42.

Starkey, K. and McKinlay, A. (1988) *Organisational Innovation. Competitive Strategy and the Management of Change in Four Major Companies*. Aldershot: Avebury, Gower.

Starkey, K. and McKinlay, A. (1989) 'Beyond Fordism? Strategic choice and labour relations in Ford UK'. *Industrial Relations Journal* 20, 2, 93–100.

Starkey, K., Wright, M. and Thompson, T. (1991) 'Flexibility, hierarchy, markets'. *British Journal of Management* 2, 165–76.

Stevens, W. (1967) *Letters*. London: Faber and Faber.

Stopford, J. M. and Turner, L. (1985) *Britain and the Multinationals*. London: Wiley.

Storey, J. (ed.) (1989) *New Perspectives on Human Resource Management*. London: Routledge.

*Strategic Management Journal* (1989) 'On Strategic Leadership'. Special issue, Summer.

Strebel, P. (1987) 'Ford of Europe'. *Journal of Management Case Studies* 3, 3, Summer, 138–57.

Tichy, N. (1973) *Managing Strategic Change*. New York: Wiley Interscience.

Tichy, N., Fombrun, C. and Devanna, M. A. (1982) 'Strategic human resource management'. *Sloan Management Review* 13(2), 47–61.

Tichy, N. M., Fombrun, C. J. and Devanna, M. A. (1984) 'The organizational context of strategic human resource management'. In C. J.

Fombrun, N. M. Tichy and M. A. Devanna (eds) (1983) *Strategic Human Resource Management*. New York: Wiley.

Toffler, A. (1980) *The Third Wave*. London: Collins.

Tolliday, S. (1991) 'Ford and "Fordism" in postwar Britain: enterprise management and the control of labour 1937–1987'. In S. Tolliday and J. Zeitlin (eds) *The Power to Manage? Employers and Industrial Relations in Comparative Historical Perspective*. London: Routledge.

Trotman, A. (1988) 'Face to face: Alex Trotman of Ford of Europe'. *European Motor Business* 14, 3–19.

Walton, R. E. (1985) 'From control to commitment: transforming work force management in the United States'. In K. B. Clark, R. H. Hayes and C. Lorenz (eds) *The Uneasy Alliance. Managing the Productivity–Technology Dilemma*. Boston, Mass.: Harvard Business School Press.

Wensley, R. (1982) 'PIMS and BCG: new horizons or false dawns'. *Strategic Management Journal* 3, 147–58.

Westley, F. and Mintzberg, H. (1989) 'Visionary leadership and strategic management'. *Strategic Management Journal*, vol. 10, Summer Special Issue, 17–32.

White, B. (1990) 'How Quality Became Job 1 at Ford'. *Canadian Business Review*, Spring, 24–7.

Williams, A., Dobson, P. and Walters, M. (1989) *Changing Culture*. London: Institute of Personnel Management.

Williams, K., Williams, J. and Haslam, C. (1987) *The Breakdown of Austin Rover. A Case Study in the Failure of Business Strategy and Industrial Policy*. Leamington Spa: Berg.

Williams, K., Cutler, T., Williams, J. and Haslam, C. (1987) 'The end of mass production?'. *Economy and Society* 16, 3, 405–39.

Williamson, O. E. (1975) *Markets and Hierarchies: Analysis and Antitrust Implications*. New York: Free Press.

Williamson, O. E. and Ouchi, W. G. (1981) 'The markets and hierarchies program of research: origins, implications, prospects'. In A. H. Van de Ven and W. F. Joyce (eds) *Perspectives on Organization Design and Behavior*. Wiley: New York.

Willman, P. and Winch, G. (1985) *Innovation and Management Control: Labour Relations at BL Cars*. Cambridge: Cambridge University Press.

Womack, J. P., Jones, D. T. and Roos, D. (1990) *The Machine that Changed the World*. London and New York: Rawson Associates/ Macmillan.

Wood, S. (1988) 'Between Fordism and flexibility? The US car industry'. In R. Hyman and W. Streek (eds) *New Technology and Industrial Relations*. Oxford: Basil Blackwell.

Wrapp, H. E. (1967) 'Good managers don't make policy decisions'. *Harvard Business Review*, September–October, 91–9.

Zaleznik, A. (1989) 'Real work'. *Harvard Business Review*, January–February, 57–64.

Zimmerman, F. (1991) *The Turnaround Experience: Real World Lessons in Revitalising Corporations*. New York: McGraw–Hill.
Zuboff, S. (1988) *In the Age of the Smart Machine. The Future of Work and Power*. Oxford: Heinemann.

# Index